The Household Finance Issues in China

Sibo Zhao · Dawei Zhao

The Household Finance Issues in China

Springer

Sibo Zhao
School of Sociology and Psychology
Central University of Finance
and Economics
Beijing, China

Dawei Zhao
FinTech Research Center
Financial Research Institute of the People's
Bank of China
Beijing, China

ISBN 978-981-97-0705-8 ISBN 978-981-97-0706-5 (eBook)
https://doi.org/10.1007/978-981-97-0706-5

This Springer imprint is published by the registered company Springer Nature Singapore Pte Ltd.
The registered company address is: 152 Beach Road, #21-01/04 Gateway East, Singapore 189721, Singapore

Paper in this product is recyclable.

Contents

Chapter 1
Research Background and Conceptual Definition of Chinese Household Finance

Over the past half century, rapid technological progress and the globalization of social finance have created tremendous economic prosperity for China while also deeply embedding Chinese households in modern financial systems, becoming an important factor affecting the productivity and quality of economic development of the entire nation. Currently, the total wealth of Chinese households is experiencing explosive growth. According to the Global Wealth Report 2022, the size of Chinese household wealth has increased to $85 trillion (about RMB 600 trillion). China's per capita wealth has reached $76,639 (about RMB 540,000), more than 10 times what it was 21 years ago. Data from the China Wealth Report 2022 also confirms that in 2021, the total amount of household wealth reached RMB 68.7 trillion, ranking second in the world, next only to the United States; household assets averaged RMB 1.34 million. On a structural level, physical assets (primarily real estate) account for 69.3% of total wealth, while financial assets account for 30.7%; financial assets of household residents are still concentrated in low-risk financial assets such as cash, demand deposits, and time deposits, accounting for about 53%, while equity assets and public funds account for about 19%.

Although real assets currently account for a much larger proportion of Chinese residents' wealth than financial assets, as the financial market continues to develop rapidly and the financial system undergoes ongoing reforms toward greater depth, the investment options available for households to allocate financial assets are also increasing. Additionally, as residents' awareness of wealth management continues to increase, personal asset allocation choices are expected to gradually shift from physical to financial assets in the coming years. Therefore, household financial market participation, household asset allocation, and its influencing factors will increasingly become focus areas for people. Research on Chinese household finance not only deepens understanding of the financial behaviors and asset allocation status of

S. Zhao and D. Zhao, *The Household Finance Issues in China*,
https://doi.org/10.1007/978-981-97-0706-5_1

Chinese households but also enhances residents' and households' awareness of financial health. Moreover, such research can contribute to the formulation and improvement of consumption policies, the adjustment of economic structure, and the prevention of household financial risks, providing guidance for improving the living welfare of Chinese households and the growth of their property income.

1.1 The Relevant Concepts and Connotations of Household Finance

1.1.1 Household Finance

At the American Finance Association's 2006 Annual Meeting, American economist John Campbell provided a systematic discussion of household finance and placed it alongside corporate finance and asset pricing as one of the three major areas of microfinance research. Since then, household finance has gradually become a new independent research direction in the development of financial economics. It focuses on how household investors use various financial tools to achieve intertemporal optimization of resources in the face of uncertainty to achieve their wealth goals of consumption smoothing and utility maximization (Gan et al. 2013; Campbell 2006).

Finance is a transactional activity. Traditional finance limits its concept to the study of the circulation of monetary capital, while modern finance extends to the study of the capitalization process of business operations. Therefore, finance is the process of reorganizing existing resources to achieve value and profit equivalent circulation. Financial development plays a significant role in promoting social and economic progress.

The decision-making authority for individual economic behavior primarily lies with households, which carries out daily economic life and significant social activities. Similar to corporate finance, government finance, and personal finance, household finance is the process of intertemporal optimization of resources by microeconomic entities through capital markets under uncertain circumstances. Therefore, this book simply defines household finance as the process by which households, as microeconomic entities, use household funds and various financial instruments and products in the financial market to seek increases in household wealth. However, it is important to note that distinguishing between household finance and personal finance can be challenging in certain cases. This is due to the fact that a residential household comprises individuals, and often a specific individual, such as the head of the household, represents the financial behavior of the entire household. Therefore, this book posits that households consisting of individual entities or represented by a particular individual (i.e., the head of the household) exhibit unity from an execution perspective.

However, household finance is different from personal finance, which selects financial behaviors based on individual asset cost–benefit characteristics and pursues the goal of maximizing profits. Household finance is a financial activity conducted at the household level. It must consider long-term but limited lifecycles and achieve certain returns based on reasonable risk, overall economic stability, and savings for the future. Therefore, to accurately characterize Chinese household financial behavior, it is necessary to expand traditional theories and models based on Chinese practical experience (Gan et al. 2013).

1.1.2 Household Wealth, Household Assets, and Household Asset Allocation

From an economic perspective, the concept of household wealth usually refers to a household's net assets or the average net worth of households in a specific geographical area, mainly including financial assets, property values, and productive assets. Household annual income is the main economic source of household wealth, mainly including members' working income, rental income from household properties, and financial investment returns. Part of household wealth can be viewed as the portion of all household members' annual income that is not consumed but accumulated. However, the creation of "household income" resulting from changes in production, labor, and ownership opportunities cannot be equated with "household wealth accumulation" entirely because different households have different consumption behaviors or investment strategies (He and Xia 2012).

Assets are the basic components of household wealth and the foundation of household wealth stability. Currently, the academic community includes "cash and demand deposits, time deposits, bonds, stocks, funds, wealth management products, trusts, industrial investments, real estate, cars, individual housing provident fund accounts, individual social security accounts, and individual health insurance accounts" into the concept of household assets. With the slowdown of economic growth and the deceleration of labor income, such as wages, the proportion of property income, such as investment, gradually increases. Therefore, achieving effective asset allocation is beneficial to enhancing the level of household wealth accumulation.

There are significant differences between household asset allocation and institutional asset allocation, as the latter possesses high professionalism and may achieve scientifically reasonable asset allocation through regulatory means. Although classic theories suggest that households should make investment decisions based on their estimations of asset cost and revenue characteristics, as well as their own risk tolerance levels and that households should invest a certain proportion of their wealth in risky assets (Dow and Werlang 1992), the purpose of household asset allocation is intergenerational inheritance, and its structure has significant continuity, as some parents want to leave a portion of their assets to their children. Therefore, it is difficult to achieve rational investment, which also determines the complexity and heterogeneity of household asset allocation. Studying household asset allocation can not only better realize household wealth preservation, appreciation, and risk resistance but also benefit the economic and financial development of the whole country.

1.1.3 Household Financial Assets and Financial Asset Selection

With the continuous development of China's financial markets, financial products have become more diverse and complex, and households are increasingly participating actively in the financial markets.

Household financial assets come from converting a portion of household savings into financial products for investment, including operating assets such as cash and cash equivalents, stocks, bank deposits, funds, options, futures, and other financial instruments such as bonds. These form household financial assets that are distinct from physical assets such as real estate, cars, valuables, and antiques. According to risk theory, people often view household deposits and government bonds as risk-free financial assets, while stocks, funds, and bonds with uncertain future returns that may result in principal losses are considered risky financial assets.

A diversified range of risky financial assets also brings a diversified asset portfolio. Therefore, in studying household participation in the financial market, how to ensure that risks are minimized while achieving comparable yields becomes an important research issue. Modern portfolio theory suggests that when investors make financial asset decisions, they should diversify their investments and not concentrate them on a single asset. Holding a more diversified asset portfolio can effectively reduce investment risk.

Therefore, this book believes that household financial asset selection is the behavior of households, constrained by conditions, to obtain maximum economic profits through appropriate financial strategies and the selection of appropriate financial instruments.

1.1.4 Financial Health

The Center for Financial Services Innovation (CFSI) in the United States introduced the concept of financial health in 2015 to measure whether consumers are in good financial or fiscal states. Financial health includes subjective and objective variables related to consumption, saving, borrowing, and planning. Since then, the concept of financial health has increasingly penetrated into various interdisciplinary research fields, such as economics. According to Newcomb (2018), financial health is different from wealth maximization, and consumers should enhance their ability to think long-term and improve their satisfaction with their financial state by increasing their financial well-being under the premise of economic stability. Garman and Forgue (2018) argue that family financial health should not only consider the stability of family assets but also have a certain degree of consumption freedom. They propose evaluating family financial health from three aspects: financial asset situation, asset allocation method, and consumption habits.

In 2019, the China Academy of Financial Inclusion (CAFI) released the "China Inclusive Finance Development Report," which officially put forward the concept of "financial health." Financial health refers to individuals or households using financial tools to select appropriate financial behaviors, managing income, expenses, debts, emergencies, risks, assets, and other aspects to meet daily and long-term financial needs, cope with financial shocks, seize development opportunities, and ensure personal or family financial well-being is maximized. CAFI's study believes that financial health should include subjective and objective variables related to consumption, savings, borrowing, and planning. Therefore, this book adopts the concept of financial health from the "China Inclusive Finance Development Report" and specifically refers to the welfare status of families or the ability of enterprises' sustainable development.

1.2 The Importance and Necessity of Developing Household Financial Health

The 6th Plenary Session of the 19th Communist Party of China emphasized the need to "promote the comprehensive development of people and achieve more significant substantive progress in common prosperity for all the people." The growth and structural changes of household financial assets play an irreplaceable role in promoting common prosperity. The household is an important subject in the Chinese financial market, and the accumulation of household wealth provides more and more families with the opportunity and ability to purchase financial products and obtain risk protection and property income. At the same time, promoting the development of family finance can also serve as an important lever to promote current economic and social development, contributing important financial forces to the high-quality development of the economy and the stability of the social structure. Therefore, vigorously developing family finance to enable more families to enjoy the dividends brought by financial development should be a strategic development direction during the "14th Five-Year Plan" period for the financial industry.

Firstly, developing family finance can further improve people's living standards. China's economic and social development has always adhered to the concept of "people-oriented" and "putting the people at the center," and the Party and the government have always regarded "realizing the comprehensive development of people and achieving common prosperity" as the ultimate goal of development. Finance is an important means to promote economic development and social progress, aiming to provide financial means for social improvement, human progress, and common prosperity through various financial means and tools. Currently, the main contradiction in Chinese society is between the growing need for a better life and imbalanced and insufficient development. Finance is an important means to improve people's quality of life and meet their needs. Throughout the history of China's financial industry development, the concept of "people-oriented" and "putting the people at the center" has been consistent, and this concept will also become an essential guide for the development of China's financial industry in the future. The development of family finance has not only economic benefits but also social benefits, which can create more harmonious and healthy living conditions and living environments for the people, greatly enrich people's material and spiritual lifestyles, and help improve people's living standards.

Secondly, developing family finance contributes to the formation of new driving forces for economic and social development. The financial industry should serve social and economic development, especially in the context of the development of inclusive finance. The financial industry should make it a priority to ensure that families can enjoy the dividends of financial development and that the rights and interests of financial consumers are guaranteed. In the era of digital economy development, ensuring that families have stable, low-cost, and convenient channels for financial consumption and providing financial products and services that match their consumption and risk tolerance levels is crucial for establishing a harmonious, orderly, healthy, and sustainable financial industry model between the financial industry, financial institutions, and families. Furthermore, establishing a harmonious and symbiotic connection between the financial system, the economic system, and the social system and creating an innovative model that can influence economic and social development by adjusting family financial behavior can promote the co-development of finance, economy, and society and ultimately provide new driving forces for economic and social development.

Thirdly, developing family finance helps to achieve high-quality development. Currently, China's economic and social development is in a new development stage where the focus has shifted from development speed to development quality. High-quality development has become the core trend of China's current and future development. To achieve high-quality development, attention must be paid to human development and the common prosperity of the people. To achieve these goals, it is necessary to continuously promote the development of family finance, enrich family financial behavior, enable more families to benefit from the financial product and service consumption, and comprehensively protect the rights and interests of financial consumers. It is necessary to meet the needs of high-quality development through a series of institutional designs and protection measures to promote the development of family finance.

In summary, developing family finance not only contributes to promoting economic and social development but also helps to build a harmonious ecological environment for financial, economic, and social development. Moreover, it optimizes the process and method of the operation and allocation of disposable funds within households in the context of expanding financial dividends and safeguarding the rights and interests of financial consumers. The full realization of the important role of family finance in the operation of the economic and social system is of special significance for the achievement of the goals of China's new era of economic and social development.

1.3 The Importance of Developing Household Finance in the Post-COVID-19 Era

In the post-COVID-19 era, the recovery and transformation of the economy and society depend on the revitalization and development of family finance, which urgently requires comprehensive and effective support from the financial industry. The COVID-19 pandemic is both a catalyst and a touchstone for the development of family finance. While it has created a crisis, it also presents an opportune moment for accelerating the development of family finance. The financial regulatory authorities in China should contemplate and practice potential strategies to turn the crisis into an opportunity. The significant meaning and functional role of developing family finance in the post-COVID-19 era can be summarized as follows.

Firstly, in the post-COVID-19 era, the importance of developing family finance has become even more prominent. To effectively cope with the impact of the COVID-19 pandemic on China's economic and social development and achieve high-quality development, it is necessary to have significant financial support and comprehensive financial tools. Developing family finance is a robust engine for China's economy and society to overcome the impact of the COVID-19 pandemic in the current and future periods.

Secondly, the outbreak of COVID-19 may have caused significant short-term financial impacts for many Chinese households, but in the longer term, it has created a window of opportunity for rapid recovery and development. In the short term, the pandemic has caused many businesses to shut down, resulting in reduced or no income for many households. However, as production and life gradually return to normal in the post-COVID-19 era, China's economy is expected to experience significant growth. From this perspective, household income is likely to increase, and the disposable income available for household investment and financial management will also increase, leading to rapid growth in family finance. In particular, as various industries recover and develop in the post-COVID-19 era, a significant amount of capital investment will be required, providing a wide range of investment opportunities for households.

Thirdly, the global outbreak of COVID-19 has had a profound impact on China's economic and social development, as well as posing significant challenges to the development of financial institutions. In particular, financial institutions are facing enormous operational challenges due to multi-pronged pressures such as the narrowing of net interest margins, increasing non-performing assets, and declining credit demand. From the perspective of China's current economic and social environment, on the one hand, the COVID-19 epidemic prevention and control measures have achieved significant decisive victories, and the resumption of work and production has steadily progressed. The operation of the social economy is orderly and has entered a new phase of transformation and upgrading. On the other hand, the COVID-19 epidemic is still in a scattered and sporadic state, and the epidemic prevention and control situation is still difficult. Social and economic development still faces considerable downward pressure. Under this background, "How to meet the needs of family finance? How to design financial products and services that better meet the needs of family development? How to fully protect the rights and interests of financial consumers?" have become significant issues that financial institutions need to pay attention to. Therefore, in the post-COVID-19 era, financial institutions must actively grasp policy positioning, seize new opportunities for family finance development, fully exploit digital means, give full play to their own advantages, and make contributions to family finance.

1.4 The Importance and Necessity of Conducting Research on Issues Related to Household Finance

Deepening the understanding of family financial issues, safeguarding the financial health of families, and achieving important goals such as maintaining financial stability, ensuring proper operation of financial institutions, and protecting the rights and interests of financial consumers play an important role in pushing these objectives. However, with the rapid development of China's financial market, the number of family financial transactions is increasing, financial instruments are becoming more complex, and the macro environment is facing many uncertainties. Therefore, conducting in-depth research on family finance in China has strong practical significance and theoretical value.

Firstly, it is necessary to deepen our understanding of family financial issues. Currently, the influence of financialization in society continues to expand. The over-reliance of families on financial sources of wealth and the overly simplistic structure of financial asset allocation has become prominent contradictions and issues in China's goal of achieving "common prosperity." This book uses quantitative research data to better understand how changes in the external environment of China's economic transformation and development have led to changes in family financial behavior and how these changes in micro-level family behavior are feedback to the macroeconomy.

Secondly, it is necessary to promote theoretical modeling research on family finance. China's household wealth growth has entered a new development cycle of structural differentiation. The increasing empirical findings and deeper understanding of family behavior motivation require more insightful models, especially those closely integrated with the reality of China, to better understand the internal mechanisms of family financial issues, thus providing the foundational tools for family financial research.

Thirdly, it is necessary to strengthen family financial health consciousness and improve the level of family financial well-being. Research on family financial issues is of particular significance for more accurately explaining and addressing the current situation and contradictions of household finances in China. It is not only conducive to a deeper understanding of the heterogeneity of family financial behavior during the period of economic transition and the gradual optimization of asset structure but also points the way towards the rationality of asset allocation in different life stages and the innovation of financial investment tools. In terms of practical application, it can help Chinese households to enhance their financial health awareness, improve their investment strategies, control investment risks, and increase their asset yields.

1.5 The Multi-perspective Mindset: Research on Household Finance Issues

1.5.1 Concerning Research on Technological Innovation and Consumer Rights in Household Financial Consumption

With the widespread and in-depth application of digital technologies in the financial industry, such as big data and artificial intelligence, the financial technology industry has emerged as an important driver of the all-round and deep integration of finance and technology, which can expand financial services accessibility, improve service efficiency, reduce transaction costs, and enhance the financial service experience. The digital technology empowerment of household financial behavior not only enables single technology empowerment but also deepens the communication and integration between households and the financial industry through technology, which leads to an increasing level of digitization in household financial behavior. In the digital age, the entire household financial industry is facing profound transformation and innovation, with strong technological support for household financial behavior consumption, allowing households to consume financial products and services in a more convenient, low-cost, and efficient (more profitable) way.

From the perspective of household financial subjects, whether it is a single-person household or a multiple-person household, financial behavior and decision-making are actually undertaken by individual financial consumers. Therefore, strengthening the protection of financial consumer rights is an important means to enhance household financial investment confidence, improve household financial risk management capabilities, and enable households to fully enjoy the dividends of financial development. In the context of financial technology development, the application of digital technology will provide solid technical support for establishing a sound mechanism for protecting financial consumer rights and comprehensively implementing the main responsibility of financial institutions to safeguard the rights and interests of financial consumers. It also provides new opportunities for establishing a financial consumer rights protection system that includes financial regulatory agencies, self-regulatory organizations, financial institutions, and financial consumers (Cheng and Yin 2020).

1.5.2 Development of Household Finance from Different Theoretical Perspectives

The asset allocation theory and the life cycle theory of savings (Markowitz 1952; Merton 1969) and expenditure in modern financial economics (Modigliani and Brumberg 1954; Friedman 1957) involve the study of family financial issues. These theories are built on the assumption of complete rationality, future time preference, and good self-control of individuals, suggesting that rational households can make reasonable asset allocation through diversified investment based on the risk-return matching principle. Rational households will smooth their expenditure over their entire life-cycle according to their total resource constraints, saving reasonably during their working years to cope with income decline in retirement. Therefore, in classical financial theory, rational households make reasonable asset allocation and savings and expenditure arrangements, and there are no abnormal issues.

However, with the continuous deepening of household finance surveys and empirical research, researchers have revealed many "anomalies" or "abnormal phenomena" that cannot be explained by classic family finance theories. For example, the limited participation of households in stock market investment (Heaton and Lucas 2000), severe lack of portfolio diversification (Polkovnichenko 2005), the mystery of consumption and income growth synchronism (Battistin et al. 2009), and overtrading (Barber and Odean 2001). Behavioral finance, which was developed based on the research of Tversky and Kahneman (1974) focuses on explaining such anomalies from factors such as cognitive biases, framing dependence, and emotions and has led to the development of the behavioral life cycle theory (Shefrin and Thaler 1988) and the behavioral asset allocation theory (Shefrin and Statman 2000). These theories focus on the cognitive and behavioral biases of humans in financial decision-making processes and how these biases affect the quality and efficiency of household financial decisions.

Compared with the investment theories that have developed under the Western liberal market, Chinese residents show more "social" characteristics in financial investment, influenced by factors such as family relationships, social environment, and psychological factors. Domestic scholars have conducted in-depth research and discussion on the fruitful results emerging from the study of Chinese family finance. For example, Li Xindan et al. systematically reviewed recent research on family investment and consumption decision-making from the perspective of behavioral finance (Li et al. 2011), and Wu Weixing et al. summarized the impact of investment opportunities, background risks, social security, and wealth effects from the perspective of asset allocation on household finance research (Wu et al. 2015). Wang Yu et al. analyzed the theoretical mechanisms of the relationship between social capital and household financial participation (Wang and Wang 2019). The exploration of these micro-internal factors provides important references for proposing better suggestions to optimize household finance and helping families to better optimize their wealth structure.

1.5.3 Research on the Factors Influencing Chinese Household Financial Behavior

Among the various factors influencing household financial investments, scholars both domestically and internationally have focused on investigating demographic and economic factors within families. As for demographic factors, most studies indicate that higher levels of education and marriage have a significant positive impact on household financial investment behavior (Wang and Wu 2014; Liao 2017; Luo and Liang 2020).

In terms of economic factors within families, some foreign scholars have found that family wealth has a positive effect on their participation in financial investments (Liu 2015); Chinese scholars, such as Weixing Wu, have also discovered that both wealth and income have a significant positive impact and that increased family wealth significantly increases the likelihood of participating in risky assets and the depth of such participation. In addition to income and wealth, housing is also an important economic feature of families (Wu et al. 2011). Research has found a significant "crowding-out effect" of household property investment on the proportion of risky financial asset investment (He and He 2018; Gao et al. 2020), which means that, under the circumstance of a certain level of household assets, if real estate is invested, the proportion of investment in risky financial assets will decrease. However, there are also studies that have come to the opposite conclusion. Scholars have found that real estate investment does not exhibit a "crowding-out effect" on the investment of risk assets in urban households in China; instead, there is a complementary rather than substitutionary relationship between real estate and household financial asset investment. This means that real estate has a positive impact on holding risk assets and that resident households may use housing ownership to achieve a diversified investment portfolio, thereby increasing their holdings of risky financial assets.

The theory of household risk management focuses on how families manage risk to protect their wealth. Specifically, under the perspective of asset allocation, research on household finance has incorporated the concept of background risk, which includes the health status of household members. It has been suggested that the existence of background risk, as it cannot be effectively diversified through investment portfolios, will reduce the holding of risky assets. In particular, household investment decisions can be influenced by asset allocation, disposable resources, and risk attitudes. For example, Smith believes that health status and the resources individuals can dispose of are positively correlated, and therefore poor health may mean insufficient disposable wealth, leading to lower investment in financial products (Smith and Love 2010). Goldman and Maestas also point out in their research that individuals with poor health are more likely to increase future medical expenses, which will decrease the asset risk brought by financial investment (Goldman and Maestas 2013). Edwards has particularly confirmed the relationship between health status and risk attitudes, pointing out that uncertain health risks will encourage investors to be more risk-averse and influence household investment behavior (Edwards 2010). In contrast to the traditional economic understanding of health, Grossman proposed a human capital model of health demand, which sees health for the first time as "health capital" that is distinct from other forms of human capital. Health determines the time one can spend on market and non-market activities and the possible returns. The health capital inherited by genetics will depreciate with age. To offset this depreciation, people will increase health investments through medical expenditures, among other ways. Given that people can rationally predict their life expectancy, the healthier an individual is, the higher the likelihood of engaging in household investment behavior (Grossman 1972). In addition, health capital not only exists at the individual level, but changes in family health can also have significant effects on the economic and psychological status of household members, thereby influencing household investment decisions.

1.5.4 Research on Financial Literacy and Household Financial Health

Financial literacy has become an essential aspect of household financial research. Researchers have found that the level of financial literacy in a household is closely related to the household's financial decisions, savings, and investment behavior. Therefore, improving household financial literacy has become one of the key policy objectives of many national governments. Financial literacy is an essential indicator of individual ability, and compared with education and previous work experience, financial literacy reflects people's ability to understand financial knowledge and use it to allocate resources effectively for financial security (Wang and Yang 2014; Yin et al. 2015). Improving financial literacy can help reduce the likelihood of individual or household financial exclusion, which can then affect household investment behavior. Correll believes that financial knowledge increasingly affects people's lives, and the level of financial knowledge is an essential factor in whether residents can be included in the financial system (Corr 2006). Zeng et al. found that households with higher levels of financial knowledge are more likely to participate in financial markets and invest in a wider range of financial assets (Zeng et al. 2015). The level of financial literacy affects household participation in financial markets and the allocation ratio of risky assets and can also affect entrepreneurial behavior through its impact on credit financing (Hastings and Tejeda-Ashton 2008; Lü and Wu 2017).

Existing research shows that improving financial literacy can effectively improve a household's preferences for loan channels, improve their formal credit demand, and increase the availability of formal credit (Su and Kong 2019; Jia et al. 2021), thereby improving household financial health.

With the development of behavioral finance research, the concept of financial health has emerged. The Financial Health Network of the United States introduced this concept in 2015 as a measure of whether financial consumers are in good financial or financial condition. They suggested that financial health should include subjective and objective variables and four aspects of content, including consumption, saving, borrowing, and planning. Newcomb believes that consumers should enhance their ability to think long-term in order to improve their financial satisfaction and achieve a high level of financial health (Newcomb 2018). In 2019, the China Inclusive Finance Research Institute first proposed the concept of financial health in its development report, stating that financial health is a higher-level pursuit of inclusive finance. The report suggests that financial health should be measured based on household asset stability (balance of income and expenses), household liquidity (savings/assets), rational planning and use of credit (debt level), use and planning of insurance (protection level), household satisfaction with the current financial situation, and confidence in future finances (personal capacity).

In recent years, micro household databases have gradually been established and improved both domestically and internationally. For example, the Southwest University of Finance and Economics and the Financial Research Institute of the People's Bank of China have conducted a national survey on household finance in China. Related reports reflect the main problems in China's household finance, such as high household savings levels, financial assets concentrated in cash, demand deposits, and time deposits, a high proportion of housing loans among household debts, and a low participation rate in consumer credit. Attention to these issues has further promoted empirical exploration of household financial health issues in China.

Based on the existing literature, research on the factors influencing financial health can be roughly classified into three categories: individual factors based on head-of-household characteristics, such as gender, marital status, educational level, health status, financial literacy, and risk attitude (Cocco 2005; Liu and Sun 2021; Chen and Li 2011);household factors focused on demographic structure, family wealth, income and expenditure, and their impacts on household financial health (Fan and Wang 2015); and macro-environmental factors including urban–rural differences, natural disasters, and the COVID-19 pandemic, and their mechanisms and pathways affecting household financial health (Zhang 2020). These studies provide an important research foundation for the further development of household financial health.

1.5.5 Regarding Risk Attitudes, Investment Behavior, and Entrepreneurial Activity

Traditional investment theory holds that risk attitudes are determinant factors in individual investment behavior. For example, Paiella and Gusio found a significant negative correlation between households' risk aversion and investment in risky assets and that risk-averse households invest less in risky assets than risk-seeking households (Paiella and Guiso 2004). Risk aversion theory, in particular, suggests that individuals who tend to be risk-seeking are willing to switch careers at lower critical wage levels, making them more likely to become entrepreneurs, while risk-averse individuals tend to prefer stable income under an employment relationship. Thus, entrepreneurs' distinct risk preferences and achievement desires are the main reasons why they engage in entrepreneurship. Under the same market wage level, differences in individuals' attitudes toward risk have led to differences in career choices.

In the 1940s, Knight's research showed a positive relationship between risk attitude and entrepreneurship; individuals with a high-risk preference tend to be more active in entrepreneurship (Knight 1942). Kirzner and Lafontaine proposed the risk aversion theory of entrepreneurship, suggesting that risk-averse individuals prefer wage employment to entrepreneurship because of their lower economic return expectations (Kihlstrom and Laffont 1979). However, the opposition argues that the individual psychological level of risk attitude tends to be unstable and does not substantially affect entrepreneurial activities. There is no significant difference in risk attitude between entrepreneurs and non-entrepreneurs; the former is simply more optimistic about risk and more likely to make seemingly risky decisions (Caliendo et al. 2009). In the context of Chinese society, researchers have only recently begun to focus on the relationship between risk attitude and entrepreneurship. Due to differences in target groups and social conditions, the conclusions of the aforementioned Western countries' research need further verification. Lv et al. analyzed the relationship between individual risk attitudes and family entrepreneurship in the Chinese social context and found that despite the slight differences in the impact of individual risk attitudes on entrepreneurship in different strong/weak social relation structures, they generally have a positive impact on entrepreneurship, and individuals who prefer risk are more likely to become entrepreneurs (Lü et al. 2018). However, Chen's study of "returning home to start a business" migrant workers found that risk-averse farmers have lower investment return expectations, smaller scale, and lower difficulty of returning home for entrepreneurship and perform more returning home entrepreneurship behavior than risk-takers (Chen 2009). Other researchers have defined the concepts of risk preference and risk tendency based on "personal traits" and "behavior trends," respectively, and found that risk preference as a stable personal trait does not have a significant effect on entrepreneurship, while high-risk tendency in behavioral decision-making can significantly increase individuals' likelihood of participating in entrepreneurship, and risk perception plays a bridging role in this process (Ma et al. 2010). Previous research has provided a lot of empirical evidence for the study of risk attitudes; although the differences in results for different groups have been large, the basic significance of the impact of risk attitudes on entrepreneurship has been recognized.

In summary, current research on Chinese household finance is focused on urban or rural households' asset allocation, wealth inequality, financial fragility, and related topics, which have promoted the development of micro-level household finance. However, these studies often rely excessively on numerical techniques for solving and deriving theoretical models within the inherent economic theory framework. Additionally, they tend to overlook social and cultural analyses of the individual heterogeneity that exists within macro structures and provide limited research on new concepts such as household financial health. Consequently, this book expands upon existing research to explore and apply household finance related issues. Doing so will promote the development of household finance theory, help individuals resist inflationary risk, achieve household planning objectives, and realize asset preservation and moderate growth, thereby continuing to progress toward comprehensive prosperity and common wealth.

References

Barber BM, Odean T (2001) The internet and the investor. J Econ Perspect 15(1):41–54

Battistin E, Blundell R, Lewbel A (2009) Why is consumption more log normal than income? Gibrat's law revisited. J Polit Econ 117(6):1140–1154

Caliendo M, Fossen FM, Kritikos AS (2009) Risk attitudes of nascent entrepreneurs—new evidence from an experimentally validated survey. Small Bus Econ 32(2):153–167

Campbell JY (2006) Household finance. J Financ 61(4):1553–1604

Chen BK, Li T (2011) Urban household's assets and liabilities in China: facts and causes. Econ Res J 46:55–66+79

Chen B (2009) An empirical study on the impact of risk attitude on returning home entrepreneurial behavior. Management World 3:84–91

Cheng XJ, Yin ZT (2020) Exploration of internet consumer finance innovation development and regulation. Finance Account Monthly 3:147–153

Cocco JF (2005) Portfolio choice in the presence of housing. Rev Finan Stud 18(2):535–567

Corr C (2006) Financial exclusion in Ireland: an exploratory study and policy review. Combat Poverty Agency, Research Series, Dublin

Dow J, Werlang SRC (1992) Excess volatility of stock prices and Knightian Uncertainty. Eur Econ Rev 36:631–638

Edwards RD (2010) Optimal portfolio choice when utility depends on health. Int J Econ Theory 6(2):205–225

Fan GZ, Wang HY (2015) Household demographic structure and household demand for life insurance: empirical research based on the data of China household finance survey. J Finan Res 421:170–189

Friedman M (1957) A theory of the consumption function. Princeton University Press, Princeton

Gan L, Yin Z, Jia N et al (2013) Analysis of household assets and housing demand in China. Financial Res 4:1–14

Gao Y, Zhang Y, Song Q (2020) The crowding out effect of housing assets on family risk asset investment. Econ Manage Rev 36(04):106–121

Goldman D, Maestas N (2013) Medical expenditure risk and household portfolio choice. J Appl Economet 28(4):527–550

Grossman M (1972) The demand for health: a theoretical and empirical investigation. NBER working paper, No. 119
Hastings JS, Tejeda-Ashton L (2008) Financial literacy, information, and demand elasticity: survey and experimental evidence from Mexico. National Bureau of Economic Research
He Y, He X (2018) Health and the level of participation in family risk financial asset investment. J South China Normal Univ 2:135–142
He X, Xia F (2012) China's institutional transformation and urban household wealth distribution gap. Econ Res 2:28–40
Heaton J, Lucas D (2000) Portfolio choice and asset prices: the importance of entrepreneurial risk. J Financ 55(3):1163–1198
Jia L, Tan W, Abulmuni. (2021). Financial literacy, family wealth, and family entrepreneurial decisions. Southwest Finance 1:83–96
Kihlstrom RE, Laffont JJ (1979) A general equilibrium entrepreneurial theory of firm formation based on risk aversion. J Polit Econ 87(4):719–748
Knight FH (1942) Profit and entrepreneurial functions. J Econ History 2(S1):126–132
Li XD, Xiao BQ, Yu HH, Song JH (2011) Survey of household finance. J Manage Sci 14(4): 74–85
Liao J (2017) Marital status and residents' financial investment preferences. Southern Finance 11:23–32
Liu P, Sun LJ (2021) Financial literacy and family financial health research—based on the 2017 China household finance survey. Res World 10:16–25
Liu J (2015) Heterogeneity of urban Chinese households and investment in risk financial assets. Econ Issues 3:51–55+60
Lü J, Guo P, Cheng J (2018) The influence of social relation and heterogeneity of risk preference on family entrepreneurship activity. Res Finan Dev 10:22–28
Lü XL, Wu WX (2017) The impact of financial exclusion on family investment portfolios: an analysis based on Chinese data. Shanghai Finance 6:34–41
Luo W, Liang J (2020) Financial literacy and family risk asset investment decision—an empirical study based on CHFS 2017 data. J Finan Theory Pract 11:45–56
Ma K, Qin RF, Hu P (2010) The relationship of risk propensity and entrepreneurial decision: the mediating role of risk perception. Forecasting, 29(1):42–48
Markowitz H (1952) Portfolio selection. J Finance 7(1):77–91
Merton RC (1969) Lifetime portfolio selection under uncertainty: the continuous-time case. Rev Econ Stat 51:247–257
Modigliani EF, Brumberg R (1954) Utility Analysis and the consumption function: an interpretation of cross-section data. In: Post Keynesian economics. Rutgers University Press, New Brunswick
Newcomb S (2018) When more is less: rethinking financial health. J Family Consum Sci 110(2):7–13
Paiella M, Guiso L (2004) The role of risk aversion in predicting individual behaviour. CEPR Discuss Papers No. 4591
Polkovnichenko V (2005) Household portfolio diversification: a case for rank-dependent preferences. Rev Finan Stud 18(4):1467–1502
Shefrin H, Statman M (2000) Behavioral portfolio theory. J Finan Quant Anal 35(2):127–151
Shefrin HM, Thaler RH (1988) The behavioral life-cycle hypothesis. Econ Inq 26(4):609–643
Smith PA, Love DA (2010) Does health affect portfolio choice. Health Electr 19(12):1441–1460
Su LL, Kong R (2019) The interaction mechanisms between farmers' financial literacy and the development of rural factors market. China Rural Observ 2:61–77
Tversky A, Kahneman D (1974) Judgment under uncertainty: heuristics and biases: biases in judgments reveal some heuristics of thinking under uncertainty. Science 185(4157):1124–1131
Wang Y, Wang SQ (2019) A literature review on the mechanism of social capital affecting family financial behavior. Res Finan Dev 12:47–52
Wang YX, Yang SH (2014) New progress in theoretical study of financial literacy. Shanghai Finance 3:26–33+116.

Wang J, Wu W (2014) The impact of marriage on family risk asset selection. Nankai Econ Res 3:100–112

Wu W, Rong P, Xu Q (2011) Health and family asset selection. Econ Res J 46(S1):43–54

Wu WX, Wang ZZ, Wu K (2015) Household finance: a literature review based on the asset allocation. Sci Decis 4:69–94

Yin ZC, Song QY, Wu Y, Peng CY (2015) Financial knowledge, entrepreneurial decision and motivation. Management World 1:87–98

Zeng Z, He Q, Wu Y, Yin Z (2015) Financial knowledge and diversity of family investment portfolio. The Economist 6:88–96

Zhang H (2020) The institutional difficulties and countermeasures of financial health of inclusive finance people—a case study of productive farmers. Rural Finance Res 12:46–51

Chapter 2
Household Finance in the Digital Technology Era

As digital technologies continue to permeate the financial sector, the FinTech industry has entered a phase of rapid evolution. Presently, these technologies serve as a pivotal catalyst, broadening the reach of financial services, optimizing their efficiency, diminishing transaction costs, elevating the overall user experience, and fostering innovation in financial products and services. However, alongside these advantages, the application of digital technologies also introduces a spectrum of new risks and challenges (Zhao et al. 2023).

2.1 Environmental Analysis of Household Finance in China in the Digital Technology Era

Household financial behaviors play a pivotal role in both the economic cycle and the broader financial system. Encouraging household financial investment stands as a strategic imperative, continuously fueling the potential for domestic consumption demand. Simultaneously, safeguarding the financial well-being of households forms a foundational element in ensuring the robust development of the economy and finance.

Household financial behaviors are integral to both the economic cycle and the broader financial system. The promotion of household financial investment remains a crucial strategy, continually stimulating domestic consumption demand. Concurrently, ensuring the financial well-being of households stands as a foundational aspect in nurturing the robust development of the economy and finance. In 2021, loose monetary policies implemented by numerous countries globally spurred a sustained surge in global financial assets. According to pertinent data, Chinese households amassed total financial assets of 3.2 trillion euros in 2021, marking a significant milestone by surpassing 50% of the entire financial assets within the Asian region for the first time. Notably, the global share of these assets surged from 7.2% in 2011 to 13.6% in

S. Zhao and D. Zhao, *The Household Finance Issues in China*,
https://doi.org/10.1007/978-981-97-0706-5_2

2021. Moreover, China's per capita net financial assets soared to 1.54 million euros, significantly surpassing the average level across the Asian region (Allianz 2022).

Despite the substantial impact of the COVID-19 pandemic on China's social production and residents' lives, the total household financial assets in the country have sustained steady growth, showcasing remarkable resilience. This resilience primarily stems from China's longstanding policies aimed at enriching its populace, alongside consistent growth in household income and the ongoing optimization of income structures.

As efforts to control the COVID-19 pandemic move toward precision and standardization, there's an anticipated continuation of steady growth in China's household financial assets and per capita net financial assets in the foreseeable future.

Several key factors contribute to the robust and sustainable development of household finance in China within the current economic and social landscape. Firstly, on an economic scale, the continuous expansion of China's overall economy and resident wealth has increased the resources available for households to invest in financial assets. Secondly, within the societal context, the healthy evolution of China's investment and wealth management market, augmented household investment awareness, and growing wealth of household investment experience serve as pivotal drivers for household finance development. Thirdly, within the policy framework, China has consistently introduced laws and regulations, ensuring institutional support for the stable and standardized functioning of financial markets. This has bolstered public confidence in investment and wealth management markets. Lastly, within the technological realm, the rapid advancement of digital technologies not only offers diverse financial investment channels for households but also furnishes sophisticated technical support. This support aids households in understanding their risk profiles, mitigating financial investment risks, and enhancing their financial investment acumen.

2.1.1 *Economic Climate: Steady Economic Growth and the Sustained Rise in Residents' Disposable Income Have Laid a Solid Material Foundation for Household Financial Behaviors*

In recent years, China's economy has seen steady growth, accompanied by the continuous consolidation of the social wealth foundation. This economic upturn has enabled households to allocate more funds toward investments, thereby establishing a robust base for household financial activities.

Since 2015, both China's GDP and resident deposits have exhibited consistent growth. Even amidst the challenging circumstances of the COVID-19 pandemic in 2020, China's economy displayed remarkable resilience. Notably, the GDP surged to 101.36 trillion yuan, marking a 2.3% increase from 2019. China stood out as the sole major global economy to achieve positive economic growth during that period. Building upon this momentum, China's economy continued its steadfast expansion in 2022, reaching a GDP of 121.02 trillion yuan alongside resident deposits totaling 120 trillion yuan. Noteworthy is the fact that the 2022 resident deposits were approximately 2.17 times higher than those in 2015, boasting an average annual growth rate slightly surpassing the GDP growth rate. The concurrent rise in GDP and resident deposits signifies a tangible increase in total social wealth and disposable income among residents, undoubtedly shaping the trajectory of household finance (Zhao 2021).

2.1.2 *Social Context: Characterized by the Robust Growth of the Financial Market and the Continuous Enhancement of Household Investment Skills, Plays a Pivotal Role in Fostering the Development of Household Finance*

The steady and methodical growth within the investment and wealth management market has cultivated a favorable social milieu and market atmosphere conducive to the development of household finance in China.

Firstly, the advancement of China's financial sector, notably the ascent of FinTech, has empowered numerous technology firms to capitalize on their technological prowess and distribution channels, thereby expanding the array of financial services. This proliferation has enriched the financial landscape in China, offering its citizens a diverse spectrum of financial products to engage with.

Secondly, the social fabric surrounding investment and wealth management in China undergoes continual enhancement. As individuals gain more exposure to investment practices, the investment acumen among Chinese residents sees a concurrent rise, fostering an increasingly informed populace regarding investment opportunities (Zhang 2020). Chinese residents' tolerance for losses in investment and wealth management has increased, fostering the investment and wealth management philosophy of "careful investment and self-risk management". The investment and wealth management landscape among Chinese residents have witnessed a notable shift, marked by an increased tolerance for investment losses, fostering a philosophy emphasizing "careful investment and self-risk management." This transformation is evident in their consumption patterns, as residents gravitate towards a more prudent approach. Rather than blindly pursuing high returns, they now seek tailored investment and wealth management products aligned with their individual financial capacities and risk tolerance.

Thirdly, A key driving force behind this change lies in the accumulation of rich experience among Chinese residents in investment and wealth management. Especially in the digital era, numerous channels have emerged, facilitating the acquisition and dissemination of knowledge and experiences in this domain. This collective knowledge-sharing fosters a continuous enhancement of households' investment and wealth management capabilities.

Fourth, the concerted efforts of financial regulators, institutions, and research bodies deserve acknowledgment. Their consistent tracking, investigations, and research into the financial behaviors of Chinese residents provide a theoretical foundation. This support aims to further the healthy and sustainable development of the financial market in China, fostering a positive and mutually beneficial relationship between residents and the financial market.

2.1.3 Policy Environment: The Chinese Government Has Issued a Series of Relevant Policies, and Household Financial Behaviors Are Becoming More Standardized

In recent years, the Chinese government has implemented numerous policies to further regulate the investment and wealth management market. The policy framework has been continuously refined, providing institutional safeguards to guide the development of the investment and wealth management sector and incentivize household investments.

Despite meeting households' investment and wealth management needs due to the rapid growth of China's asset management sector, it is crucial not to overlook issues such as irregular development, multi-layer nesting, rigid payment structures, evasion of financial supervision, and macro-control avoidance in asset management businesses. In April 2018, the PBOC, CBIRC, CSRC and SAFE jointly issued *Guiding Opinions on Regulating the Asset Management Business of Financial Institutions*, focusing on regulating the asset management business of financial institutions, unifying the supervision standards of similar asset management products, effectively preventing and controlling financial risks. Subsequently, Chinese financial regulators have successively issued institutional regulations, such as *Administrative Measures for the Supervision and Management of Financial Business of Commercial Banks*, *Administrative Measures for the Management of Financial Subsidiaries of Commercial Banks*, *Interim Measures for the Management of Financial Product Sales of Financial Companies*, *Notice on Regulating the Management of Cash Management Financial Products*, and *Administrative Measures for the Liquidity Risk Management of Financial Products of Financial Companies*, which provide institutional guarantees for promoting the healthy and stable development of the investment and wealth management market.

Furthermore, the financial regulatory authority has implemented a range of regulatory measures. These measures serve to enhance investors' understanding of investment and wealth management products, enabling them to make informed decisions based on their individual circumstances. Additionally, they encourage financial institutions to adhere to standardized practices, safeguarding investors' rights and interests while refining the regulatory framework governing investment and wealth management product sales and operations in order to ensure compliance.

2.1.4 Technological Environment: The Rise of Digital Technologies Has Provided Robust Technical Support for the Advancement of Household Finance

Digital technologies are deeply integrated within the household finance industry, providing robust technical support for household financial behaviors and enabling households to conveniently consume financial products and services at lower costs, with increased efficiency and profitability. Currently, the application of digital technologies is continuously enhancing the relationship between households and the financial industry, leading to a growing prevalence of digitized financial behaviors.

In the era of digitalization, profound changes are anticipated in the entire household finance industry encompassing technological advancements and innovative scenario construction. Particularly during the COVID-19 pandemic, significant transformations have occurred in both social production and family lifestyles. The rise of contactless living styles has increasingly relied on internet-based solutions, further amplifying the demand for financial digitalization. The online model exemplified by the online economy and contactless economy has gained widespread acceptance in the financial industry, emphasizing the value of online channels. Household finance will leverage these online channels to continually enhance its level of digitalization while achieving breakthroughs in business models and product innovation.

2.2 The Advancement of Digital Technologies Brings New Opportunities to Household Finance

With the integration of digital technologies and the household finance industry, financial services are becoming increasingly diverse, and a variety of innovative financial business models are emerging. This not only enhances the accessibility of financial services, reduces financial transaction costs, improves financial transaction efficiency, and enhances the financial service experience, but also provides technical support for households to enjoy the benefits brought by the development of finance industry (Lu and Yao 2015).

On the one hand, the widespread use of digital technologies in the finance industry has enabled household financial behaviors to break through geographical restrictions. Households no longer need to visit physical branches and can now complete financial transactions through contactless and online business models. On the other hand, household financial behaviors can also break through time constraints, allowing households to rely on the internet for 7*24 access to financial products and services (Zhao 2018).

2.2.1 The Utilization of Digital Technologies Can Help Financial Institutions Reduce Operational Costs, Allowing Them to Allocate More Resources Towards Enhancing the Financial Services Experience for Households

In the digital technology era, financial institutions are vigorously expanding their online channels to provide financial services, significantly reducing costs associated with physical branch construction, operation, and daily maintenance. Additionally, by leveraging the advantages of online channels, financial institutions do not need to employ a large number of staff, saving substantial expenses such as personnel salaries, social security, and training fee. Financial institutions can utilize savings all above to invest in technologies research and development, enhancing data analysis and risk control capabilities, improving internal management and operational processes, thereby enhancing the overall financial services experience.

2.2.2 Digital Technologies Help Financial Institutions Expand Service Scope and Increase the Accessibility of Financial Services

The prominent advantage brought by digital technologies to the finance industry lies in channels (such as e-commerce platforms, social apps, media apps, etc.), the diversified, convenient, and low-cost channels can help households quickly obtain financial support. In addition, the application of digital technologies enables financial institutions to serve more vulnerable households with inclusive loans.

2.2.3 Digital Technologies Help Financial Institutions Improve Service Efficiency and Quickly Respond to Financial Needs

On one hand, digital technologies facilitate online processing of financial transactions, enabling households to swiftly conduct financial operations through PC or mobile applications, thereby saving time and reducing the need for physical presence at traditional bank branches. On the other hand, digital technology has significantly enhanced the efficiency of financial institutions in handling financial activities. Particularly in terms of lending operations, when a household applies for a loan, financial institutions can promptly ascertain the available loan amount within 5 s and disburse it within 30 min, effectively catering to temporary and urgent financial requirements.

2.2.4 Digital Technologies Help Financial Institutions Create New Scenarios and Effectively Help Households to Overcome Liquidity Constraints

The financial needs of households have become increasingly diverse, and there is a gradual shift from offline to online consumption scenarios. Currently, digital technologies can harness the trend of contextualization to connect household financial requirements with available financial resources through e-commerce platforms, social apps, media apps, and other channels, thereby offering real-time financial services to households. Simultaneously, digitally-based financial services can permeate work, social interaction, shopping, and learning contexts by attentively addressing household financial needs in real-time and providing timely and adaptable financial support.

2.2.5 Digital Technologies Make Financial Business Models More Flexible and Provide Diverse Financial Services to Households

Households can conveniently apply for loans online, eliminating the need for paper documentation. Financial institutions have the capability to offer unsecured credit loans without requiring collateral or guarantees from households. Leveraging big data analysis technology, financial institutions can conduct comprehensive assessments of household creditworthiness, risk profile, and actual borrowing needs. This enables them to provide suitable loan amounts promptly, simplifying and expediting the loan application process for households. Furthermore, digital technologies allow financial institutions to offer interest-bearing loan products that cater to daily cash flow management and unforeseen financial emergencies.

2.2.6 Digital Technologies Can Help Households Improve Financial Literacy and Further Enhance Risk Management Skill by Self-Profiling

On one hand, households can access financial knowledge anytime and anywhere through diverse scenarios, share investment experiences via forums, blogs, and official websites, obtain information on fraud cases through anti-fraud apps, and promptly learn lessons to safeguard their financial rights. On the other hand, households can utilize big data technology to assess their own risk tolerance and select suitable financial services based on disparities in education level, work experience, income level, investment experience, debt situation, and risk tolerance. For households with high risk tolerance levels along with stable income sources, good credit history and extensive financial expertise; they may opt for high-risk/high-yield investment products or increase loan amounts as per their financial needs while enjoying relatively low interest rates due to their favorable credit records. Conversely for households with low risk tolerance levels or unstable/inadequate income sources coupled with frequent credit defaults and limited financial experience; it is advisable for them to choose stable investment options while prudently avoiding high-risk investments. They should borrow moderately according to household requirements.

Additionally, households can monitor real-time changes in their own risk tolerance levels, income status, debt situations, credit conditions etc., using digital technologies. They are able to profile themselves at any given time using big data analysis technology enabling them to adjust their investment strategies continuously thereby enhancing their skills in managing risks (Wu 2014).

2.3 The Application of Digital Technologies in the Finance Industry Poses Risks to Household Finance

The proliferation and implementation of digital technologies in the finance industry have not altered the fundamental nature of intertemporal transactions and credit exchanges. Consequently, the risks inherent in the finance industry manifest themselves within the realm of FinTech, giving rise to novel risk characteristics. As previously mentioned, while digital technologies provide significant impetus for the advancement of the finance industry, they also engender a series of new risks (Sun et al. 2020). Similarly, household finance inevitably necessitates addressing the risks and challenges posed by digital technologies.

2.3.1 Digital Technologies Amplify the Impact of Financial Risks, Thereby Exacerbating Household Vulnerabilities

On the one hand, BigTechs and FinTechs have begun to provide financial services, financial service providers are becoming more diversified, and multiple entities and businesses are interconnected, making financial risks more complex and covert. Especially the application of digital technologies in the finance industry makes financial products and services more complex, far beyond the scope of household financial knowledge, posing obstacles for households to choose financial products. On the other hand, financial institutions rely on digital technologies to provide 7*24 financial services, which has invisibly amplified the impact of financial risks. Especially, financial risks are more likely to trigger social risks, causing adverse effects on a larger scale and exposing household financial security to greater risks.

2.3.2 The Illegal and Irregular Operation of Some FinTechs is the Main Factor Threatening Household Financial Security

Although the application of digital technologies will bring new risks to the finance industry and pose more threats to household financial security, it should be clearly recognized that digital technologies are neutral. Currently, the main threat to household finance is still caused by the illegal and irregular operation of FinTechs. Especially when the COVID-19 has led to a slowdown in economic growth, insufficient financial supervision, and a lack of risk awareness of financial consumers, the illegal and irregular operation of FinTechs will pose a serious threat to household financial behaviors, which will not only lead to the loss of household financial assets, but also affect the safety of other household assets. In this situation, the focus of future financial supervision should be on rectifying and cracking down on illegal and irregular business activities of FinTechs, creating a healthy, standardized and competitive market environment for FinTechs that operate in accordance with the law.

2.3.3 Technical and Data Risks May Affect Household Financial Experience

Financial institutions meet the needs of households through internet channels, relying on digital technologies to offer fast and cost-effective financial services. The Internet, along with a reliable trading platform system architecture and mobile applications, serves as essential infrastructure for financial institutions to deliver financial services. However, technical selection errors, outdated technology, hacker attacks, and incompatibility between platform systems and hardware can lead to significant resource wastage and efficiency losses for these institutions. In extreme cases, such technical errors may even impact the normal repayment behavior of households and have adverse effects on their creditworthiness. Particularly concerning artificial intelligence (AI) technology which is still in its nascent stage of development; its relevance-based algorithms can result in unpredictable decisions lacking logical reasoning. If an AI algorithm is hacked into, it not only affects the financial experience of households but also poses a substantial threat to the security of their financial assets. Currently, big data analysis plays a crucial role as a reference point for both financial institutions and household financial decision-making processes. However, erroneous or flawed data can have immeasurable negative impacts on both parties involved. Moreover, even if the data used is accurate and reliable, big data analysis alone may not provide appropriate recommendations or suggestions for making sound financial decisions by households.

Over-reliance on big data analysis technology could potentially lead to errors in financial decision-making that result in losses of household financial assets. Particularly when big data analysis technology is extensively employed by financial institutions and households, the convergence of data, algorithms, and operational mechanisms inherent in this technology tends to lead to nearly identical financial decisions, thereby potentially impacting the normal financial returns for households. Furthermore, there may exist risks associated with data storage, transmission, and utilization processes. The operational errors committed by financial institutions and their personnel pose a significant threat to the security of household data.

2.3.4 Household Financial Rights Protection Faces Severe Challenges

The widespread application of digital technologies in the finance industry has enabled more households to enjoy the benefits of financial development, but it has also brought about problems such as information leakage and excessive debt. The protection of household financial rights is facing severe challenges. Firstly, online and mobile payments provide the possibility for criminals to steal information and data from households. Through various apps, e-commerce platforms, and payment platforms, not only can the identity information households be collected, but also the consumption habits, payment preferences, social network and other behavioral data of households can be gathered. Once technical defects or employee dereliction occur, the privacy of households will face significant risks of leakage. Secondly, the behaviors of excessive collection of information about households still exists. Thirdly, digital technologies have lowered the threshold for financial services. Low income or non-income households can also apply for loans. Due to the lack of income or unstable income, these households may face difficulties in repaying their debts, thus burdening them with heavy debts. Especially during risk outbreaks, these households have poor risk resistance and are more susceptible to risk shocks.

2.3.5 Insufficient Preventive Intervention Measures May Lead to Irreversible Losses of Household Financial Assets

Due to limited regulatory resources and inadequate supervision measures, financial risk management still primarily focuses on post-event management, resulting in a relatively weak ability to provide early warning and prevention. The integration of digital technologies with the finance industry has significantly accelerated the pace of financial innovation, thereby causing financial supervision to lag behind. Owing to the absence of effective pre-event and mid-event management methods, financial regulators can only take action after an outbreak occurs. However, this approach fails to eliminate economic losses and adverse effects experienced by households, potentially leading to irreversible damage to household financial assets.

2.3.6 The Monopolistic Risk Brought About by Digital Technologies May Infringe upon Household Financial Rights

The application of digital technologies in the finance industry undoubtedly benefits greatly in improving the efficiency of financial services, but it is also difficult to avoid some BigTechs and FinTechs transforming their technological advantages into monopoly advantages, leading to the misuse of household information, exaggerating the returns of financial products while weakening risks, inducing households to consume financial products that do not match their risk tolerance, inducing households to excessively apply for loans, obstructing fair competition through monopolistic data, by leveraging the advantages of channel monopolies, aim to enhance the stickiness of households, thereby influencing their choices in channels, products and services.

2.4 The Trends and Prospects of Utilizing Digital Technologies to Promote the Development of Household Finance

On one hand, in the era of digital technology, financial institutions can further integrate advanced technologies into their business and operational management systems, effectively leveraging the transformative potential of digital technology to drive the advancement of household finance. On the other hand, financial regulators should also prioritize the adoption of digital technologies in the domain of financial supervision, fostering a harmonious and stable environment for the development of household finance.

2.4.1 Financial Institutions Can Deeply Cultivate Internet Channels and Further Enhance Household Financial Services Experience

The COVID-19 pandemic has significantly impacted the offline operations of financial institutions. On February 14, 2020, the China Banking and Insurance Regulatory Commission (CBIRC) issued a *Notice on Further Improving Financial Services for Epidemic Prevention and Control*, mandating financial institutions to prioritize technological applications, innovate financial services, enhance the efficiency of online financial services, actively promote digital business models, optimize contactless service provisions, and offer secure and convenient "At Home" financial services. Under policy guidance, financial institutions can fully leverage digital technologies' advantages in providing online financial products and enhancing their service capabilities while cultivating internet channels. They should also introduce diverse online financial services that cater to various household needs by offering contactless solutions (CBIRC 2020).

2.4.2 Financial Institutions Can Provide One-Stop Financial Services to Households on a Cloud Platform

Financial institutions can use digital technologies to integrate resources and build a comprehensive household financial service platform that includes financial education, investment and wealth management, lending, income and expenditure management, credit evaluation, insurance, and many other financial services. In business practice, financial institutions can use digital technologies to launch personalized financial products and financial education plans, providing households with one-stop financial services. In addition, financial institutions can leverage their channel advantages to create a one-stop platform which includes daily services, social networking, e-commerce, catering, entertainment, travel, and tourism, organically connecting the production and living needs of households with the supply of funds.

2.4.3 Financial Institutions Can Use Big Data Technology to Profile Households and Manage the Entire Process of Household Financial Services

Financial institutions can establish an anti-fraud system based on big data technology, and use internet and apps to send relevant information to households at any time, effectively improving the efficiency and accuracy of risk management. Financial institutions can use big data technology to profile households, evaluate household risk levels based on factors such as income, debt situation, risk tolerance, investment and financial management level, credit level, etc., and use this as the basis for promoting financial products to them. At the same time, the profile results can also be used as the basis for whether to lend and determine the lending amount. Financial institutions can also leverage big data risk control technology to further improve the proactivity, timeliness, and accuracy of risk management. They can conduct post event monitoring and risk warning on households' investment and lending businesses. When households purchase financial products that do not match their risk tolerance, or when their lending amount exceeds the risk tolerance threshold, financial institutions can promptly issue warning information to households, reminding them to consume financial products rationally.

2.4.4 Financial Institutions Can Use Artificial Intelligence Technology to Further Reduce Costs and Increase Efficiency

Financial institutions can leverage artificial intelligence technology to optimize the business models of household investment, wealth management, and loans, thereby reducing labor costs, effectively controlling risks, and enhancing the overall experience of household financial services. For instance, recurrent neural networks can be employed for efficient identification of key information in documents. By accurately identifying crucial details amidst vast amounts of household data and information, financial institutions can significantly improve their operational efficiency. Autoencoder technology ensures the security of financial services while also reducing risk identification time, making financial services more convenient and efficient. Deep reinforcement learning technology can be utilized for optimal allocation of financial resources by eliminating manual judgment interference based on specific data features associated with households; this enhances the effectiveness of financial resource allocation.

2.4.5 Financial Institutions Can Use Blockchain Technology to Provide Household Financial Services and Solve Problems Such as Information Asymmetry and Default Disposal

The characteristics of blockchain technology, such as its transparency, immutability, and adherence to contractual principles, align closely with the inherent requirements for the development of household finance. Firstly, blockchain technology enables transparent information disclosure that truthfully reflects households' income and debt situation, risk tolerance, investment skills, credit level, and other relevant information. This not only enhances the efficiency and accuracy of financial product promotion and loan approval but also mitigates the adverse effects of information asymmetry on investment and lending decisions. Secondly, smart contracts in loan transactions can enforce predetermined purposes for loan funds usage by households, thereby reducing default risks. In purchasing financial products, smart contracts ensure that financial institutions allocate investments according to agreed-upon terms while guaranteeing that invested entities utilize funds as intended. Consequently, this further minimizes the likelihood of risk occurrence and safeguards fund safety. Lastly but importantly, records pertaining to compliance and contract breaches are meticulously documented within a blockchain system which aids in establishing credit histories for households while forming a solid foundation for future consumption of financial products.

2.4.6 Financial Regulators Should Rectify Unfair Competition on FinTech Platforms

Financial regulators should focus on regulating the improper operation and competitive behavior of FinTech platforms. High risk and high-yield financial products should strictly adhere to investor suitability standards and obey more information disclosure requirements. Financial regulators should promptly eliminate the behavior of FinTech platforms providing high return financial products through self-owned subsidies. In response to the strong concealment of illegal and irregular activities in FinTech industry, financial regulators should leverage the role of social supervision, establish a reporting system, and provide clues for FinTech regulation. Implement the reward and punishment system to increase the cost of illegal and irregular operations. Strengthen the sharing mechanism of information on dishonesty and complaints.

2.4.7 *Financial Regulators Can Address the Risks in Financial Industry by SupTech Innovation*

Based on digital technologies, financial regulators can explore and establish a SupTech framework, timely collect, analyze, and report data, predict potential risks, and provide warning services. Also, financial regulators can collect behavioral data from financial service platforms and households, promptly detect illegal and irregular business activities, monitor suspicious fund flows, investigate problematic websites and apps, thus provide security protection services to various financial platforms.

2.4.8 *Financial Regulators Can Use Sandbox to Verify and Analyze the Applicability of Digital Technologies in Household Finance*

The sandbox plays a crucial role in verifying and analyzing the security and applicability of digital technology in household finance. Through conducting sandbox testing, it enables monitoring of the operational status of digital technologies in household financial services and timely identification of technical vulnerabilities. It comprehensively verifies whether the implementation of new digital technologies infringes upon households' financial rights and triggers new risk and security issues, thereby limiting the potential risks associated with the application of digital technologies to the development of household finance within a defined scope.

References

Allianz (2022) Allianz global wealth report 2022

CBIRC (2020) Notice on further improving financial services for epidemic prevention and control. http: //www.gov.cn/zhengce/zhengceku/202-02/16/content_5479561.htm

Lu L, Yao Y (2015) New financial era. CITIC Press, Beijing, pp 3–35

Sun G et al (2020) Blue book on regulatory science and technology: China regulatory science and technology development report. Social Science Literature Publishing House, Beijing, pp 1–36

Wu X (2014) Research on the direction and path of Internet financial supervision. Jilin Finan Res 9:1–8

Zhang W (2020) Promoting the transformation of residents' savings into stock market investment. China Economic Times

Zhao D, Yuan J, Chen W (2023) FinTech and SupTech in China. Springer Singapore, pp 93–94

Zhao D (2018) Research on risk and supervision of internet banking in China. Zhejiang Finance 1:3–8

Zhao D (2021) Research on issues related to internet consumer finance in China—based on the perspective of financial consumer rights protection. Financial Theory Pract 8:49–56

Chapter 3
FinTech, Household Finance and Financial Consumer Protection: Opportunities, Challenges and Countermeasures

Financial consumers are the main participants in the financial market and the main driving force for the healthy, orderly and sustainable development of the financial industry. Whether it is a one-person household or a multi-person household, financial behaviors and decisions are actually undertaken by individual financial consumers. Therefore, strengthening of financial consumers protection is an important means to boost household financial investment confidence, enhance household financial risk management capabilities, and allow households to fully enjoy the benefits of financial development. In order to protect the legitimate rights of financial consumers, regulate the behaviors of financial institutions in providing financial products, maintain a fair and just market environment, and promote the healthy and stable development of the financial market, The Chinese government has successively issued a series of guidelines and management measures, including *Guiding Opinions of the General Office of the State Council on Strengthening Financial Consumers Protection* (GOSC 2015), *Implementation Measures of the People's Bank of China on Financial Consumers Protection* (PBOC 2020), and *Measures for the Administration of Consumer Protection in Banking and Insurance Institutions* (CBIRC 2022). In addition, local governments of China have also taken the lead in formulating local financial consumer protection guidelines based on their own actual conditions, basically establishing a financial consumer protection policy system that is in line with China's national conditions and covers a wide range of areas.

Currently, with the emergence of FinTech, digital technologies not only provide technical support for strengthening financial consumer protection, but also exposes financial consumers to new risks (Yin 2020). In view of this, based on clarifying the new opportunities and challenges faced by financial consumer protection in the FinTech era, it is of great theoretical value and practical significance to study how to further strengthen financial consumer protection and promote the development of household finance.

S. Zhao and D. Zhao, *The Household Finance Issues in China*,
https://doi.org/10.1007/978-981-97-0706-5_3

3.1 New Opportunities for Financial Consumer Protection in the FinTech Era

In the context FinTech Era, the application of digital technologies will provide solid technical support for establishing and improving the financial consumer protection mechanism, comprehensively implementing the primary responsibility of financial institutions to protect financial consumers, and also provide new opportunities for establishing a financial consumer protection system that includes financial regulators, self-regulatory organizations, financial institutions, and financial consumers (Cheng and Yin 2020).

3.1.1 The Application of Digital Technologies Can Fully Protect Financial Consumers

3.1.1.1 The Application of Digital Technologies is Conducive to the Establishment of a Financial Consumer Suitability System

Financial institutions can use big data technology to accurately profile financial consumers, divide them into different types of groups based on factors such as risk tolerance, risk perception level, and risk preference, then match different types of financial products with different types of financial consumer groups based on the complexity, risk level and return level of financial products (Bai 2020). In addition, it is necessary to dynamically adjust the division of financial consumer groups based on the change of their income level, financial situation, risk preference and accumulation of financial management experience, to ensure that households can maximize their benefits from financial development.

3.1.1.2 The Application of Digital Technologies Helps to Protect the Property Security Rights of Financial Consumers

On the one hand, the application of digital technologies in the compliance business of financial institutions can ensure the security of financial products, effectively avoid the illegal business activities of financial institutions, and thus protect the property security of financial consumers. On the other hand, with the development and popularization of SupTech, financial regulators can timely and accurately detect the behaviors that infringe the property security of financial consumers, achieve “early detection and early intervention”.

3.1.1.3 The Application of Digital Technologies Helps to Ensure that Financial Consumers to Be Informed the Details of Financial Products

According to the requirements of disclosure, financial institutions need to clearly indicate relevant information about financial products on their websites and apps, and at the same time remind financial consumers that there may be risks in financial consumption. When promoting financial products, financial institutions should not promise to guarantee principal and profit, exaggerate profits excessively, or conceal potential risks, in order to avoid false advertising that misleads financial consumers in making decisions. Financial consumers can verify the information and data of financial institutions and financial products services through various ways, and reasonably match risks and returns on the basis of fully understand relevant information.

3.1.1.4 The Application of Digital Technologies Helps to Ensure that Financial Consumers Can Choose Financial Products Freely

The application of digital technologies in the finance industry has greatly expanded the accessibility of financial services, enabling financial consumers to freely choose financial products at a lower cost. At the same time, financial services have completed a shift towards customer centricity, and financial institutions (especially FinTechs) have begun to design more personalized financial products around the needs of financial consumers. Financial consumers can continuously improve their financial literacy through diverse ways (websites, forums, Weibo, apps, and WeChat groups, etc.), forming the foundation to exercise their autonomy of choice.

3.1.1.5 The Application of Digital Technologies Helps to Ensure Fair Transactions for Financial Consumers

In the FinTech era, it is necessary for financial regulators to guide financial institutions to correctly utilize digital technologies to protect financial consumers, guide financial institutions to use digital technology to further eliminate transactions that violate the principle of fairness, and reasonably clarify financial consumer responsibility.

3.1.1.6 The Application of Digital Technologies Helps to Ensure that Financial Consumers Can Claim Compensation in Accordance with the Law

The application of digital technologies has created diverse and low-cost channels for financial consumers to claim compensation in accordance with the law. In the past, when the legitimate rights of financial consumers are infringed upon, the cost of legal compensation for financial consumers is higher and may require more time and energy. In the FinTech era, financial consumers can fulfill their claims in a low-cost, fast and convenient way through various channels such as online human customer service, intelligent customer service, feedback emails, and customer evaluations. When claims are obstructed, financial consumers can seek support and assistance from financial regulators and self-regulatory organizations through internet financial information reporting platforms and others. At the same time, the application of digital technologies can enable financial consumers to check the progress of their claims anytime and anywhere, improve the quality and efficiency of complaint handling, and place the handling of incidents of infringement of financial consumer rights under widespread public supervision.

3.1.1.7 The Application of Digital Technologies Helps to Ensure that Financial Consumers Can Be Educated

Financial regulators, financial institutions, and self-regulatory organizations can use internet channels to educate financial consumers at a lower cost, which can maximize the accessibility, breadth, and sustainability of financial consumer education. Big data technology can be used to push the urgently needed financial knowledge to financial consumers and meet their urgent financial consumption needs. Targeted promotion of financial knowledge can be provided to elderly population, students and low-income groups. When financial consumers purchase financial products through websites or apps, they can be educated about the relevant knowledge of the products and given risk warnings in the form of pop ups. In addition, the application of digital technologies also enables financial consumers to obtain the financial knowledge they need at a lower cost or even for free, in a diversified and timely manner.

3.1.1.8 The Application of Digital Technologies Helps to Ensure that Financial Consumers Can Be Respected

As mentioned earlier, in the FinTech era, financial products are designed and provided with a customer-centric approach, which better meets the needs of financial consumers. At the same time, the extensive application of digital technologies enables financial institutions (or FinTechs) to fully respect the personal dignity and ethnic customs of financial consumers when designing financial products, and effectively avoid discriminatory treatment based on gender, age, race, ethnicity, or nationality of financial consumers.

3.1.1.9 The Application of Digital Technologies Helps to Ensure the Information Security of Financial Consumers

There are frequent risk events of excessive collection, abuse, and leakage of information, which seriously affect the information security of financial consumers. Financial regulators and financial institutions have an obligation to use technological means to strengthen financial consumer information protection. First, it is possible to consider strengthening the research on storage servers, using secure backup technology methods to ensure the storage security of financial consumer information. Second, consider establishing a data lifecycle management system based on digital technologies, covering the entire process of data collection, data transmission, data storage, data usage, data deletion, and data destruction, etc. Third, consider enhancing terminal protection capabilities, effectively responding to network attacks, and avoiding data and information leakage. Finally, using advanced data encryption and digital desensitization technologies ensures both data security and usability.

3.2 New Challenges for Financial Consumer Protection in the FinTech Era

As previously mentioned, the application of digital technologies can facilitate the advancement of financial consumer protection and foster the sound and systematic development of the household finance industry. However, it is imperative to acknowledge that certain financial institutions (particularly FinTechs) have harnessed digital technologies to undertake a substantial amount of business and service innovation, surpassing the existing capacity of financial regulation. Simultaneously, these innovative behaviors have engendered significant transformations in the nature, transmission channels, and security boundaries of financial risks, thereby presenting novel challenges to safeguarding financial consumers.

3.2.1 Regulatory Vacuum and Regulatory Arbitrage Risks Threaten the Rights of Financial Consumers

In the context of rapid development of FinTech, BigTechs provide financial services but are not regulated by financial regulators. In addition, BigTechs do not bear credit risks but charge high fees, posing new challenges to financial consumer protection. Some BigTechs, utilizing advanced internet technology and user information, jointly invest with banks to provide small and short-term online credit loans to financial consumers nationwide, which may cause the following risks:

First, BigTechs engage in financial services but are not regulated, resulting in regulatory arbitrage risks. BigTechs participate in joint loan business, and the financial products they provide are not fundamentally different from the small loans provided by banks. However, there is currently a lack of clear rules and requirements for the capital, provisions, liquidity of BigTechs, which creates unfair competition with licensed financial institutions. At the same time, due to the fact that BigTechs have mastered the most critical risk control models, they actually undertake a series of core functions such as credit evaluation, risk pricing, and post loan management. These core risk functions are also detached from financial supervision, providing the possibility of infringing on financial consumers.

Second, the leverage ratio has exceeded regulatory requirements. According to the *Notice on Strengthening the Supervision and Management of Small Loan Companies*, the total leverage scale of small loan companies shall not exceed 5 times their net assets (CBIRC 2020). However, in practical operation, the leverage ratio of some BigTechs has exceeded regulatory requirements. Once the funding chain breaks, financial consumers (especially fund security) will not be protected.

Third, some small loan companies have indirectly broken through restrictions on cross regional operations, increasing risk spillovers. Small loan companies should provide financial services within the provincial-level administrative region where they are registered. However, some FinTechs break through the limitations of regional business scope by conducting joint loans with commercial banks, invisibly amplifying the risks faced by financial consumers.

Finally, Banks become funding channels, making it difficult to effectively identify financial risks. In the process of online joint loans, FinTechs are responsible for pre loan review, post loan management, collection and preservation. Cooperative banks lack first-hand information on financial consumer payment scenarios, and their ability to control loan flows is limited. Banks play more of a role as funding channels, unable to effectively identify risks and assume responsibility for protecting financial consumers.

3.2.2 Some FinTechs Have Become Systemically Important Financial Institutions, Harboring Significant Cross Risk and Contagion Risk

Several FinTech companies have significantly penetrated the financial industry through equity investments and other strategic approaches. The group's cross-industry and cross-domain financial products are intricately intertwined, exhibiting a strong correlation and heightened procyclicality. Furthermore, owing to their extensive network coverage, convergence of business models and algorithms, there is an accelerated transmission of financial risk contagion that can rapidly escalate into systemic risks within a short timeframe, posing a substantial threat to financial consumers (Zhou 2020).

FinTech companies not only offer financial services, but also engage in diverse sectors such as social networking, e-commerce, media, and search engines. Typically targeting individuals who are underserved by traditional financial institutions, these consumers often lack expertise in finance and investment decision-making while exhibiting a pronounced herd mentality. During periods of significant market fluctuations or reversals, there is a propensity for triggering collective irrational behavior among this group, leading to the rapid propagation of risks and the emergence of systemic financial risks.

3.2.3 Inducing Low-Income Financial Consumers to Over-Borrow Can Easily Lead to Debt Repayment Risks

Certain FinTech companies have introduced online lending products specifically targeting young individuals and low-income groups, featuring minimal application requirements, streamlined review processes, enhanced efficiency, and the convenience of applying anytime and anywhere through mobile internet access. Undoubtedly, the availability of online loans may lead financial consumers to overlook their risk tolerance and income levels, thereby increasing their inclination towards excessive borrowing. However, these financial consumers often possess unstable incomes and lack collateral; consequently, they are more susceptible to falling into a cycle of accumulating new debts in order to repay old ones.

3.2.4 Due to the Advantages of Data and Customer Resources, Oligopoly and Unfair Competition Are Prominent

Financial consumers require technical and financial support from BigTechs, yet they lack the capacity to negotiate on an equitable basis and are compelled to adhere to service regulations formulated by BigTechs, thereby making concessions in terms of choice. BigTechs gain market share through unfair competition via direct subsidies or cross-subsidies (derived from other businesses), positioning themselves as winners. They subsequently eliminate competitors (including potential ones) through collaborations and mergers while leveraging advanced technologies to fortify their dominant market position, further solidifying their advantages and establishing monopolies. Consequently, financial consumers encounter the predicament of limited alternatives or choosing between only two options, ultimately being coerced into consuming the financial products and services provided exclusively by BigTechs (Zhou and Shi 2018).

3.2.5 *Data Monopoly and Information Security Risks Are Intertwined and Exist for a Long Time*

Data constitutes the fundamental asset in the FinTech era, and both FinTechs and BigTechs inherently possess a proclivity to capitalize on data. In recent years, instances of illicit activities, criminal behavior, as well as encroachments upon personal privacy have become increasingly prevalent.

Firstly, FinTechs and BigTechs amass a substantial volume of data and information from financial consumers while delivering financial services, thereby posing a significant privacy threat to these individuals. In March 2020, Southern Metropolis Daily and China Financial Certification Center conducted an assessment on 143 internet finance applications, revealing that these apps frequently collect user data and information unrelated to the realm of finance.

Secondly, FinTechs and BigTechs frequently utilize data and information without obtaining proper authorization from financial consumers, thereby analyzing their consumption preferences in order to selectively promote financial products and advertisements.

Thirdly, the risk of data leakage persists for a long time. Most financial data is bound to financial consumers and involves the flow of funds, once these data are improperly stored or subjected to network attacks, it may lead to data leakage, it can lead to privacy leakage of financial consumers, causing property damage and personal safety hazards.

Finally, If FinTechs and BigTechs disregard the historical underpinnings of financial services and blindly pursue unverified technological innovations, particularly those lacking rigorous validation, the implementation of such systems may give rise to critical technical flaws and algorithmic vulnerabilities, leading to widespread systemic risks. These risks not only compromise the service experience for financial consumers but also pose a detrimental impact on their financial asset security (Chen et al. 2020).

3.2.6 *The Confusion Between Regulators and Regulated Institutions*

At present, some local governments in China have collaborated with FinTechs and BigTechs to develop SupTech systems. For example, Beijing has collaborated with Ant Group to develop the *Beijing Financial Risk Control Cockpit*, and Shenzhen Financial Office has collaborated with Tencent to develop the *Lingkun Financial Security Big Data Regulatory Platform*. The misplaced relationship of FinTechs and BigTechs, may conceal its infringement of financial consumers (Zhao and Li 2021).

On one hand, due to the intricate nature of software systems, it becomes challenging for financial regulators to comprehend the fundamental algorithms and rules underlying the technologies employed by FinTechs and BigTechs when collecting data and information from financial consumers through big data and cloud computing technology. Consequently, identifying potential system vulnerabilities or backdoors that may exist within these technologies becomes arduous, thereby impeding timely prevention, detection, and handling of any infringements on financial consumers perpetrated by FinTechs and BigTechs.

On the other hand, integrating machine learning and artificial intelligence technologies into daily compliance management enables FinTechs and BigTechs to effectively meet regulatory requirements in safeguarding financial consumers at both technical and systemic levels while avoiding regulatory penalties. Furthermore, this integration facilitates identification of existing loopholes within the protection system (Zhao 2019).

3.2.7 Some FinTechs and BigTechs Use Media and Social Influence to Guide and Control the Emotions and Behaviors of Financial Consumers

Currently, certain FinTechs and BigTechs encompass a wide array of industries, offering not only financial services but also financial infrastructure (including SupTech and regulatory platforms), as well as media, social software, and e-commerce platforms. Leveraging diverse channels to their advantage, these FinTechs and BigTechs not only wield the influence of online discourse but also possess the potential to shape the emotions and behaviors of financial consumers. Consequently, they may exert control over public opinion, thereby undermining the harmonious atmosphere surrounding the protection of financial consumers.

3.3 The Application of Digital Technologies in Financial Consumer Protection

3.3.1 Enrich Financial Consumer Protection Measures with Digital Technologies

To safeguard the interests of financial consumers, concerted efforts should be made to enhance precision and delve into the root causes of infringements. Adhering to the principle of employing distinct approaches for different rights and subjects, targeted and differentiated protection measures ought to be implemented in order to diversify avenues for safeguarding financial consumers. With the continuous advancement of FinTech, not only are FinTechs and BigTechs venturing into providing financial services, but non-financial institutions are also leveraging technological means to offer more convenient and cost-effective financial services. However, this inevitably introduces new risks and challenges to the financial industry. In light of this situation, it is imperative to collaborate between financial institutions and non-financial entities in ensuring consumer protection within the realm of finance. Under the guidance of regulatory bodies and self-regulatory organizations, exploring a diversified integration among various stakeholders based on digital technologies becomes essential in providing technical support that caters specifically to the genuine needs of financial consumers while effectively addressing issues such as infringement upon their rights (Zeng and Liu 2020).

3.3.2 Utilize Big Data Technology and Artificial Intelligence to Achieve Accurate Profiling, Precise Positioning and Efficiency Protection

First, utilizing big data technology to comprehensively and accurately collect information and data on incidents of infringement of financial consumer rights, providing a basis for efficiency protection. Big data technology can collect multidimensional information on infringement incidents from multiple channels, including the information of the infringing subjects and the affected financial consumers, the detailed information of the infringement, and applicable laws and regulations and previous cases. In addition, big data technology can also help financial regulators and industry self-regulatory organizations establish information inquiry system to verify whether institutions providing financial services have records of infringement of financial consumer rights.

Second, using artificial intelligence to provide suggestions for carrying out efficiency protection. Based on comprehensive and accurate access to data and information on infringement incidents, artificial intelligence can assist financial regulators and financial institutions in establishing an information evaluation system that can accurately identify infringement incidents, determine the protection methods, reducing the subjective impact of human evaluation and intervention, and enhancing the scientific and credibility of financial consumer protection.

Third, big data technology can be used to timely grasp the changes in financial consumer protection. When financial institutions have obvious illegal and irregular business operations, risks occur in related parties, and negative public opinion continues to increase, artificial intelligence can send early warning prompts to financial consumers in the first time, suggesting that financial consumers pay attention to the risk situation in a timely manner to avoid property losses. Similarly, when financial institutions promptly correct illegal and irregular business operations, have sufficient funds and no negative reflections, artificial intelligence can also send prompt messages to financial consumers in a timely manner, remove previous warning prompts, and truly implement precise positioning of infringement incidents and efficiency financial consumer protection.

3.3.3 Based on Blockchain and Smart Contracts, Effectively Protect Financial Consumers

The characteristics of blockchain, such as immutability, openness and transparency, can ensure the authenticity and effectiveness of financial consumption records, can reduce or prevent the infringement incidents. On the one hand, every node on the blockchain stores a copy of all transaction records, and the cost of modifying records will be very high. It is possible to modify information only if it has more than 51% of the computing power of the entire network, and the cost of modification may far exceed the expected benefits. Therefore, blockchain can ensure that every recorded financial consumption information is unaltered, authentic, and effective, providing a reliable basis for handling infringement incidents. On the other hand, blockchain is an open accounting technology, with transparent transaction information, ensuring that all transactions are accessible and conducive to financial regulators to fully grasp the detailed information of infringement incidents, and achieve comprehensive and full-process supervision of financial consumer protection. In addition, the application of smart contracts can also ensure funds security. Based on smart contracts, a string of codes is attached to each sum of money used for financial consumption. When the use of the funds complies with the plan, the transaction is automatically executed. When there is a violation of the original fund usage plan, the smart contract will automatically terminate the transaction and freeze the funds, then record the violation information and send warning information to financial regulators, self-regulatory organizations, and financial consumers, thus ensuring that the funds are not occupied or used for other purposes, and fully protecting funds security (Zhao 2016).

3.3.4 Improve the Supporting Measures for Financial Consumer Protection Through Digital Technologies

First, the application of internet channels, big data and artificial intelligence technology, can help financial regulators and financial institutions further smooth financial consumer protection channels, enrich the tools and means for protection and reduce the cost.

Second, financial regulators or self-regulatory organizations can consider establishing a financial institutions rating system based on big data technology, and according to the history of financial consumer protection, conduct a rating and disclose it to financial consumers on relevant platforms., providing a reference basis for financial consumers to choose financial institutions.

Third, the application of digital technologies can improve financial literacy, so that financial consumers can enjoy the benefits of financial development. Financial regulators and financial institutions can carry out targeted financial publicity and education through the Internet or offline channels, providing intellectual support for financial consumers.

Finally, a platform which includes financial regulators, self-regulatory organizations, financial institutions and financial consumers, should be established to strengthen coordination among various entities and provide organizational support for financial consumer protection.

3.4 Suggestions for Promoting Financial Consumer Protection in the FinTech Era

In recent years, the integration of digital technologies and finance has gradually positioned digital technologies as the core driving force behind financial innovation. This transformation brings significant benefits in terms of expanding the coverage, enhancing efficiency, and reducing costs associated with financial services. However, it also introduces a range of new risks to the financial industry, thereby posing fresh challenges for safeguarding financial consumers. Presently, an increasing number of FinTechs and BigTechs are leveraging their technological prowess and contextual advantages to offer diverse financial services. Consequently, the boundaries between different types of financial service institutions are becoming increasingly blurred. This phenomenon not only conceals and complicates financial risks but also amplifies their dissemination speed across a wider spectrum, ultimately elevating both overall vulnerability within the financial system and systemic risk probability. As such circumstances intensify, there is an urgent need to explore a macro policy framework along with practical approaches that align with China's rapidly evolving FinTech landscape while ensuring robust protection for financial consumers.

3.4.1 Strengthen Prudential Management, Prevent Systemic Risks, and Optimize the Overall Environment for Financial Consumer Protection

Some FinTechs and BigTechs are developing into systemically important financial institutions that are too big to fail, should be brought under the financial regulatory framework. Separate the industrial and financial sectors from the mechanism, bring licensed financial institutions and financial services into the financial regulatory framework. Strictly implement penetrating supervision on all financial businesses. At the same time, it is necessary to establish a set of micro and macro prudential supervision indicators applicable to the new FinTech industry, so as to provide a positive and healthy overall social atmosphere for further optimizing financial consumer protection.

3.4.2 *Strict Market Access and Comprehensive Functional Supervision Should Be Implemented to Reduce the Probability of Incidents that Infringe on Financial Consumers*

Adhere to the principle of *Only Licensed Financial Institutions Can Provide Financial Services, and Regulatory Consistency to Maintain Fair Competition and Prevent Regulatory Arbitrage*, FinTech business supervision should be carried out according to relevant business categories, adhering to the principle of. For example, for small loan companies that carry out joint loans, they are not allowed to carry out loan business across provincial administrative regions. In a single joint loan, the proportion of capital contribution of small loan companies is clearly restricted, additional minimum shareholder capital contribution requirements are set for joint loans. Specific requirements are put forward for financial institutions from the aspects of institutional norms and business operations to prevent some FinTechs from breaking the policy bottom line, resulting in infringement of financial consumer.

3.4.3 *Financial Regulators Should Guide Technology Companies to Provide Technical Support for Financial Institutions to Improve Financial Consumer Protection*

Financial regulators should guide technology companies to provide technical support to the financial industry, not only providing financial institutions with technology and business solutions such as customer acquisition channel, refined operations, real-time big data risk control system, and full-process cost reduction and efficiency improvement, but also starting cooperation in strengthening financial consumer protection. Technology companies should strive to return to the "best practice" of technology export, comprehensively help financial institutions to enhance their ability to serve financial consumers, and ultimately achieve the goal of better protecting financial consumers.

3.4.4 *Financial Regulators Can Establish a Technology-Driven Regulatory System, Use Technological Means to Address the Risks and Protect Financial Consumers in the FinTech Era*

First, financial regulators can establish a comprehensive and sound data collection system, focusing on the continuous operation ability and risk control ability of financial institutions. Second, financial regulators can build a big data analysis and risk warning mechanism, to detect and prevent financial risks in advance, providing a basis for protecting financial consumers. Third, financial regulators can improve the supporting measures for financial consumer protection, focusing on the supervision of the technical infrastructure and information systems of financial institutions, and requiring the establishment of network security facilities and management systems such as firewalls, intrusion detection, data encryption, and disaster recovery.

3.4.5 Financial Regulators Should Strengthen Data Management, Establish a Mechanism for Data Flow and Price Formation, and Fully Protect the Security of Financial Consumer Information

Data ownership is a fundamental issue in the market-oriented allocation of data. Currently, most countries in the world have not accurately defined the ownership of data property. In the FinTech era, BigTechs actually have control over data. They should further clarify their data rights in all aspects, ensure fair and reasonable allocation of data production factors, and promote a sound mechanism for data circulation and price formation, providing institutional guarantees for ensuring the information and data security of financial consumers. In addition, when promoting the construction of relevant infrastructure, full consideration should be given to big data technology, and as an important infrastructure for financial institutions, it should be planned and developed to internalize the protection of financial consumer information and data security into the management philosophy and culture.

3.4.6 Financial Regulators Should Monitor the Business Behavior of Financial Institutions to Ensure Their Stable Operation and Further Reduce the Probability of Incidents that Infringe on Financial Consumer

It is necessary for financial regulators and self-regulatory organizations to monitor the business behavior of financial institutions in real-time. Based on regional industry cloud platforms, similar financial institutions can be included in corresponding cloud platforms for real-time monitoring and management. Through digital technologies, information comparison between enterprises of different scales can be achieved, and abnormal operations can be detected in a timely manner. Through big data platforms, financial regulators can collect operational information of financial institutions in real-time, achieve efficient and comprehensive analysis and processing of operational risk information, and timely discover illegal and irregular business clues. By using blockchain technology, financial regulators, self-regulatory organizations, and financial institutions can simultaneously go online, achieving searchable information and traceable transactions, and eliminating false information and advertising.

3.4.7 All Types of Financial Institutions Should Strengthen Publicity and Education on Financial Consumption

To enhance the financial decision-making ability, risk awareness, and contractual spirit of financial consumers, all types of financial institutions should strengthen financial publicity and education, advocate a rational consumption culture, guard against blind comparison, advanced consumption, and excessive borrowing. For the issue of infringement on financial consumers, financial regulators should not only investigate licensed financial institutions, but also conduct extended investigations on relevant technical service providers. In response to oligopolistic monopolistic behavior, special investigations should be organized to investigate whether the relevant companies have abused their dominant market position. Strengthen anti-monopoly and anti-unfair competition law enforcement, prevent winners from taking all, and fully protect the independent choice and fair-trading rights of financial consumers.

References

Bai Z (2020) Research on the socio-economic value of digital inclusive financial development. Stat Manage 2020(8):112–121

CBIRC (2020) Notice on strengthening the supervision and management of small loan companies. https://www.cbirc.gov.cn/cn/view/pages/ItemDetail.html?docId=929448&itemId=928

CBIRC (2022) Measures for the administration of consumer protection in banking and insurance institutions. https://www.cbirc.gov.cn/cn/view/pages/ItemDetail.html?docId=1087560&itemId=915&generaltype=0

Chen Y, Wang Y, Zhang Q (2020) China's fintech regulatory challenges and responses. Finan Theory Pract 2020(1):49–56

Cheng X, Yin Z (2020) Innovative development and supervision of internet consumer finance. Financial Monthly 2020(3):147–153

GOSC (2015) Guiding opinions of the general office of the state council on strengthening financial consumers protection. https://www.gov.cn/zhengce/content/2015-11/13/content_10289.htm

PBOC (2020) Implementation measures of the people's bank of China on financial consumers protection. http://www.pbc.gov.cn/tiaofasi/144941/144957/4099060/index.html

Yin Y (2020) Constructing a financial consumer protection system in the era of FinTech. Contemp Finan 2020(Z1):46–49

Zeng G, Liu W (2020) Strengthening financial consumer protection and promoting the return of finance to its origin. https://baijiahao.baidu.com/s?id=1678668845010676273&wfr=spider&for=pc

Zhao D (2016) Can blockchain save P2P lending? Finan Theory Pract 2016(9):41–44

Zhao D (2019) The ability and inability of SupTech. Tsinghua Finan Rev 2019(5):54–56

Zhao D, Li J (2021) Intelligent finance era. People's Daily Press, Beijing, pp 59–67

Zhou L, Shi F (2018) Research on market failure, behavior supervision and financial consumer protection. Res Finan Supervis 2018(8):84–93
Zhou J (2020) Big internet companies' financial business is more likely to trigger systemic risks. Financial Times

Chapter 4
Risk Attitude, Health Status, and Household Financial Investment Behavior

With the vigorous development of the Chinese financial market, family financial transactions have been increasing, and financial products continue to permeate into social production and daily life. The accumulation of family wealth allows more and more families the opportunity and ability to purchase financial products, thereby obtaining risk protection and property income. Family financial investment behavior refers to the financial behavior of investing family assets into various financial products to achieve value preservation and appreciation. This behavior has a significant impact on individual living standards and the overall strength of the country. Since the 1970s, research on family finance has been continuously deepening. Scholars generally believe that Chinese family financial investment behavior has the characteristics of "heterogeneity" and "limitedness", that is, different families show significant differences in financial asset investment behavior, such as the proportion of financial assets in total wealth, types of held financial assets, and the proportion of risky financial assets. At the same time, the participation of family risk assets in the market is very limited in terms of breadth and depth (Chen and Liu 2014).

4.1 Origin, Connotation, and Influencing Factors of Family Financial Investment Behavior

Family financial investment behavior refers to a series of investment activities undertaken by families using existing assets to obtain additional returns, in addition to obtaining returns through labor. This allows for the reutilization of family economic resources, thereby obtaining more economic value (Gao 2009). Campbell (2006) proposed the concept of family finance, suggesting that the participation in the family financial market, family asset selection, and their influencing factors are among the most important issues in family finance research. He believes that the

S. Zhao and D. Zhao, *The Household Finance Issues in China*,
https://doi.org/10.1007/978-981-97-0706-5_4

most effective way for family asset maximization is for family investment decision-makers to allocate family assets reasonably through financial markets and financial instruments. This marks a new stage in family finance research (Campbell 2006). Subsequently, the concept of family finance and related research have increasingly become the focus of attention for domestic and foreign scholars. Traditional investment theories suggest that families make investment decisions based on estimates of asset cost-return characteristics and their own risk-taking capacity, and that families should invest a certain proportion of their wealth in risky assets (Dow and da Costa Werlang 1992). However, the "heterogeneity" and "limited participation" phenomena observed in Chinese family financial investment behavior cannot be explained by traditional investment theories. Compared to what traditional theories state about family investment decisions depending on factors such as the returns and risks of asset portfolios and the family's own risk attitude, modern Chinese families, influenced by traditional Chinese savings culture, exhibit greater complexity in financial investment, including influences from family relationships, social environment, and psychological factors (Hillesland 2019; Park and Suh 2019; He et al. 2020; Zhang and Liang 2020). Among the many factors influencing family financial investment, scholars have focused on exploring demographic and economic factors. In terms of demographic factors, most studies indicate that higher education levels and marital status have a significant positive impact on family financial investment behaviour (Wang and Wu 2014; Liao 2017; Luo and Liang 2020).

In terms of household economic factors, some foreign scholars have found that wealth plays a positive role in encouraging families to participate in financial investments (Liu 2015). Domestic scholars like Wu et al. (2011) also conducted studies and found that both wealth and income have significant positive effects. An increase in family wealth will significantly enhance the likelihood and depth of their participation in risky assets. In addition to wealth and income, housing is also a crucial economic characteristic of households (Wu et al. 2011). Some studies have discovered a notable "crowding out effect" of family real estate investment on the proportion of investments in risky financial assets (He and He 2018; Gao et al. 2020), which means that, under certain circumstances of family assets, if real estate is invested in, the proportion of investments in risky financial assets will decrease. However, there are studies that have yielded contrary conclusions. Domestic scholars found that real estate does not exhibit a "crowding out effect" on the investment in risky assets of Chinese urban families. Real estate and family risk financial assets have a complementary relationship rather than a substitutive one, which implies that real estate has a positive impact on the holding of risky assets. Resident families may be using real estate holdings to achieve a diversified investment portfolio, thereby increasing the holding of risky financial assets. Given the potential impact of variables such as gender, age, marital status, education level, family income, and housing on the dependent variable, it is necessary to incorporate them into the statistical model. These relevant variables that are likely to have an impact can be included as control variables in the model for a better linear fit, aiming to enhance the accuracy and explanatory power of the empirical results (He et al. 2020).

4.2 Theoretical and Empirical Research on Household Financial Investment Behavior

The theoretical and empirical research on household financial investment behavior has been a focal point for scholars both domestically and internationally over the past half-century. Studies have primarily focused on demographic factors and objective economic variables influencing family financial investments, such as gender, age, education level, marital status, employment status, income level, and property ownership (Wei et al. 2014; Wang and Wu 2014). In 2019, the "China Household Finance Survey Report" demonstrated that Chinese households exhibit a structurally uniform financial asset allocation pattern. Savings levels are relatively high, predominantly concentrated in cash, current deposits, and fixed-term deposits, accounting for nearly ninety percent. Real estate investments hold a significant proportion, with disparities existing between urban and rural residents. For urban households, the net value of real estate constitutes 71.35% of per capita family wealth, whereas for rural households, this proportion is only 52.28%. A singular financial asset structure is detrimental to balancing asset risks for resident families and hinders the potential for value appreciation. Among the reasons for households diverting funds from other financial assets due to savings, "dealing with unexpected events and medical expenses" accounts for nearly half at 48.19%, while "reluctance to take investment risks" constitutes 13.82%. This underscores the importance of discussing the relationship between the health status of family members and their financial investment behavior, a variable crucial for exploration beyond known factors influencing family financial investments.

Recognizing the significant impact of health status on family financial investment behavior, the academic community has conducted a series of studies. Particularly, in the context of asset allocation, considering health status as part of background risk, it is pointed out that background risk, as it cannot be effectively diversified through investment portfolios, will reduce the holding of risky assets. Specifically, it mainly influences residents' family investment decisions from three aspects: asset allocation, disposable resources, and risk attitude. For instance, Smith and Love (2010) argues that health status is positively correlated with an individual's disposable resources. Therefore, poor health may imply insufficient disposable wealth, leading to a reduction in investments in financial products (Smith and Love 2010). Goldman and Maestas (2013) also note in their research that individuals with poor health are more likely to incur higher future medical expenses. Hence, investors will reduce asset risk brought about by financial investments (Goldman and Maestas 2013). Edwards (2010) particularly confirms the relationship between health status and risk attitude, pointing out that uncertain health risks promote investors to be more risk-averse, thereby influencing family investment behaviour (Edwards 2010). Differing from the traditional economic understanding of health, Grossman (1972) introduced the human capital model of health demand, where health is considered as "health capital" distinct from other forms of human capital. It determines the time and potential returns that can be allocated to market and non-market activities. The inherited health capital depreciates with age, and to compensate for this depreciation, people invest in health through means like healthcare expenditure. Given that individuals can rationally anticipate their life expectancy, the healthier a person is, the more likely they are to engage in family investment behaviour (Grossman 1972). Furthermore, health capital exists not only at an individual level but also changes in family health status can have a significant impact on the economic and psychological states of family members, thus influencing family investment decisions. This forms the theoretical foundation of this chapter.

Traditional investment theory posits that risk attitude is a determining factor in individual investment behavior. Paiella and Gusio (2004) found a significant negative correlation between household risk aversion and investments in risky assets. Risk-averse households tend to allocate a significantly lower proportion of their investments to risky assets compared to risk-seeking households. However, recent research has revealed discrepancies between family financial investments and the predictions of traditional investment theory, indicating that family investment behavior is influenced by many social factors beyond risk attitude, such as the health status of family members (Paiella and Guiso 2004). Further research by Edwards (2010) discovered that the increase in health risk leads to an increase in risk aversion because individuals attempt to mitigate the impact of health risks by investing in safer assets. Domestic scholars like Liu et al. (2014) also found that the higher the level of residents' health, the greater their willingness to invest in risky assets, showing a preference for riskier financial assets (Liu et al. 2014). This suggests that health status can influence the psychological expectations and behavioral choices of family investors. Families with good health tend to exhibit stronger risk preferences, leading to an increased likelihood of investing in risky assets. Conversely, when family health is poorer, the degree of risk preference in investment tends to decrease, favoring safer financial assets.

While previous research on family financial investment behavior has explored various influencing factors, there has been relatively little research that simultaneously considers the objective and subjective levels of health status and incorporates them into the framework of investable health capital theory. In particular, there is a lack of detailed discussion on the mechanism through which risk attitude influences the relationship between health status and family financial investment behavior. Considering the combined impact of health status and risk attitude on family financial investment behavior, we employ data from the 2017 China Household Finance Survey (CHFS) to empirically analyze both factors within the same framework. This allows us to examine how health status affects family financial investment behavior by influencing risk attitude. By providing empirical evidence for understanding family financial investment behavior, this research contributes to exploring feasible measures to further promote the healthy development of the financial market in China.

4.3 Hypotheses on the Relationship Between Health Status, Risk Attitude, and Household Financial Investment Behavior

4.3.1 Research and Hypotheses on the Relationship Between Health Status and Household Financial Investment Behavior

Building on existing foreign research, Chinese scholars have conducted a series of studies on the relationship between health and household financial investment behavior in recent years. In terms of theoretical modeling, some scholars have incorporated health factors into lifecycle models or asset selection models to explore the impact of health status on household financial investment behaviour (Chen and Liu 2014; Edwards 2010; Yogo 2016). In empirical research, both domestic and international studies have primarily revolved around two core propositions: whether health status has an impact and how it affects household financial investment. On the one hand, some studies suggest that, after controlling for wealth levels and family heterogeneity, the influence of health status on household financial investment is not significant (Smith and Love 2010; Hu et al. 2015). On the other hand, other studies have found that families with poorer health and higher health risks are less likely to invest in risky financial assets and hold a lower proportion of them (Liu 2015; Liu et al. 2020).

Inconsistent conclusions in existing literature may be attributed to differences in research samples and the measurement of health status. Aside from the micro-level data being sourced from different regions and survey subjects, there are also variations in how health status is measured. Some scholars use self-rated health as a benchmark, finding that self-rated health significantly impacts the proportion of stocks and risky assets in total wealth (Wu et al. 2011). Others gauge the overall health status of a family by the proportion of non-healthy members in the total household population. Since non-healthy individuals must allocate a portion of their resources for health expenses, and the returns on both health consumption and health products are uncertain, the proportion of non-healthy individuals in a family affects the risk preference and allocation of family investments.

Studies have found that poorer family health status has a significantly negative effect on the proportion of risky financial assets in the family's investment portfolio (He and He 2018). Existing research indicates that if the objective health expenditure amount is used as an endogenous variable to measure health status, urban residents with higher health expenditure hold more financial assets and risky assets, while the opposite is true in rural areas. This gives health expenditure the characteristics of a "luxury good" (Smith and Love 2010). The author believes that the difference in health expenditure between urban and rural residents may be due to variations in participation rates and coverage of medical insurance in China's urban and rural areas. In rural households, health expenditure for medical treatment and health care depends more on whether there is a surplus in the family economy, making health expenditure a "luxury." This also, to some extent, indicates the important role of health expenditure in improving health status. Based on the above discussions, this chapter proposes the following hypotheses:

Hypothesis 1 Health status has a significant positive impact on household financial investment behavior; families with better health status are more inclined to invest in financial assets.

Hypothesis 1a Families with household heads who rate their health status higher are more likely to invest in financial assets.

Hypothesis 1b Families with better overall health status (a lower proportion of non-healthy members in the total household population) are more likely to invest in financial assets.

Hypothesis 1c Families with higher health expenditure are more likely to invest in financial assets.

4.3.2 The Study and Hypotheses on the Relationship Between Risk Attitude and Household Financial Investment Behavior

The academic community has a long history of studying the relationship between risk attitude and household financial investment behavior. Risk attitude is a psychological inclination when facing uncertain risks, indicating the degree of preference (or aversion) towards risk. It manifests as three situations: risk preference, risk aversion, and risk neutrality (Warneryd 1996). In financial investment decision-making with characteristics of uncertainty, preference relationships are established among different probability distributions. The convexity or concavity of the utility function can reflect the investor's risk preference. Different risk subjects have different risk functions, and people generally exhibit risk aversion (or risk aversion), which is also one of the basic assumptions of traditional investment theory. Behavioral finance theory posits that investors' rationality is limited. Building on this theory, Shefrin and Statman (2000) proposed the Behavioral Portfolio Theory, suggesting that investors make investment decisions based on their investment goals and risk attitudes, forming a pyramid of financial products ranging from low to high risk (Shefrin and Statman 2000). Abundant research indicates that families with risk preferences are more likely to participate in the financial market and invest in risky financial assets, while risk-averse families, due to risk aversion, are less likely to participate in the financial market (Paiella and Guiso 2004; Luo and Liang 2020). However, some studies have arrived at different conclusions, finding that risk attitude does not have a significant impact on the participation rate in stocks and risky financial assets (Li and Guo 2009). Therefore, this chapter proposes the following hypothesis.

Hypothesis 2 As risk preference increases, the likelihood of households participating in the financial market significantly increases. Families with a preference for risk may have a higher proportion of investments in risky assets.

Currently, most studies on household financial investment behavior from the perspective of risk attitude consider the independent influence of risk attitude, but overlook the potential impact of health status on the relationship between risk attitude and household financial investment behavior. Residents with poor health in families tend to be conservative in the investment process and lean towards risk-averse investments. For families, the utility derived from using family wealth for investment is far less than the utility derived from maintaining health. Therefore, when there are family members with poor health in the family, the family will consider potential future medical expenses in the investment decision-making process to mitigate potential health risks, thereby reducing risk preference and avoiding investment in risky financial assets (Love and Perozek 2007). Therefore, this chapter proposes the following hypotheses.

Hypothesis 3 Health status exerts an intermediary effect on household financial investment behavior through its impact on risk attitude.

Hypothesis 3a The self-rated health status of the household head exerts an intermediary effect on household financial investment behavior through its impact on risk attitude.

Hypothesis 3b The overall health status of the family (the proportion of non-healthy members in the total household population, as self-rated) exerts an intermediary effect on household financial investment behavior through its impact on risk attitude.

Hypothesis 3c Family health expenditure exerts an intermediary effect on household financial investment behavior through its impact on risk attitude.

This chapter comprehensively measures health status (including individual health, family member health, and health expenditure), highlighting the simultaneous influence of health as both background risk and health capital on the financial investment behavior of Chinese residents. With health status controlled for, it examines how risk attitude significantly influences people's household financial investment behavior. Furthermore, it verifies whether risk attitude plays an intermediary role in the relationship between health status and household financial investment behavior, empirically testing whether risk attitude is an important transmission channel for health status. At the same time, it investigates how health status and risk attitude

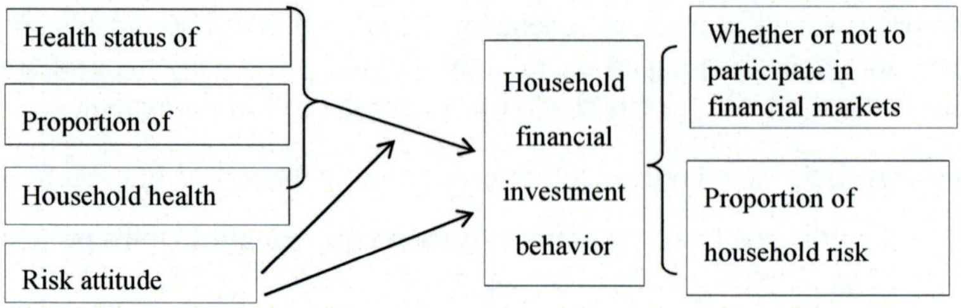

Fig. 4.1 Research framework of this chapter

affect household financial investment behavior under gender differences, providing new insights for a better understanding of residents' asset allocation behavior.

Based on the above discussions, this chapter establishes the following research framework (see Fig. 4.1).

4.4 Empirical Study Based on the 2017 China Household Finance Survey

4.4.1 Data

The data used in this chapter comes from the 2017 China Household Finance Survey (CHFS). The CHFS employed a scientific random sampling method, collecting data from a total of 40,011 households, covering 29 provinces, 355 districts and counties, and 1428 communities nationwide. It is representative at the national, provincial, and some sub-provincial city levels. This project was conducted by the China Household Finance Survey and Research Center of Southwestern University of Finance and Economics as a nationwide survey. Its main purpose is to collect relevant information about micro-level household finance, including housing assets and financial wealth, debts and credit constraints, income, consumption, social security and insurance, intergenerational transfer payments, demographic characteristics, employment, payment habits, and other related information. These rich data provide the empirical analysis for this chapter. The unit of analysis for the family financial investment behavior in this chapter is the household rather than the individual. After removing samples with missing key variables, the analyzed sample consists of 27,841 households with valid information.

4.4.2 Variables

4.4.2.1 Dependent Variables

The focus of the study is family financial investment behavior, which will be measured through two variables based on previous literature: family participation in the financial market and family asset selection. According to the CHFS data, family financial assets mainly consist of stocks, funds, financial wealth management products, financial derivatives, bonds, gold, non-RMB assets, current deposits and fixed deposits, cash, and lending. Family risk financial assets mainly include stocks, funds, financial wealth management products, financial derivatives, bonds, gold, non-RMB assets, and lending. Family participation in the financial market is a binary variable, measured by whether the family invests in risk assets in the financial market. If the respondent holds any type of risk asset, the variable takes the value of 1; otherwise, it takes the value of 0. The proportion of family risk assets is a continuous variable, measured by the proportion of family risk assets to total financial assets. The value ranges from 0 to 1.

4.4.2.2 Independent Variables

The core independent variables are health condition and risk attitude. Health indicators are measured at both the household head level and the household level, constructing three health condition measurement indicators: (1) The household head's health condition is measured through the head's personal self-rated health, divided into five dimensions: very poor, poor, fair, good, and very good; (2) Household-level health takes into account both subjective and objective health indicators. Following the approach of He and He (2018), the overall health condition of the household is measured by the proportion of non-healthy members in the household population (i.e., members who self-rate their health as poor or very poor); (3) The household health investment indicator is represented by the sum of family medical expenses and family health care expenses. Health condition is an investable asset, determined by both innate endowment and postnatal investment. For example, investments in health care expenses for maintaining health reflect the degree of importance that family members attach to health (Grossman 1972). The analysis shows that the higher the proportion of family members self-rating as non-healthy, the more family health expenses there are. The risk attitude variable is divided into three categories: risk preference, risk aversion, and risk neutrality.[1] "High-risk, high-return projects" and "slightly high-risk, slightly high-return projects" are defined as risk preference; "average-risk, average-return projects" are defined as risk neutrality; "slightly low-risk, slightly low-return projects" and "unwilling to take any risk" are defined as risk aversion.

---

[1] The question in the CHFS questionnaire measuring risk attitude is: If you have a sum of money to invest, which type of investment would you prefer?

4.4.2.3 Control Variables

To better control for the influence of other relevant factors on family financial investment behavior, this chapter selects variables from three levels: household head characteristics, family characteristics, and regional characteristics, as control variables. Among them, household head characteristic variables include gender, age, marital status, and education level. Referring to the research of Zhou and Liu (2014), considering the important correlation between health status and medical insurance, it is necessary to include medical insurance in the model when studying the impact of health status on family financial investment behaviour (Zhou and Liu 2014). Therefore, family characteristic variables include family income, whether they own their own housing, and whether they participate in medical insurance. Regional characteristic variables are measured by urban–rural type and regional variables. In addition, considering the nonlinear impact of the age variable, the model also introduces the square of age to characterize this feature. Marital status is defined as a binary dummy variable, with the marital statuses of "married," "remarried," and "cohabiting" defined as "partnered" with a value of 1, while other marital statuses are assigned a value of 0. Education level is a grouped variable, divided into four categories: primary school and below, junior high school, high school, and college and above. Variables such as owning one's own housing and having medical insurance are binary dummy variables, with "yes" assigned a value of 1 and "no" assigned a value of 0.

Table 4.1 shows the descriptive statistical results of the relevant variables studied in this chapter. The data shows that among the 27,841 samples studied in this chapter, 31.2% of families participated in the financial market, with an average proportion of risk assets of 16.1%. Risk-averse families had the highest proportion at 68.6%, indicating that Chinese families have a relatively low participation rate in the financial market and a low proportion of risk assets in total financial assets. Families with good health conditions accounted for the highest proportion at 37.7%; the proportion of families with self-assessed non-healthy members was 20.6%, and the family's health expenses within a year were 0.862 million yuan, indicating that the overall health condition of the sample is relatively good. The average income of the families was 10.306 million yuan, with 83.9% of families owning their own homes, and 95.1% of families having medical insurance. Male household heads accounted for 79.2% of the sample, with an average age of 54 years. Households with partners accounted for 86%. Urban families accounted for 73.4%, with respective proportions in the eastern, central, and western regions being 52.4, 25.6, and 21.9%.

4.4.3 Models

To assess household financial investment behavior from the perspectives of market participation and asset selection, two dependent variables, "Household Financial Market Participation" and "Proportion of Household Risk Assets," were constructed. Based on micro-data from the 2017 China Household Finance Survey (CHFS), Logit

Table 4.1 Descriptive statistics of variables

Variables	Mean	Standard deviation	Min	Max
Financial market participation	0.312	0.464	0	1
Proportion of risk assets	0.161	0.297	0	1
Head of household's health status				
Very poor	0.017	0.130	0	1
Poor	0.093	0.291	0	1
Fair	0.357	0.479	0	1
Good	0.377	0.485	0	1
Very good	0.155	0..362	0	1
Family member health condition	0.206	0.388	0	1
Health expenditure (in 10,000 RMB)	0.862	2.579	0	60
Risk attitude				
Risk preference	0.107	0.309	0	1
Risk aversion	0.686	0.464	0	1
Risk neutral	0.207	0.405	0	1
Family income (in 10,000 RMB)	10.306	20.711	0	500
Owns house	0.839	0.368	0	1
Medical insurance	0.951	0.217	0	1
Head of household gender	0.792	0.406	0	1
Head of household age	53.988	13.992	18	90
Square of head of household age	3110.432	1529.638	324	8100
Head of household has a partner	0.860	0.347	0	1
Head of household education level				
Elementary school or below	0.251	0.433	0	1
Junior high school	0.256	0.437	0	1
High school	0.217	0.412	0	1
College or above	0.191	0.393	0	1
Urban	0.734	0.442	0	1
Region				
Eastern	0.524	0.499	0	1
Central	0.256	0.437	0	1
Western	0.219	0.414	0	1

and Tobit models were employed, while controlling for other influencing factors, to empirically study the relationship between health status, risk attitude, and household participation in the financial market as well as the proportion of risk assets. When examining household participation in the financial market, a Logit model was used in this chapter. The regression equation takes the form:

$$\text{Finance}_i = \alpha + \beta_1 \text{Health}_i + \beta_2 \text{Risk}_i + \beta_3 \text{X}_i + \varepsilon_i \quad (4.1)$$

where, for the surveyed household represented by i, α is the intercept term. Finance_ i, the dependent variable representing household financial market participation, is a dummy variable; 1 denotes participation in the financial market, while 0 indicates non-participation. Health_i represents health status, with the main variables being the head of the household's health status, overall family health status, and family health expenditures. Risk_i denotes risk attitude, and Xi represents control variables that may influence household market participation, including family characteristics, head of household characteristics, and regional variables. ε_i is the error term, representing unobservable factors in the model, and follows a logistic distribution.

When examining household financial asset selection, the dependent variable is the proportion of household risk assets. Since various financial asset variables for households may be equal to zero, the Tobit model is used to address the issue of zero accumulation due to many households not holding risk financial assets. In this case of censored data, the Tobit model is applied to analyze the impact of health status and risk attitude on the proportion of household risk assets. The regression equation for the Tobit model is as follows:

$$\text{Risk\_weight}_i = \alpha + \beta_1 \text{Health}_i + \beta_2 \text{Risk}_i + \beta_3 \text{X}_i + \varepsilon_i \quad (4.2)$$

The Tobit model regression formula is similar to the Logit model, except that Risk_weight_i, representing the proportion of risk assets, denotes the amount of risk assets owned by the surveyed household. It is constrained to be within the range of (0, 1), indicating the proportion of risk assets to total financial assets held by the household. ε_i is the error term, following a standard normal distribution.

4.5 Family Financial Investment Behavior Choices Under Different Health Conditions

Health status is an important influencing factor in household financial market participation and asset selection, and it varies among different families. CHFS categorizes self-assessed health status into five dimensions, thereby dividing the sample into five levels: very poor, poor, fair, good, and very good, for a brief analysis, as shown in Table 4.2.

In families with extremely poor health conditions, only 63 households participate in the family financial market. As the health condition improves, the participation rate in the family financial market gradually increases, rising from 13.21 to 38.01%. Correspondingly, the proportion of risk assets also increases from 7.09 to 19.83%. It can be observed that there is a positive correlation between health status and whether a family participates in the financial market, as well as the proportion of risk assets held. The better the health condition of the family, the higher the likelihood of

Table 4.2 Family financial investment choices under different health conditions

Health condition	Participation in financial markets		Not participating in financial markets		Risk asset proportion	
	Number of households	Percentage (%)	Number of households	Percentage (%)	Mean (%)	Standard deviation
Very poor	63	13.21	414	86.79	7.09	0.220
Poor	524	20.19	2071	79.81	10.35	0.255
Fair	2790	28.05	7158	71.95	13.92	0.282
Good	3709	35.32	6792	64.68	18.35	0.309
Very good	1642	38.01	2678	61.99	19.83	0.317

participating in the financial market and the greater the proportion of risk financial assets held.

4.6 Family Financial Investment Behavior Choices Under Different Risk Attitudes by Gender

Consistent with previous research findings, this chapter's results indicate that the higher the risk preference, the more inclined the family is to engage in financial investment. As shown in Table 4.3, families with a risk preference exhibit the highest participation rate in the financial market and the highest proportion of risk assets. Specifically, for families where the head is male, the participation rate in the financial market is 49.73%, and the proportion of risk assets is 27.14%. For families where the head is female, the participation rate is 53.85%, and the proportion of risk assets is 31.80%. Meanwhile, there are also differences in the choice of financial investment behavior based on risk attitudes and gender. Previous studies have found gender differences in risk attitudes, leading to differential choices in investment behaviour (Croson and Gneezy 2009). In risk-preference families, compared to males, females have relatively higher participation rates in the financial market and higher proportions of risk assets, which contradicts the general conclusion that females are more risk-averse in investment decisions (Barber and Odean 2001). In risk-neutral families, the differences between males and females are not significant. In risk-averse families, males tend to be more involved in the financial market and hold a relatively higher proportion of risk assets.

Table 4.3 Family financial investment behavior choices under different risk attitudes by gender

Risk attitude	Participation rate in financial markets		Proportion of risk assets	
	Male (%)	Female (%)	Male (%)	Female (%)
Risk preference	49.73	53.85	27.14	31.80
Risk neutral	41.82	42.24	22.09	23.62
Risk aversion	25.42	24.29	12.39	11.86

4.7 Family Financial Investment Behavior Choices Among Different Groups

Due to the existence of family heterogeneity, there are differences in family financial investment behavior among different groups. As shown in Table 4.4, under different marital statuses, families with partners have higher participation rates and higher proportions of risk assets in the financial market compared to single-parent families. In terms of education levels, as the educational level of the head of the household increases, there is a greater likelihood of family participation in the financial market and a higher proportion of investment in risk assets. Regarding home ownership, families with self-owned houses participate relatively less in the financial market, avoiding investments in risky financial assets. In terms of medical insurance, families with medical insurance have a higher participation rate in the financial market and tend to increase the proportion of risk assets. Sample data indicates a positive correlation between having a partner, education level, medical insurance, and family financial investment behavior, while home ownership shows a negative correlation with family financial investment behavior. Additionally, there are significant differences between urban and rural areas, with urban families having nearly twice the participation rate and proportion of risk assets in the financial market compared to rural families. Among different regions, compared to the central and western regions, families in the eastern region have the highest participation rate in the financial market and the highest proportion of risk assets.

4.8 Health Condition, Risk Attitude, and Family Financial Investment Behavior

4.8.1 Analysis of Family Participation in Financial Markets

When analyzing the factors influencing family participation in financial markets, especially the impact of health condition and risk attitude on the likelihood of family participation, a Logit model was employed. The regression results of this model are shown in Table 4.5.

Table 4.4 Family financial investment behavior choices for different groups

Variables	Participation rate in financial markets		Proportion of risk assets	
	Households	Percentage (%)	Mean	Standard deviation
Marital status				
With partner	7680	32.07	16.30	0.297
Without partner	1048	26.89	14.62	0.293
Educational level of head of household				
Primary school or below	1020	14.61	7.55	0.223
Junior high school	2563	26.95	13.79	0.281
Senior high school	2265	37.57	18.11	0.308
College and above	2880	54.10	28.95	0.345
Own housing				
Yes	7141	30.59	15.45	0.292
No	1587	35.35	19.21	0.317
Medical insurance				
Yes	8393	31.71	16.23	0.297
No	335	24.36	12.71	0.279
Urban–rural classification				
Urban	7431	36.34	18.65	0.312
Rural	1297	17.54	8.89	0.234
Region				
Eastern	5172	35.43	18.12	0.309
Central	1825	25.59	13.01	0.273
Western	1731	28.33	14.69	0.289

The (1) column presents the regression results considering only the control variables' impact on the probability of family participation in financial markets. The results show that family income, medical insurance, male head of household, age, education level, and urban residence have a significant positive impact on family participation in financial markets. On the other hand, owning a house, age squared, and marital status have a significant negative impact on family participation. In terms of regions, compared to the eastern region, families in the central and western regions have a lower probability of participating in financial markets.

The (2) column and (3) column sequentially include the health condition and risk attitude variables in the regression results. The results show that after including the risk attitude variable, the regression results of health condition and other control variables remain consistent with the previous conclusions. However, the marginal effects of health condition-related variables have changed.

Regarding health condition, the head of the household's health condition has a positive impact on family participation in financial markets, significant at the 10%

Table 4.5 Empirical analysis of financial market participation

Variables	Logit		
	(1)	(2)	(3)
Health condition of household head			
Poor		1.412**	1.434**
		(0.213)	(0.217)
Fair		1.281*	1.308*
		(0.190)	(0.194)
Good		1.347**	1.364**
		(0.201)	(0.204)
Very good		1.413**	1.433**
		(0.214)	(0.218)
Health condition of family members		0.717***	0.732***
		(0.036)	(0.037)
ln (health expenditure)		1.030***	1.031***
		(0.004)	(0.004)
Risk attitude			
Risk preference			1.385***
			(0.068)
Risk aversion			0.681***
			(0.024)
ln (household income)	1.528***	1.501***	1.478***
	(0.022)	(0.022)	(0.021)
Own housing	0.867***	0.859***	0.862***
	(0.034)	(0.034)	(0.034)
Medical insurance	1.255***	1.233***	1.245***
	(0.088)	(0.086)	(0.088)
Male household head	1.113***	1.117***	1.098***
	(0.041)	(0.041)	(0.041)
Age of household head	1.016**	1.020***	1.027***
	(0.007)	(0.007)	(0.007)
Square of age of household head	1.000***	1.000***	1.000***
	(0.000)	(0.000)	(0.000)
Household head with partner	0.924*	0.906**	0.929*
	(0.044)	(0.043)	(0.044)
Educational level of household head			
Junior high school	1.476***	1.452***	1.463***
	(0.064)	(0.063)	(0.064)
Senior high school	2.057***	2.001***	1.965***

(continued)

Table 4.5 (continued)

Variables	Logit		
	(1)	(2)	(3)
	(0.096)	(0.094)	(0.092)
College and above	2.798***	2.679***	2.520***
	(0.143)	(0.138)	(0.131)
Urban	1.426***	1.382***	1.375***
	(0.056)	(0.054)	(0.054)
Region			
Central	0.815***	0.828***	0.836***
	(0.028)	(0.029)	(0.030)
Western	0.917**	0.921**	0.916**
	(0.033)	(0.034)	(0.034)
Observations	27,841	27,841	27,841
Pseudo R^2	0.122	0.125	0.134

Note *, **, and *** indicate significance at the 10%, 5%, and 1% confidence levels, respectively. The table reports estimated marginal effects, with standard errors in parentheses

level. The overall health risk of the family has a significant negative impact on family participation, with a marginal effect of 0.283. This indicates that as the proportion of family members with poor self-rated health increases, the family is more inclined not to participate in financial markets. Maintaining health requires investment in healthcare costs, and investing in healthcare can help people achieve good health. Family health expenditure has a significant positive impact on family participation in financial markets.

The more health expenditure, the higher the subjective life expectancy, reflecting a higher expected level of life. According to Friedman's Permanent Income Hypothesis, residents' consumption levels depend on their permanent income. As age increases, non-risk income decreases, especially after retirement, which may exhibit a "cliff-like" decline. Therefore, to ensure individual consumption levels or future quality of life, it is more likely to accumulate wealth at the current stage, such as participating in investments in risk assets to obtain additional income. This validates the first research hypothesis of this chapter, that health condition has a significant positive impact on family financial investment behavior.

The full model results show that risk attitude significantly affects whether families participate in financial markets at the 1% level. Compared to risk-neutral families, risk-loving families have a significantly increased probability of participating in financial markets by 38.5%, while risk-averse families have a significantly decreased probability of 31.9%. This indicates that the likelihood of family investing in financial assets significantly increases with the degree of risk preference, validating hypothesis 2.

After introducing the risk attitude variable, the marginal effect and significance level of the head of the household's health condition have increased, indicating that risk attitude is a suppressor variable between the head of the household's self-rated health condition and family participation in financial markets. Hypothesis 3a is not supported, suggesting that the impact of the head of the household's self-rated health condition on family financial investment behavior is to some extent overshadowed by risk attitude, exerting a greater promotion effect on family participation in financial markets than expected. The marginal effect of family member health condition is slightly reduced after adding the risk attitude variable, decreasing from 28.3 to 26.8%, indicating that risk attitude plays an intermediary role between family member health condition and family participation in financial markets. This validates hypothesis 3b. The marginal effect of family health expenditure does not change significantly after adding the risk attitude variable, indicating that there may be no mediating effect of risk attitude between family health expenditure and family participation in financial markets. Hypothesis 3c is not supported. This performance may be because the family health expenditure studied in this chapter is not expected to occur, and therefore, it does not have an impact on current risk attitude.

The regression results of control variables are consistent with the (1) column. In terms of family-level variables, with an increase in income, the probability of family participation in financial markets increases, in line with the "wealth theory." Families who own houses are less willing to participate in financial markets, showing a significant negative relationship. The impact of property on financial market participation is primarily due to "substitution effect" and "crowding-out effect." Medical insurance significantly promotes family participation in financial markets. Insured families are more inclined to participate in financial investments compared to uninsured families, indicating that medical insurance can weaken the impact of health risks on family participation in financial markets. Participating in medical insurance is an effective way for families to reduce health risks because medical insurance can change the expected uncertainty of the family's future, reduce the potential for large medical expenses in the future, and thereby inhibit the adverse effects of health risks on family financial asset investment.

In terms of head of household characteristics, the head of household's gender has a significant impact on family participation in financial markets. Families with male heads of households are more inclined to invest in financial markets compared to those with female heads. Age and the probability of family participation in financial markets have a significant positive relationship and exhibit a significant quadratic nonlinear impact, indicating that the probability of family participation in financial markets shows an increasing-then-decreasing trend with age, in line with the "life cycle theory." Some previous studies believed that marriage is a form of safety asset, and married families are more willing to invest in financial markets compared to single families. However, this study indicates that having a partner has a significant negative impact on whether families participate in financial markets. Families with partners are less inclined to invest in financial assets. This is consistent with the findings of Hu et al. (2015). On one hand, it may be because single families have lighter burdens and stronger risk resistance, so they are more willing to invest in financial assets. On the other hand, families with partners bear greater responsibilities and are more cautious and conservative when investing in financial markets, tending to avoid risks. Due to inconsistent conclusions in existing literature, the impact of marriage on family participation in financial markets requires further verification in future research. Education level significantly promotes family participation in financial markets. The higher the education level of the head of household, the deeper the understanding of financial knowledge and risk-return, thereby promoting family financial investment. In terms of regional variables, compared to rural families, urban families have a significantly increased probability of participating in financial markets. Compared to the eastern region, families in the central and western regions have a significantly lower probability of participating in financial markets.

4.8.2 Analysis of Proportion of Risk Assets

When determining the factors influencing the proportion of risk assets held by families, this chapter employs the Tobit model for empirical analysis. The model aims to identify the factors affecting the proportion of risk assets held by families within their total financial assets, particularly considering factors such as health condition and risk attitude. The regression results of this model are shown in Table 4.6.

Regarding the core explanatory variables, the results are consistent with those of the Logit model. Overall, health condition and risk attitude significantly impact the proportion of risk assets held by families, aligning with Hypotheses 1 and 2.

Specifically, apart from the general health condition, the health condition of the head of the household significantly influences at the 5% level. The health condition of family members and family health expenditures have a significant impact on the proportion of risk assets at the 1% level. This suggests that the better the health condition of households, the higher the expenditure on health, and the greater the proportion of investment in risk assets. This further underscores the positive utility of health as a special form of human capital. Maintaining health condition relies on investment in health expenditures.

The influence of risk attitude on the proportion of risk assets is also significant at the 1% level. Compared to risk-neutral families, risk-averse families have a significantly lower proportion of risk assets, below 16.2%. Risk-seeking families, on the other hand, have a significantly higher proportion, above 9.9%. After incorporating the risk attitude variable, the marginal effect of the head's health condition increases. This indicates an inhibitory effect of risk attitude. Risk attitude does not mediate between the head's health condition and the proportion of risk assets. Thus, Hypothesis 3a in this chapter is not confirmed.

After including the risk attitude variable, the marginal effect of family members' health condition decreases by 1.2%. This suggests that risk attitude plays a partial mediating role between family members' health condition and the proportion of investment in risk assets. The higher the proportion of self-assessed non-healthy members in the family, the more conservative the family's risk attitude tends to be,

Table 4.6 Empirical analysis of proportion of risk assets

Variables	Tobit		
	(1)	(2)	(3)
Health condition of household head			
Poor		0.109**	0.115**
		(0.055)	(0.054)
Fair		0.071*	0.080*
		(0.054)	(0.053)
Good		0.112**	0.117**
		(0.054)	(0.054)
Very good		0.122**	0.127**
		(0.055)	(0.055)
Health condition of family members		– 0.130***	– 0.118***
		(0.019)	(0.019)
ln (health expenditure)		0.010***	0.010***
		(0.002)	(0.002)
Risk attitude			
Risk preference			0.099***
			(0.018)
Risk aversion			– 0.162***
			(0.013)
ln (household income)	0.126***	0.120***	0.114***
	(0.005)	(0.005)	(0.005)
Own housing	– 0.064***	– 0.067***	– 0.065***
	(0.015)	(0.015)	(0.015)
Medical insurance	0.086***	0.081***	0.083***
	(0.026)	(0.026)	(0.026)
Male household head	0.034**	0.034**	0.027**
	(0.014)	(0.014)	(0.014)
Age of household head	– 0.001	0.001	0.003
	(0.003)	(0.003)	(0.000)
Square of age of household head	– 0.000***	– 0.000***	– 0.000***
	(0.000)	(0.000)	(0.000)
Household head with partner	– 0.030*	– 0.039**	– 0.030*
	(0.018)	(0.018)	(0.018)
Educational level of household head			
Junior high school	0.140***	0.134***	0.134***
	(0.016)	(0.016)	(0.016)
Senior high school	0.238***	0.225***	0.211***

(continued)

Table 4.6 (continued)

Variables	Tobit		
	(1)	(2)	(3)
	(0.018)	(0.018)	(0.018)
College and above	0.375***	0.355***	0.321***
	(0.019)	(0.020)	(0.019)
Urban	0.141***	0.127***	0.121***
	(0.015)	(0.015)	(0.015)
Region			
Central	– 0.074***	– 0.065***	– 0.060***
	(0.013)	(0.013)	(0.013)
Western	– 0.039***	– 0.035***	– 0.036***
	(0.014)	(0.014)	(0.014)
Observations	27,841	27,841	27,841
Pseudo R^2	0.103	0.106	0.114

Note *, **, ***indicate significance at the 10%, 5%, 1% confidence levels, respectively. The table reports estimated marginal effects, with standard errors in parentheses

resulting in a reduction in the proportion of investment in risk assets. This verifies Hypothesis 3b. The marginal effect of family health expenditures remains unchanged after including the risk attitude variable. This indicates that risk attitude does not mediate between family health expenditures and the proportion of investment in risk assets. Therefore, Hypothesis 3c is not supported.

In terms of control variables, family income continues to have a significant positive impact on the proportion of risk assets, consistent with the "wealth effect". The proportion of risk assets significantly increases with the increase in family income. Owning a residential property has a significant negative impact on the proportion of risk assets, exhibiting a "crowding out effect". This means that investment in housing reduces the proportion of investment in financial risk assets. Medical insurance has a significant promoting effect on the proportion of risk assets. Families with medical insurance are more willing to increase the proportion of investment in risk assets. Medical insurance can to some extent compensate for the economic costs associated with health risks, further promoting family participation in risk investment.

In contrast to the regression results of the Logit model, the age of the head of the household does not have a significant impact on the proportion of risk assets. However, the impact of other characteristics of the head of the household follows the same pattern as in the Logit model. Urban–rural type and regional variables have a significant impact on the proportion of risk assets. Urban families have a higher proportion of risk assets compared to rural families. Families in the central and western regions have a lower proportion of risk assets compared to families in the eastern region.

4.8.3 Test of the Mediating Effect of Risk Attitude

The stepwise regression method was used to preliminarily explore whether the health condition of the household head, the health condition of family members, and family health expenditures affect household financial investment behavior through their influence on risk attitude. It was found that risk attitude exerts a suppressive effect between the health condition of the household head and household financial investment behavior. There is no mediating effect between family health expenditures and household financial investment behavior. Instead, it is only the health condition of family members that exerts a mediating effect on household financial investment behavior through its influence on risk attitude. To further examine the existence of the mediating effect of risk attitude, this chapter employs the KHB detection method for a secondary examination of the mediating effect and estimates the contribution of the mediating effect.

The results of the mediation test between risk attitude, family member health condition (proportion of self-assessed non-healthy members), and family participation in the financial market as well as the proportion of risk assets are shown in columns (1) and (2) of Table 4.7. The results indicate that whether in terms of the probability of family participation in the financial market or the impact on the proportion of risk assets, the total effect, direct effect, and mediating effect of family member health condition are all significant. This suggests that risk attitude plays a mediating role between the two. Upon further decomposition of the mediating effect, it is found that family member health condition has a negative effect on risk attitude, while risk attitude has a positive effect on family participation in the financial market and the proportion of risk assets. This implies a negative correlation between family member health condition and risk attitude. This is because when the proportion of non-healthy family members is higher, the family faces greater health risks, causing them to be less willing to engage in financial investment and reduce their holdings of risk assets, turning to safer investments. Therefore, risk attitude partially mediates between family member health condition (proportion of self-assessed non-healthy members) and family participation in the financial market as well as the proportion of risk assets: 6.59% of the impact of family member health condition on family participation in the financial market is achieved through risk attitude, and 7.08% of the impact of family member health condition on the proportion of risk assets is achieved through risk attitude.

Different genders have different risk attitudes, leading to different financial investment decisions. To study the gender differences in the impact of health status and risk attitudes on household financial investment behavior, this chapter divides the full sample into two sub-samples by gender for regression analysis based on Model (1) and Model (2). Table 4.8 presents the regression results of the gender differences in the impact on household financial market participation and the proportion of household risk assets.

In the case of poor health status for the household head, the likelihood of financial market participation and the proportion of risk assets are significantly higher for

Table 4.7 Mediation effects test of risk attitude

Variables	Financial market participation	Risk asset ratio
	Family member health condition	Family member health condition
Direct effect	– 0.279***	– 0.106***
Mediation effect	– 0.020**	– 0.008**
Confidence interval lower bound	– 0.036	– 0.015
Confidence interval upper bound	– 0.004	– 0.001
Contribution rate (%)	6.59	7.08
Total effect	– 0.299***	– 0.114***

Note *, **, and *** respectively indicate significance at the 10, 5, and 1% confidence levels. Control variables are the same as in Table 4.5

Table 4.8 Gender differences in household financial investment behavior

Variables	Financial market participation rate		Proportion of risk assets	
	Male (1)	Female (2)	Male (3)	Female (4)
Head of household health condition				
Poor	1.348*	1.966*	0.105*	0.155
	(0.227)	(0.711)	(0.062)	(0.117)
Fair	1.186	1.937*	0.059	0.143
	(0.195)	(0.704)	(0.060)	(0.118)
Good	1.241	2.025*	0.089	0.208*
	(0.205)	(0.740)	(0.060)	(0.119)
Excellent	1.301	2.142*	0.096	0.234*
	(0.219)	(0.797)	(0.061)	(0.121)
Family member health condition	0.740***	0.691***	– 0.116***	– 0.127***
	(0.041)	(0.090)	(0.021)	(0.049)
ln (health expenditure)	1.029***	1.038***	0.010***	0.011***
	(0.005)	(0.010)	(0.002)	(0.003)
Risk attitude				
Risk preference	1.312***	1.694***	0.076***	0.183***
	(0.072)	(0.191)	(0.020)	(0.040)
Risk aversion	0.687***	0.653*	– 0.156***	– 0.180***
	(0.027)	(0.510)	(0.015)	(0.029)
Observations	22,041	5800	22,041	5800
Pseudo R^2	0.129	0.159	0.109	0.136

Note *, **, and *** indicate significance at the 10%, 5%, and 1% confidence levels respectively. Values in parentheses are standard errors. Control variables are the same as in Table 4.5

male-headed households at the 10% level. For female-headed households, regardless of their health status, there is a significant impact on their participation in the financial market. However, the proportion of risk assets for female-headed households is significantly higher only when their health status is good or very good. There is no gender difference in the impact of family member health status and family health expenditures on financial market participation and the proportion of risk assets. They are both significant at the 1% level, indicating that investments in healthcare have the same improvement effect on the health status of both males and females. Risk attitudes have a significant impact on male and female household heads' participation in the financial market and the proportion of investment in risk assets, both at the 1% level, with a relatively higher marginal effect in female-headed households. The results indicate that better health status does not necessarily lead to increased participation in the financial market; this depends on the specific level of the household head's health. Compared to male-headed households, risk attitudes have a greater impact on the financial investment decisions of female-headed households.

4.9 Urban–Rural Disparities in the Influence of Health Status and Risk Attitudes on Household Participation in Financial Markets

To verify the robustness of the empirical results, this chapter divides the full sample into urban and rural samples for subgroup analysis. According to the data in Table 4.9, overall, good health status promotes household participation in financial markets and increases the proportion of household investments in risk assets. At the same time, as risk preferences increase, the likelihood of household participation in financial markets and the proportion of investments in risk assets significantly rise. The disparity in health expenditures between urban and rural residents may be attributed to the differences in the participation rate and coverage of medical insurance enjoyed by urban and rural residents in China. In rural households, health expenditures for medical visits and healthcare are more dependent on whether there is a surplus in the household economy. Therefore, health expenditures also become a "luxury". Given that the impact of various explanatory variables on financial market participation and the proportion of risk assets is relatively consistent, it indicates that the estimation results in this chapter are robust.

Table 4.9 Health status, risk attitudes, and household financial investment behavior: robustness test (urban and rural sample regression)

Variables	Market participation rate		Risk asset proportion	
	Urban (1)	Rural (2)	Urban (3)	Rural (4)
Head of household health				
Poor	1.377*	1.613*	0.107*	0.148
	(0.242)	(0.505)	(0.063)	(0.122)
Fair	1.199	1.540	0.068	0.097
	(0.207)	(0.467)	(0.062)	(0.118)
Good	1.196	1.954**	0.092	0.195*
	(0.208)	(0.598)	(0.062)	(0.120)
Very good	1.284	1.851**	0.108*	0.178*
	(0.227)	(0.579)	(0.063)	(0.123)
Family member health	0.700***	0.810*	− 0.122***	− 0.115***
	(0.044)	(0.073)	(0.023)	(0.040)
ln (health expenditure)	1.034***	1.012	0.011***	0.005
	(0.005)	(0.010)	(0.002)	(0.004)
Risk attitude				
Risk preference	1.500***	0.931	0.115***	− 0.015
	(0.081)	(0.122)	(0.019)	(0.059)
Risk aversion	0.639***	0.858*	− 0.182***	− 0.083**
	(0.025)	(0.072)	(0.014)	(0.038)
Observations	20,448	7393	20,448	7393
Pseudo R^2	0.116	0.098	0.098	0.086

Note *, **, and *** denote significance at the 10%, 5%, and 1% levels respectively. Standard errors are reported in parentheses. Control variables are the same as in Table 4.5

4.10 Recommendations for Promoting the Healthy Development of China's Household Financial Market

Based on the 2017 China Household Finance Survey data, this chapter explores the relationship between health status, risk attitudes, and household financial investment behavior. Building on previous research, health status is operationalized from both subjective and objective perspectives. The findings confirm that at the household level, good health status, considered as an investable health capital, has a significant positive impact on household participation in financial markets and asset selection. From a theoretical perspective, economic theory assumes that household investors are rational and seek to achieve intertemporal optimization of resources to maximize long-term utility. More expenditure on health reflects greater investment in one's health over time, implying an expectation of a longer lifespan. Consequently, as individuals age, non-risky income may decrease, particularly after retirement, potentially leading to a precipitous drop. According to the Friedman permanent income hypothesis, the level of resident consumption depends on their permanent income. In order to ensure their consumption level or future quality of life, individuals are more likely to accumulate wealth in the current stage. This may involve investing in risk assets to gain additional returns. Additionally, when controlling for health status, as risk preferences increase, the likelihood of household participation in financial markets and the proportion of investments in risk assets also significantly increase.

The study found that compared to female household heads, male household heads are more inclined to participate in household financial markets and invest in risk assets. However, it is worth noting that there is a significant gender difference in the impact of household health status on financial investment behavior. In cases where the household head's health status is good or very good, women have a significantly higher proportion of risk assets compared to men. The influence of risk attitudes is greater for female household heads. The study also further identifies the impact of the "wealth effect" and the "crowding-out effect" on household investment in financial assets. As income increases, there is a greater likelihood of household participation in financial markets and a higher proportion of investments in risk assets, showing a significant positive impact, indicative of the "wealth effect". Owning a home suppresses household participation in financial markets and reduces the proportion of investments in risk assets, demonstrating a significant negative impact, indicative of the "crowding-out effect". Additionally, participating in medical insurance can reduce the economic burden of health risks. Therefore, insured households are more likely to invest in financial assets and have a relatively higher proportion of risk asset holdings.

The study elaborates in detail on the mechanisms through which health status and risk attitudes influence household financial investment behavior. It also provides a new perspective from the standpoint of financial sociology, highlighting how health is increasingly valued as a form of capital by investors. This offers a better understanding of household asset allocation and achieving asset appreciation. For financial institutions, designing products and financial innovations tailored to families with different health statuses and risk attitudes, and optimizing resource allocation across society through market segmentation, can be beneficial. At the macro level, the research findings can reflect residents' reasonable expectations regarding their lifespan and risk management. Therefore, they have certain guiding significance for deepening medical system reform, promoting the rational allocation of medical resources and healthcare expenditure, further improving the overall health level of the population, and reducing household health risks. By increasing the breadth and depth of household participation in financial markets, China's household financial market can be further developed in a healthy market.

References

Barber BM, Odean T (2001) Boys will be boys: gender, overconfidence, and common stock investment. Quart J Econ 116(1):261–292

Campbell JY (2006) Household finance. J Finance 61(4):1553–1604

Chen Q, Liu W (2014) The impact of health expenditure on residents' asset selection behavior: a discussion based on the homogeneity and heterogeneity debate. Shanghai Econ Res 2014(06):111–118

Croson R, Gneezy U (2009) Gender differences in preferences. J Econ Literature 47(2):448–474

Dow JS, da Costa Werlang SR (1992) Uncertainty aversion, risk aversion, and the optimal choice of portfolio. J Econometr Soc 60(1):197–204

Edwards RD (2010) Optimal portfolio choice when utility depends on health. Int J Econ Theory 6(2):205–225

Gao Y, Zhang Y, Song Q (2020) Crowding out effect of housing assets on family risk asset investment. Econ Manage Rev 36(4):106–121

Gao S (2009) Household financial investment and risk avoidance under financial crisis. J Hubei Univ Technol 24(3):59–60+65

Goldman D, Maestas N (2013) Medical Expenditure Risk and Household Portfolio Choice. J Appl Economet 28(4):527–550

Grossman M (1972) The demand for health: a theoretical and empirical investigation. NBER Working Paper, No. 119

He Y, He X (2018) Health and the degree of participation in family risk financial asset investment. J South China Normal Univ 2:135–142

He X, Xu M, Zheng L (2020) Real estate, social security, and financial risk investment of Chinese urban residents' families: an empirical study with relative deprivation and subjective well-being as mediators. Jianghuai Forum 1:98–109

Hillesland M (2019) Gender differences in risk behavior: an analysis of asset allocation decisions in Ghana. World Dev 117:127–137

Hu Z, Wang C, Zang R (2015) Family heterogeneity and financial asset allocation behavior: an empirical study based on urban Chinese families. Modern Manage 35(2):16–18

Li T, Guo J (2009) Risk Attitude and Stock Investment. Econ Res 44(2):56–67

Liao J (2017) Marital status and residents' financial investment preferences. Southern Finance 11:23–32

Liu X, Cheng Z, Zhang Q (2014) Resident health and financial investment preferences. Econ Res 49(S1):77–88

Liu H, Deng Y, Peng G (2020) Study on financial literacy, risk preference, and family risk asset allocation behavior. Contemp Econ 11:56–59

Liu J (2015) Heterogeneity of urban Chinese resident families and investment in risky financial assets. Econ Issues (3):51–55+60

Love DA, Perozek MG (2007) Should the old play it safe? Portfolio choice with uncertain medical expenses. Working paper

Luo W, Liang J (2020) Financial literacy and household risk asset investment decision: an empirical study based on CHFS 2017 data. Financial Theory Pract 11:45–56

Paiella M, Guiso L (2004) The role of risk aversion in predicting individual behaviour. CEPR discussion papers, no. 4591

Park JS, Suh D (2019) Uncertainty and household portfolio choice: evidence from South Korea. Econ Lett 180:21–24

Shefrin H, Statman M (2000) Behavioral portfolio theory. Cambridge University Press

Smith PA, Love DA (2010) Does health affect portfolio choice. Health Electron 19(12):1441–1460

Wang J, Wu W (2014) The influence of marriage on family risk asset selection. Nankai Econ Stud 3:100–112

Warneryd KE (1996) Risk attitudes and risky behavior. J Econ Psychol 17(6):749–770

Wei X, Zhang Y, Wu W et al (2014) Study on influencing factors of financial asset allocation in Chinese resident families. Manage Rev 26(7):20–28

Wu W, Rong P, Xu Q (2011) Health and family asset selection. Econ Res 46(S1):43–54

Yogo M (2016) Portfolio choice in retirement: health risk and the demand for annuities, housing and risky assets. J Monet Econ 80(6):17–34

Zhang J, Liang L (2020) An empirical study on the influence of family heterogeneity on financial asset allocation. J Chongqing Univ 23(1):1–11

Zhou Q, Liu G (2014) Health shocks: what role does the current medical insurance system play? Econ Rev 6:78–90

Chapter 5
Housing Types, Financial Literacy, and Household Financial Investment Behavior

It is well known that the past decade has been a golden period for Chinese real estate development in China. Houses, as a major asset class, have become a guarantee for the appreciation of residents' wealth. In recent years, guided by the policy of "housing for living, not for speculation," the contribution of real estate to wealth is decreasing. Chinese households are gradually shifting their asset allocation from physical assets like real estate towards financial assets. Citic Securities predicts that Chinese households will transfer $18 trillion USD into financial products over the next nine years. This structural shift in asset allocation is beneficial not only for increasing household property income but also for adjusting income distribution gaps and promoting macroeconomic growth. In this chapter, the author will focus on exploring the impact mechanism of housing types and financial literacy on household financial investment behavior at the micro level.

5.1 Characteristics of the Asset Allocation Structure of Residential Household Financial Assets

With the substantial growth of disposable income for urban and rural residents in China, asset allocation has become an important part of family investment decisions. The main focus of Chinese household asset allocation is on housing investment, with the participation and involvement rates in financial risk assets remaining relatively low internationally (Wu and Lv 2013). Since the implementation of the commercialization reform of housing in China at the end of the twentieth century, and the cancellation of the welfare housing allocation policy, the housing market has developed rapidly, and housing prices have continued to rise. The homeownership rate of residential households has increased rapidly. According to the "China Household Wealth Survey Report 2019," the structure of household financial asset allocation

S. Zhao and D. Zhao, *The Household Finance Issues in China*,
https://doi.org/10.1007/978-981-97-0706-5_5

shows a characteristic of singularity: household savings are relatively high, concentrated in cash, current deposits, and fixed-term deposits, accounting for nearly 90% of household financial assets. In terms of property composition, 93.03% of residential households own at least one property; there is a certain difference in net property value between urban and rural residential households, with urban households accounting for 71.35% of per capita wealth, while rural households account for 52.28%. A single financial asset structure is not conducive to balancing household asset risks and is difficult to achieve value preservation and appreciation (China Household Wealth Survey Report 2019). Additionally, there are significant differences in housing composition between urban and rural residential households. Urban households mainly purchase newly built commercial housing, accounting for 36.26%, while the proportions of self-built housing and purchasing second-hand housing are 24.43% and 10.97% respectively. Rural households are primarily engaged in self-built housing, accounting for 53.18%, with the proportion of self-built housing being nearly twice that of urban households. The proportions of purchasing newly built commercial housing and second-hand housing are 21.81% and 6.73% respectively. At the same time, the net value growth of Chinese real estate is mainly attributed to the value appreciation of newly built commercial housing and second-hand housing. Therefore, the difference in net property value of Chinese residential households reflects to some extent the difference in housing composition among residential households.

The advancement of urbanization has led to significant urban–rural differences in financial investment for Chinese residential households. From a micro perspective, this urban–rural difference mainly stems from the differences in income levels, housing, education levels, and financial literacy between urban and rural households, which in turn affect household financial investments. Household income is closely related to regional economic development. The duality of urban and rural economic development leads to higher incomes for urban households compared to rural households. Scholars have also found that household income has a significant positive impact on the likelihood and depth of household participation in financial investment (Faig and Nolan 2009; Wachter and Yogo 2010; He et al. 2019; Dan 2019). Housing is another important economic factor for families. Compared to rural households, urban households face greater pressure in the process of urbanization to purchase commercial housing, while rural households primarily engage in self-built housing. Studies have found that owning a home can significantly reduce the participation rate in the financial market and the proportion of financial asset holdings (He and He 2018; Gao et al. 2020). Differences in education levels between urban and rural areas influence the individual education levels and financial literacy levels of Chinese residents, leading to different choices in financial assets for urban and rural families. Previous studies have also confirmed the positive impact of education levels and financial literacy on household financial investment behavior (Bertocchi et al. 2011; Liao 2017; Hu 2019). Therefore, considering the significant differences in the housing environment and financial literacy between urban and rural households, in order to ensure the effectiveness of the conclusions, this chapter, through empirical analysis, starts from the relationship between housing and urban household financial investment behavior, discusses whether housing has a "negative crowding-out effect" or a "positive wealth effect" on household financial investment behavior, and further analyzes whether financial literacy plays an intermediary role in the relationship between housing and urban household financial investment behavior. It provides empirical evidence for explaining household financial investment behavior and explores feasible measures to further promote the healthy development of the Chinese financial market.

5.2 Empirical Research and Assumptions on the Impact of Housing on Household Financial Investment Behavior

Different from other investment products in the market, housing is one of the few assets that families can invest in through loans. On the other hand, housing also has the dual attributes of consumption and investment (Yang et al. 2014), thus affecting the demand for other goods and services and directly influencing the living standards and investment levels of the household. It is worth noting that while housing can be invested or consumed through borrowing, its liquidity and diversification are not as good as financial investment products. Therefore, price fluctuations in the housing market will affect the investment behavior of household investors (Wu et al. 2015). In addition, owning a home is not only a cultural preference but also a necessary means to guard against future poverty risks. Although many families can enjoy physical income and long-term appreciation from housing investment, it is more difficult to extract asset value from housing, making it challenging to convert these fixed assets into liquid resources for consumption. Therefore, there are currently two different viewpoints in the academic community regarding the impact of housing on household financial investment behavior, namely, whether housing has a dominant "crowding-out effect" or a dominant "wealth effect." A consensus has not yet been reached.

5.2.1 Empirical Studies on the "Crowding-Out Effect"

Currently, research on housing mainly focuses on aspects such as homeownership, quantity, price, proportion in total assets, and housing loans (He et al. 2019; Cardak and Wilkins 2009). It has been pointed out that there is a significant "crowding-out effect" of household housing investment on the proportion of risky financial asset investment (Zhou and He 2019). That is, under a certain level of household assets, housing investment leads to a decrease in the proportion of investment in risky financial assets. Fratantoni's research found that owning a home brings price risk and certain repayment risk to families, thereby reducing household investment in risky assets (Fratantoni 1998). Additionally, owning a home also reduces the share of stock assets in liquid financial assets (Yao and Zhang 2005). It is worth noting that this "crowding-out effect" is more pronounced for young and poor families. Cock's research found that housing investment reduces the liquidity assets of young and lower-wealth families, displacing the share of stock asset investment, which is consistent with previous research results (Cocco 2005).

5.2.2 *Empirical Studies on the "Wealth Effect"*

Existing literature has also produced competitive research conclusions. Some scholars believe that as a significant family asset, the appreciation of housing value increases the family's wealth level, promotes investment in financial assets, and demonstrates a "wealth effect" (Tobin 1980; Chen et al. 2015). With the substantial appreciation of housing, family wealth increases, encouraging active participation in financial investment. For instance, Cardak and Wilkins (2009) found that in societies with relatively sound credit systems, housing can serve as collateral, and families with more housing are more likely to invest in risky assets. However, when measuring housing value from the perspectives of net housing value and mortgage debt for home purchase, their impacts on holding risky assets are opposite. That is, an increase in net housing value enhances the allocation of risky assets, while mortgage debt for home purchase leads to a decrease in the allocation of risky assets (Cardak and Wilkins 2009; Chetty and Szeidl 2010). Domestic scholars, such as Wu et al. (2010), measured property investment based on the proportion of housing assets to financial assets. Their research found that when housing makes up a relatively low proportion of family wealth, it exhibits a "crowding-out effect" on investment in other risky assets. However, for families that already own homes and have higher wealth levels, housing enhances the family's ability to withstand risks, and the proportion of investment in risky assets actually increases (Wu et al. 2010). Liu (2015) found that in Chinese urban families, homeownership and the quantity of housing complement each other rather than being substitutes. This means that housing has a positive impact on the holding of risky assets. It is possible that residential households use housing ownership to achieve a diversified investment portfolio, thereby increasing the holding of risky financial assets (Liu 2015). Zhang and Xie (2018) study also found that owning multiple homes does not significantly lead to a "crowding-out effect" on the financial assets of rural families (Zhang and Xie 2018).

5.2.3 *Research Hypotheses Regarding Housing Types*

Given the unique characteristics of the Chinese housing market, some scholars have found that the dual-track reform model adopted for housing marketization results in a dual nature of market transformation in the housing sector. Commercial housing gradually becomes determined by market mechanisms, while welfare housing continues under a redistribution mechanism (Wu 2017). In the real estate market, housing disparities in China mainly stem from differences in family wealth, making it difficult for low-income families to improve their housing conditions (Ren and Hu 2016). Moreover, housing net value, as a form of financial resource, holds higher value compared to self- built/expanded housing and welfare housing (Toussaint and Elsinga 2009). Therefore, considering housing value and family wealth level, this chapter proposes the following assumptions:

Hypothesis 1a Owning commercial housing significantly increases the likelihood of family investment in financial assets, demonstrating a "wealth effect."

Hypothesis 1b Owning self-built/expanded housing significantly reduces the likelihood of family investment in financial assets, demonstrating a "crowding-out effect."

5.2.4 Empirical Studies on Housing Loans

Meanwhile, housing, as a consumable or investment product, can be consumed or invested in through borrowing. Staggered payments for housing loans represent a significant aspect of household debt. It alleviates the economic burden on families purchasing homes to some extent and allows them to diversify debt risks when facing economic shocks. In recent years, the continuously rising housing prices have stimulated expectations of future price increases. As a result, the proportion of housing assets in asset allocation continues to increase for families with different levels of wealth and income. Due to higher income, high-income families have stronger purchasing and financing capabilities for housing, resulting in higher housing debt ratios and leverage ratios. Research by Wu et al. (2013) also indicates that differences in the scale of household debt led to the widening gap in household wealth and have different impacts on asset allocation. Higher-income families face lower credit constraints because their wealth accumulates more quickly. They can further refine their household financial asset allocation through mortgage financing (Wu et al. 2013). Additionally, in China, qualification criteria for housing loans include stable income, good credit, and recognized mortgage assets. Wealthier families with higher income and more assets can use financial leverage to expand the gap in housing compared to other families. Affluent families, while obtaining higher asset yields and faster wealth growth, also bear lower debt costs (Chen et al. 2008; Wu and Li 2016). High debt, high housing value, and high income exhibit a positive correlation (Ling and Garry 1998). Therefore, holding housing loans to a certain extent can reflect a family's level of wealth and investment capability, making it more likely to allocate funds to invest in risky financial assets. Hence, we include housing loans as a control variable in the model to enhance the accuracy and explanatory power of the empirical results.

5.3 Empirical Study on the Impact of Financial Literacy on Household Finance Investment Behavior and Hypotheses

Financial literacy is an important form of human capital, referring to the knowledge and ability that investors possess to effectively manage their financial resources for lifelong financial well-being (Hu and Zang 2017). In recent years, both domestic and international scholars have recognized the significant role of financial literacy in financial investment. Kroll (2006) argues that financial knowledge has an increasingly significant impact on people's lives, and the level of financial knowledge is a crucial factor in determining whether individuals can be integrated into the financial system (Corr 2006). Zeng et al. (2015) found that households with higher levels of financial knowledge are more likely to participate in the financial market and invest in a wider range of financial products (Zeng et al. 2015). Qin et al. (2018) and Hu (2019) also discovered that an improvement in financial knowledge contributes to higher household participation rates in the financial market and increased investment in risk assets (Qin et al. 2018; Hu 2016). Additionally, some scholars have identified urban–rural disparities in financial literacy due to differences in economic development, resource allocation, and financial depth between urban and rural areas. Consequently, investors face variations in financial products and services, resulting in significant differences in financial literacy between urban and rural residents, with urban residents generally having higher financial literacy than rural residents (Liu 2018).

Stiglitz and Weiss (1981) pointed out that information asymmetry in financial markets can increase the difficulties and obstacles for households to participate in financial activities, leading to some households staying away from the financial market (Stiglitz and Weiss 1981). Therefore, limited participation in financial services and activities hinders the acquisition of financial information, largely contributing to the inadequate financial knowledge of household residents, thus exerting a negative impact on their involvement in risk financial investments. In the process of purchasing commercial housing, household residents can acquire financial and investment knowledge through financial institutions, thereby enhancing their level of financial literacy and subsequently promoting investment in financial assets. Given that most existing studies on household financial investment behavior primarily consider the independent impact of housing and largely overlook the potential influence of financial literacy between housing and household financial investment behavior, this chapter proposes the following hypotheses.

Hypothesis 2a Commercial housing affects household financial investment behavior by mediating the impact of financial literacy.

Hypothesis 2b Self-built/expanded housing affects household financial investment behavior by mediating the impact of financial literacy.

Based on the above discussions, this chapter establishes the following research framework, as shown in Fig. 5.1.

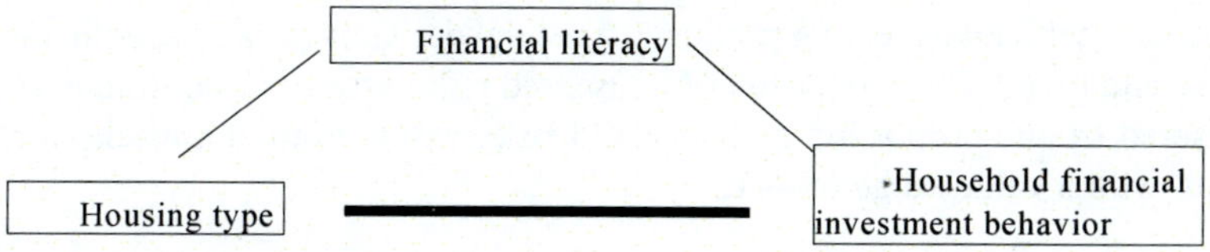

Fig. 5.1 Research framework of this chapter

5.4 Empirical Study Based on the 2017 China Household Finance Survey

5.4.1 Data

The research data comes from the 2017 China Household Finance Survey (CHFS). The survey adopts a scientific random sampling method, collecting data from 40,011 households, covering 29 provinces, 355 counties, and 1,428 communities nationwide. It has representative samples from national, provincial, and some sub-provincial cities. This project is a nationwide survey conducted by the China Household Finance Survey and Research Center of Southwestern University of Finance and Economics. Its main purpose is to collect relevant information about household finance at the micro level, including housing assets and financial wealth, debt and credit constraints, income, consumption, social security and insurance, intergenerational transfer payments, population characteristics and employment, payment habits, etc. These abundant pieces of information provide data support for empirical analysis. In this chapter, the unit of analysis for urban household financial investment behavior is households, not individuals. After removing samples with missing key variables, the analysis includes 13,050 households with valid information.

5.4.2 Variables

5.4.2.1 Dependent Variable

The focus of this chapter is on household financial investment behavior. Currently, existing studies mainly focus on household participation in the financial market and the proportion of risky assets (Hu 2019; Zhou and He 2019). Considering the urban–rural differences, rural households have a lower proportion of participation in risky financial markets, so to avoid biased estimates, this chapter only studies the financial investment behavior of urban households and uses the variable "proportion of household risky assets" to measure. CHFS data shows that household financial assets mainly consist of stocks, funds, financial wealth management products, financial derivatives, bonds, gold, non-RMB assets, current deposits, fixed deposits, cash, and loans. Household risky financial assets mainly consist of stocks, funds, financial wealth management products, financial derivatives, bonds, gold, non-RMB assets, and loans. The proportion of household risky assets is a continuous variable, measured by the proportion of household risky assets to total household financial assets, with a value range of 0–1.

5.4.2.2 Independent Variable

The core independent variable in this chapter is housing type. Housing types are divided into commercial housing, welfare housing, and self-built/expanded housing. Among them, "commercial housing" includes "purchasing new commercial housing" and "purchasing second-hand commercial housing"; "welfare housing" includes "purchasing policy-based housing," "inheritance or gift," "purchasing from the unit at a price below market value," "raising funds to build houses," "placement housing," "purchasing small property rights housing," and "other." Considering the complexity of influencing factors for welfare housing, this chapter treats it as the reference category.

5.4.2.3 Other Variables

To better control for the impact of other relevant factors on household financial investment behavior, the author selects control variables from two aspects: household characteristics and regional characteristics. Household characteristic variables include housing loans and household income. Housing loans are a binary dummy variable, with a value of 1 for "yes" and 0 for "no." Regional characteristic variables are measured by urban–rural type and regional variables. In addition, considering that there may be an intermediary effect between housing and household financial investment behavior, financial literacy is also selected as a mediator variable to be added to the regression model. Following the approach of Yin et al. (2014), financial literacy is measured by the answers to three aspects of questions regarding interest rates, inflation, and investment risk judgment, and the principal component analysis method is used to calculate the financial literacy index (Yin et al. 2014).

Table 5.1 presents the descriptive statistics of the relevant variables studied. The data shows that among the 13,050 urban samples, the mean value of the proportion of risky assets is 17%, indicating a relatively low proportion of risky assets in Chinese households' total financial assets. In terms of housing type, 32.49% are commercial housing, 35.73% are welfare housing, and 31.78% of housing is self-built/expanded. Only 6.46% of households have housing loans. The average annual income of households in the sample is 10.966 million yuan. In eastern, central, and western regions, the proportions of families are 54.3%, 24.96%, and 20.74% respectively. The average financial literacy is 0.247, indicating that the level of financial literacy among Chinese resident household investors is relatively low.

Table 5.1 Descriptive statistics of variables

Variable name	Mean/frequency	Standard deviation/ percentage	Minimum value	Maximum value
Percentage of risky assets	0.170	0.300	0	1
Housing type				
Commercial housing	4243	32.49	0	1
Self-built/extended housing	4150	31.78	0	1
Welfare housing	4666	35.73	0	1
Has housing loan				
Yes	844	6.46	0	1
No	12,215	93.54	0	1
Household income (in ten thousand yuan)	10.966	1.482	0	15.425
Region				
Eastern	7091	54.30	0	1
Central	3259	24.96	0	1
Western	2709	20.74	0	1
Financial literacy	0.247	0.915	-1.390	1.234

5.4.3 Models

To study urban household financial investment behavior, the research focuses on household asset allocation. A dependent variable, "Proportion of Household Risky Assets," is constructed. Based on microdata from the 2017 China Household Finance Survey, the Tobit model is employed to empirically investigate the relationship between housing type and the proportion of risky assets in urban households, while controlling for other influencing factors.

When examining household financial asset selection, the dependent variable is the proportion of household risky assets. As households may hold zero risky financial assets, the Tobit model is employed due to its ability to address the issue of excessive zeros in the data. In this case of truncated data, the Tobit model is used to analyze the impact of different housing types on the proportion of risky assets in urban households. The regression equation of the model is as follows:

$$\text{risk\_weighti} = \alpha + \beta\ 1\text{housei} + \beta 2\text{Xi} + \varepsilon\text{i} \tag{5.3.1}$$

$$\text{risk\_weighti} = \alpha + \beta\ 1\text{housei} + \beta 2\text{jrsyi} + \beta 3\text{Xi} + \varepsilon\text{i} \tag{5.3.2}$$

$$\text{risk\_weighti} = \begin{cases} \text{risk\_weighti}^* & \text{risk\_weighti}^* > 0 \\ 0 & \text{risk\_weighti}^* \leq 0 \end{cases}$$

where

- i represents the surveyed household. α is the intercept term.
- risk_weighti is the dependent variable, representing the proportion of risky assets.
- housei denotes the housing type.
- jrsyi represents financial literacy.
- Xi represents control variables that may affect the proportion of household risky assets.
- εi is the error term, representing unobservable factors in the model, following a standard normal distribution.

5.5 Empirical Results and Analysis

5.5.1 Empirical Analysis of the Proportion of Risky Assets

When analyzing the determining factors affecting urban household financial investment behavior, the Tobit model is used for empirical analysis. The regression results of the model (1) regarding the impact of housing type and control variables on the proportion of risky assets in urban households are shown in Table 5.2.

Model (1) provides the regression results of the impact of housing type and control variables on the proportion of risky assets in urban households. The results show that, at the 1% significance level, commercial housing significantly affects the proportion of risky assets invested by urban households, with a marginal effect of 0.096, demonstrating a "wealth effect." This implies that compared to welfare housing, urban households owning commercial housing have a significantly higher proportion of risky asset holdings, exceeding 9.6%. Possible explanations are, on the one hand, the higher value of commercial housing compared to welfare housing, suggesting that households owning commercial housing generally have higher wealth levels. On the other hand, in the process of purchasing commercial housing, families have more opportunities to participate in financial activities. Families may use housing loans to diversify the economic pressure of buying houses, thereby promoting the use of family funds for financial investment. In contrast to commercial housing, self-built/expanded housing has a significant negative impact on the proportion of risky assets invested by urban households, with a marginal effect of -0.08, exhibiting a "crowding out effect." This supports hypothesis 1b, indicating that compared to welfare housing, owning self-built/expanded housing significantly reduces the proportion of risky assets held by urban families by 8%. This may be because, relative to welfare housing, urban families need to invest a large amount of funds in building self-built or expanded housing, and most families cannot share the economic burden of housing construction through loans. The reduction in family asset liquidity significantly inhibits the

Table 5.2 Empirical analysis of risky asset percentage

Variables	(1)	(2)
Housing types		
Commercial housing	0.096***	0.081***
	(0.018)	(0.018)
Self-built/extended housing	– 0.080***	– 0.037***
	(0.019)	(0.033)
Housing loan	0.109***	0.098***
	(0.030)	(0.030)
Ln (household Income)	0.187***	0.169***
	(0.007)	(0.007)
Region		
Central	– 0.062***	– 0.056***
	(0.019)	(0.018)
Western	– 0.024	– 0.026
	(0.020)	(0.020)
Financial literacy		0.135***
		(0.009)
Observations	13,050	13,050
Pseudo R2	0.066	0.078

Note *, **, *** indicate significance at the 10%, 5%, and 1% confidence levels, respectively. The reported values in the table are the estimated marginal effects, with standard errors in parentheses

proportion of family investments in risky assets. In terms of control variables, holding housing loans and increasing family income significantly increase the proportion of family investments in risky assets. This suggests that families with housing loans and more wealth are more likely to use funds for investing in risky assets, indicating they have better investment capabilities. Compared to the eastern region, urban families in the central region have a significantly lower proportion of risky assets, and there is no significant difference in the proportion of risky assets between families in the western region and those in the eastern region.

Model (2) adds the variable of financial literacy based on model (1). The results show that after adding the financial literacy variable, the regression results of housing type and other control variables remain the same as before, but the marginal effects of each variable have all decreased. The marginal effect of commercial housing is reduced to 0.081 after adding the financial literacy variable, and the marginal effect of self-built/expanded housing is also reduced to – 0.037. This indicates that financial literacy plays an intermediary role in the relationship between housing type and the proportion of risky assets in urban families, confirming Hypotheses 2a and 2b.

Regarding family-level variables, holding housing loans and increasing income significantly increase the proportion of family investments in risky assets, in line with the "wealth theory." Urban families will purchase properties through loans and utilize other family funds for investing in risky assets, beyond repaying the loan. On the variable of regional characteristics, urban families in the eastern region have a relatively higher proportion of investments in risky assets compared to families in the central region.

5.5.2 *Test of the Mediating Effect of Financial Literacy*

Previously, we used a stepwise regression method to preliminarily explore whether housing types influence urban household financial investment behavior through financial literacy. It was found that both commercial housing and self-built/expanded housing exerted mediating effects on urban household financial investment behavior through the influence on financial literacy. To further examine whether the mediating effect of financial literacy exists, we conducted a secondary test of the mediating effect using the KHB detection method and estimated the contribution of the mediating effect.

Columns (2) and (3) of Table 5.3 present the test results of the mediating effect of financial literacy between commercial housing and self-built/expanded housing and the proportion of urban household risk assets. The results show that whether the impact of financial literacy is on commercial housing or on self-built/expanded housing, the total effect, direct effect, and mediating effect are all significant, indicating that financial literacy plays a mediating role between the two. After decomposing the mediating effect, it was found that the effect of commercial housing on financial literacy is positive, and the effect of financial literacy on the proportion of family risk assets is positive. In other words, there is a positive correlation between commercial housing and financial literacy. This is because when a family purchases commercial housing, they need to interact with financial institutions. Through this interaction, families improve their financial literacy, which in turn promotes the holding of family risk assets. On the other hand, for families choosing to self-build or expand housing, on the one hand, they are willing to use a large amount of family funds for construction rather than for investment. On the other hand, there is no way to access the financial market, and the reduction of disposable assets means that families have no opportunity to participate more in various financial activities. There is no channel to accumulate financial knowledge and skills. This conservative attitude towards avoiding financial markets is detrimental to the improvement of financial literacy, further inhibiting family risk asset investment. Therefore, financial literacy plays a partial mediating role between housing types and the proportion of family risk assets, explaining 17.36% and 56.85% of the influence of commercial housing and self-built/expanded housing on family financial investment behavior, respectively.

Table 5.3 Mediation test of financial literacy

Variable	Housing type	
	Commercial housing	Self-built/expanded housing
Total effect	0.097***	− 0.085***
Direct effect	0.080***	− 0.037*
Mediation effect	0.017***	− 0.049***
Lower confidence interval	0.005	− 0.062
Upper confidence interval	0.029	− 0.035
Contribution rate	17.36%	56.85%

Note *, **, and *** indicate significance at the 10%, 5%, and 1% confidence levels, respectively. Control variables are the same as in Table 5.2

5.6 The Relationship Between Housing Types and Urban Household Financial Investment Behavior, Along with Development Recommendations

Based on the 2017 China Household Finance Survey data, this chapter investigates the association between housing types and investment behavior of urban households in terms of finance, as well as their underlying mechanisms. The findings of this study demonstrate a "wealth effect" whereby ownership of commercial properties significantly stimulates urban household investment in risky financial assets. Conversely, ownership of self-built/expanded houses exhibits a "crowding-out effect" by substantially suppressing such investments. Furthermore, it is revealed that financial literacy partially mediates the impact of housing types on urban household finance investment behavior, influencing the proportion of risk assets held by households. Additionally, controlling for other variables, it is observed that holding housing loans and experiencing an increase in household income both exert a significant positive influence on household finance investment behavior. As households accumulate more housing loans and witness growth in income levels, they display a greater inclination towards investing in risky financial assets.

The research findings of this chapter contribute to the existing literature by offering a novel perspective on housing as a variable, examining the similarities and differences in the impact of commercial properties and self-built/expanded houses on household financial investments. Moreover, by considering the mediating role of financial literacy between housing types and household finance investment behavior, our optimized model provides deeper insights into the financial investment choices made by urban resident households.

Currently, real estate continues to hold a significant proportion in Chinese households' asset allocation. Particularly among high-net-worth households in cities like Beijing and Shanghai, housing assets constitute nearly 50% of their overall portfolio for emerging middle-class families. Therefore, maintaining a stable real estate market is crucial for wealth preservation and appreciation among households, with housing exerting a dominant "wealth effect". However, amidst increasing global economic uncertainties and heightened risks, external factors are driving changes in people's wealth management habits. Investor demands are evolving towards new trends that impose higher requirements on individuals' financial literacy to navigate diverse financial market environments. Enhancing financial literacy can partially bridge the "financial divide" among households with varying levels of wealth. Promoting fair income distribution, reinforcing financial education, and expanding inclusive finance all play pivotal roles in reducing this divide while fostering healthy development within China's financial market.

References

Bertocchi G, Brunetti M, Torricelli C (2011) Marriage and other risky assets: a portfolio approach. Soc Sci Electron Publishing 35(11):2902–2915

Cardak BA, Wilkins R (2009) The determinants of household risky asset holdings: Australian evidence on background risk and other factors. J Bank Finance 33(5):850–860

Chen Z, Chen J, Liu X (2008) Countless mansions in peace: a review and prospect of the marketization reform of China's urban housing system. World Econ Pap 1:43–54

Chen Y, Shi Y, Quan W (2015) Housing wealth, financial market participation, and household asset portfolio selection: evidence from Chinese cities. Finan Res 4:1–18

Chetty R, Szeidl A (2010) The effect of housing on portfolio choice. Nat Bureau Econ Res 72(3):1171–1212

China Household Wealth Survey Report (2019) China economic trends research institute household wealth research group. Economic Daily Press

Cocco JF (2005) Portfolio choice in the presence of housing. Rev Fin Stud 18:535–567

Corr C (2006) Financial exclusion in Ireland: an exploratory study and policy review. Dublin Combat Poverty Agency

Dan D (2019) Financial literacy and urban poverty. China Ind Econ 4:136–154

Faig M, Nolan P (2009) What explains household stock holding? J Bank Finance 30(9):2579–2597

Fratantoni MC (1998) Homeownership and investment in risky assets. J Urban Econ 44(1):27–42

Gao Y, Zhang Y, Song Q (2020) Crowding-out effect of housing assets on family risk asset investment. Econ Manag Rev 4:106–121

He Y, He X (2018) Health and the degree of participation in family risk financial asset investment. J South China Normal Univ (soc Sci Edn) 2:135–142

He Z, Shi X, Lu X (2019) Home equity and household portfolio choice: evidence from China. Int Rev Econ Financ 60(3):149–164

Hu Y (2019) The impact of financial knowledge and investment ability on Chinese household financial market participation and asset allocation. China Market 1:13–18

Hu Z, Zang R (2017) The influence of financial literacy on family financial planning: micro evidence from urban Chinese families. J Central Univ Fin Econ 2:72–83

Liao J (2017) Marital status and residents' financial investment preferences. South Fin 11:23–32

Ling DC, Garry AM (1998) Evidence on the demand for mortgage debt by owner-occupants. J Urban Econ 44(1):391–414

Liu J (2015) Heterogeneity of Chinese urban resident families and investment in risky financial assets. Econ Issues (3):51–55+60

Liu G (2018) Research on the current situation of Chinese consumer financial literacy: based on the 2017 consumer financial literacy questionnaire survey. Finan Res 3:1–20

Qin H, Li C, Wan J (2018) Financial literacy, financial asset allocation, and portfolio effectiveness. J Nanjing Univ Fin Econ 15:99–110

Ren Q, Hu R (2016) Housing inequality in urban China. Chin J Sociol 2(1):144–167
Stiglitz JE, Weiss A (1981) Credit rationing in markets with imperfect information. Am Econ Rev 71(3):393–410
Tobin J (1980) Asset accumulation and economic activity: reflections on contemporary macroeconomic theory. Economica 48(191):134–138
Toussaint J, Elsinga M (2009) Exploring "housing asset-based welfare": can the UK be held up as an example for Europe? Hous Stud 24(5):669–692
Wachter JA, Yogo M (2010) Why do household portfolio shares rise in wealth? Rev Fin Stud 23(11):3929–3965
Wu W, Li Y (2016) Family structure and financial asset allocation: an empirical study based on micro survey data. J Huazhong Univ Sci Technol (soc Sci Edn) 2:61–70
Wu W, Lv X (2013) Asset allocation of urban Chinese families and international comparisons: an analysis based on micro data. Int Fin Res 10:45–57
Wu W, Yi J, Zheng J (2010) Empirical analysis of investment structure of Chinese resident families: based on lifecycle, wealth, and housing. Econ Res S1:72–82
Wu W, Xu Q, Bai X (2013) Comparative study on group differences in debt decision-making of Chinese resident families. Fin Econ Res 39(3):19–29
Wu W, Wang Z, Wu K (2015) A review of household financial research: based on the perspective of asset allocation. Sci Decis Mak 4:69–94
Wu K (2017) Housing reform process, life course, and urban housing property acquisition (1980–2010). Sociol Stud 32(5):64–89+243–244
Yang Z, Zhang H, Zhao L (2014) The dual nature of Chinese housing: perspectives of consumption and investment. Econ Res 1:55–65
Yao R, Zhang HH (2005) Optimal consumption and portfolio choices with risky housing and borrowing constraints. Rev Fin Stud 18(1):197–239
Yin Z, Song Q, Wu Y (2014) Financial knowledge, investment experience, and household asset allocation. Econ Res 49(4):62–75
Zeng Z, He Q, Wu Y et al (2015) Financial knowledge and diversification of family investment portfolio. Economist 6:88–96
Zhang Z, Xie J (2018) Empirical study on factors influencing asset allocation of Chinese rural families. Explor Econ Issues 9:150–164
Zhou Y, He G (2019) The impact of housing on household financial asset allocation. J Zhongnan Univ Econ Law 2:76–87+159–160

Chapter 6
The Influence of Mental Accounts and Housing Wealth Effect on Household Finance Asset Allocation

"The excavator rings a thousand gold taels." With the advancement of urbanization in China, the demand for urban construction land continues to rise. Many households are involved in government land acquisition and housing demolition issues. Compensation from demolition has become one of the main ways for many families to obtain property income. According to the "Urban Housing Demolition Management Regulations" issued by the State Council in 2001 and the "Regulations on the Acquisition and Compensation of Houses on State-owned Land" issued in 2011, demolition households will "determine the compensation standards based on the market assessment price of real estate." This means that demolition compensation not only increases the disposable income of demolition households but also may stimulate them to participate more deeply in the financial market.

However, when people marvel at how lucky the demolition households are to have become overnight millionaires in the news reports, few pay attention to the situation of these people after receiving compensation. Richard Thaler first proposed the concept of mental accounts in 1980, suggesting that people have a psychological tendency to categorize and budget money during the consumption process (Thaler 1985). Later researchers pointed out that consumers categorize money into different accounts based on its different sources, such as fixed income and windfall income (Kivetz 1999). Furthermore, these different sources of wealth are irreplaceable. Under the influence of mental accounts, consumers choose to make economic decisions based on the ease with which wealth is acquired. Interestingly, this system of mental accounts often contradicts the decision-making behavior of the "rational economic man" assumed by traditional economics and is referred to as the cognitive matching effect. This means that money earned through hard work tends to be used more cautiously, while unexpectedly acquired wealth tends to be used more casually. It can be seen that the compensation from demolition is an additional income for households that does not involve labor. Due to the influence of mental accounts, demolition households are likely to classify it into an account for windfall gains, thereby triggering their motivation to participate more deeply in the financial market.

S. Zhao and D. Zhao, *The Household Finance Issues in China*,
https://doi.org/10.1007/978-981-97-0706-5_6

In fact, not all demolition households can receive millions of RMB overnight, nor do all of them have the ability to allocate their wealth reasonably after benefiting. The assets of these families have transformed from fixed forms to highly liquid cash overnight, or their original houses have been replaced by one or even several brand-new resettlement houses. This change has undoubtedly affected the allocation of household financial assets and increased the financial risk of households in terms of quality and quantity.

Existing research has discussed how the mechanism of mental accounts changes the disposable income that households expect, thereby changing the decision-making logic of household participation in the financial market. It also examines the impact of mental accounts on investment decision-making behavior or the encoding and valuation of compensation from demolition in mental accounts (Yuan and Huang 2018a). However, there are few studies that systematically analyze the relationship between compensation from demolition, mental accounts, and participation in the financial market. Wu et al. (2006) pointed out that overconfidence leads some investors who would not originally participate in the market to enter the market, or leads market participants to engage in excessive trading and purchase more risky assets (Wu et al. 2006). In other words, after receiving compensation, the level of financial market participation by demolition households may exceed the limits of their established financial literacy and risk tolerance, exposing households to excessive risk. Therefore, conducting an in-depth exploration of the impact mechanism of housing demolition experience on the allocation of financial assets of demolition households and understanding the financial market participation behavior of demolition households have important research significance for providing scientific guidance on the household asset allocation of domestic demolition households.

6.1 Research and Hypotheses Based on the Theory of Mental Accounts

The Mental Accounts Theory, proposed by economist Richard Thaler, expands on the concept of mental accounting. It suggests that individuals organize their financial decisions into different "mental accounts" based on perceived relevance, rather than viewing all money as a unified pool of funds. These mental accounts are often based on various criteria such as the source of income, the intended use of money, or emotional attachments. It helps explain why people may make financial decisions that seem irrational or suboptimal from a purely economic standpoint. It posits that consumers unconsciously allocate wealth to different mental accounts during decision-making, thereby exerting unpredictable influences on their choices. Since its introduction, the theory of mental accounts has rapidly advanced empirical research on consumption and investment decisions.

Firstly, in the field of financial investment, scholars have pointed out that individuals tend to use fixed income for savings and windfall income for risky investments.

This is because fixed income is the result of individual labor, which is hard-earned and constitutes expected income. On the other hand, windfall income is unexpected and comes from non-labor sources, making it unexpected income (Li et al. 2007). Secondly, in the field of individual consumption, the cognitive labels and emotional labels of mental accounts also have a significant impact on consumption decisions. Different emotional labels for "windfall gains" will influence an individual's inclination towards either indulgent consumption or indulgent avoidance (Li et al. 2012). Yuan and Huang (2018b) also pointed out through empirical analysis that housing demolition leads to significant differences between demolition and non-demolition households in terms of money sources and ownership. Demolition households tend to use non-precious resources, windfall income, for consumption (Yuan and Huang 2018b).

The above studies further indicate that compared to people's relatively stable non-risky income (such as wages), the promulgation of demolition policies and the distribution of demolition compensation are often unexpected for demolition households. There are also differences in the effort exerted by the household and the difficulty in obtaining these two different sources of income. Therefore, under the influence of mental accounts, demolition households often assign higher value to wage income categorized as fixed income accounts, and tend to be more conservative in spending. On the other hand, they hold a higher risk tolerance for housing demolition compensation categorized as windfall income accounts, thereby increasing the probability of household participation in the financial market. Based on the above, the following hypotheses are proposed:

Hypothesis 1 Demolition experience (monetary compensation) will significantly increase the proportion of household financial assets invested.

Hypothesis 2 Demolition experience (monetary compensation) will significantly increase the likelihood of investment in household financial assets.

6.2 Research and Hypotheses Based on Housing Wealth Effect

The impact of housing wealth on household finance asset allocation is contingent upon the interplay between the wealth effect (where property appreciation stimulates investment in household finance) and the risk effect (where property ownership diminishes asset liquidity). However, existing studies have shown that property quantity has a significant wealth effect. Simultaneously, housing wealth significantly increases the probability of household participation in financial markets and also increases the proportion of household holdings in risk assets (Chen et al. 2014). Considering that households receiving housing compensation through demolition typically acquire better conditions (often newly built housing planned by the government), households receiving housing compensation may also increase their investment in risk financial assets. In the current research on the impact of demolition experience on household asset allocation, there has been no distinction made regarding the compensation method. The explanatory logic is often based on the assumption that "demolition households receive monetary compensation." However, the logic of how housing compensation and monetary compensation affect household finance asset allocation is different. Therefore, in order to thoroughly investigate the impact of demolition experience on household finance asset allocation, this study will categorize households that receive housing compensation separately based on the compensation method, and delve into the situation of household finance asset allocation when obtaining housing compensation. Based on this, the following hypotheses are proposed.

Hypothesis 3 Demolition experience (housing compensation) significantly increases the proportion of household investments in risky financial assets.

Hypothesis 4 Demolition experience (housing compensation) significantly increases the likelihood of investment in household financial assets.

6.3 The Impact of Financial Knowledge on Household Financial Asset Allocation

Currently, there is a substantial body of literature, both domestically and internationally, discussing the influence of financial knowledge on household financial asset allocation from various perspectives. On one hand, a higher level of financial knowledge aids residents in understanding financial markets and products. On the other hand, there is a significant positive correlation between financial knowledge and risk preference, thereby affecting residents' allocation behavior towards risky financial products. Bernheim and Garrett (2003) found that residents who received financial education tend to save more (Bernheim and Garrett 2003). Calvet et al. (2009) conducted a study on Swedish data and discovered that households with lower educational levels make more investment mistakes (Calvet et al. 2009). Zhang and Yin (2016) pointed out that financial knowledge can significantly reduce the probability of household financial exclusion, thus increasing the demand for household finance (Zhang and Yin 2016). Additionally, numerous studies suggest that financial knowledge significantly influences the allocation behavior of household financial assets, especially risky financial assets. Based on this review, it can be hypothesized that the financial knowledge level of heads of households in relocation families will impact their allocation behavior of financial assets. Therefore, the following hypothesis is proposed.

Hypothesis 5 The higher the financial knowledge level of the head of a relocation family, the more likely they are to engage in investment in risky financial assets.

6.4 Empirical Analysis Based on the 2017 China Household Finance Survey

6.4.1 Data

The China Household Finance Survey has been conducted since 2009, with a survey conducted every two years. It has been successfully implemented nationwide four times in 2011, 2013, 2015, and 2017. The sample of the fourth survey in 2017 covers 29 provinces (autonomous regions, municipalities directly under the central government), 355 counties (districts, county-level cities), and 1428 villages (neighborhoods/communities) nationwide, with a sample size of 40,011 households. After excluding some samples that are invalid due to missing core variable data, there are 25,554 remaining households. Among them, 1046 households experienced relocation and received monetary compensation, while 1137 households experienced relocation and received housing compensation.

6.4.2 Variables

6.4.2.1 Dependent Variables

Participation in risk financial asset investment, and the proportion of household risk financial assets to total financial assets. Household risk financial assets include stocks, funds, financial derivatives, non-RMB assets, etc. The sum of savings (including household current deposits and fixed deposits) and household risk financial assets will roughly equal all the financial assets held by the household.

6.4.2.2 Independent Variables

Experience of household demolition. If no experience of demolition, assign a value of 0. If experienced demolition, assign a value of 1. Categories of household demolition experience (based on compensation type) are as follows: if no experience of demolition, assign a value of 0; if experienced demolition with monetary compensation, assign a value of 1; if experienced demolition with housing compensation, assign a value of 2.

6.4.2.3 Control Variables

These mainly include two categories: household characteristics and head of household characteristics. Household characteristics comprise total household income, total asset level, quantity of self-owned homes, and urban–rural dummy variables.

Head of household characteristics include whether they have social insurance, years of education, physical condition, risk preference, trust in strangers, and financial knowledge, etc. Specifically, when the head of the household has any one of the old-age insurance, unemployment insurance, and medical insurance, "social insurance" is assigned a value of 1; otherwise, it is assigned a value of 0. Physical condition is assessed using the Likert 5-point scale, with "very good" as 1, "good" as 2, "average" as 3, "poor" as 4, and "very poor" as 5. Years of education are calculated based on the Chinese education system, specifically following the calculation of 6 years for primary school, 3 years for junior high school, 3 years for high school, 2 years for technical secondary school, 3 years for junior college, 4 years for undergraduate, 3 years for master's degree, and 3 years for doctorate. Risk preference is categorized into five levels based on the respondent's answer to "If you have funds available for investment, which type of investment project would you prefer?" Specifically, high risk preference is 1, slightly high risk preference is 2, neutral is 3, slightly low risk preference is 4, and lowest risk preference (unwilling to take any risk) is 5. Trust is categorized into five levels based on the respondent's answer to "How much do you trust strangers?" Specifically, very trusting is 1, moderately trusting is 2, neutral is 3, moderately distrustful is 4, and very distrustful is 5.

As for the measurement of financial knowledge, there is currently no unified method. For direct measurement, existing literature mainly adopts methods of setting subjective and objective questions and directly summing up the scores, or constructing financial literacy indicators through factor analysis and principal component analysis, etc. The direct summation method organizes the answers to each question, with correct answers assigned 1 and incorrect answers assigned 0, ensuring that the overall ranking of financial literacy remains unchanged. Therefore, following the approach of Luo (2020), the study selects 11 questions from the CHFS questionnaire that reflect respondents' financial knowledge and uses the summation method to obtain the final financial knowledge indicator (Luo and Liang 2020). The questions and score processing used in this chapter are shown in Table 6.1.

6.4.3 Models

In this chapter, the dependent variable, "Proportion of Household Risk Assets," is constructed. Based on microdata from the 2017 China Household Finance Survey, the Tobit model is employed to empirically study the relationship between household demolition experience and the proportion of household risk assets, while controlling for other influencing factors. Due to the large number of zero values in the dependent variable possibly caused by many households not holding risk assets, the Tobit model is used for regression analysis. The Tobit model refers to a type of model where the dependent variable is approximately continuously distributed on the positive values but includes a portion of observations with a probability of 0. It is also known as a censored regression model or a truncated regression model, belonging to a type of regression with a restricted dependent variable. For the model with "Whether

Table 6.1 Survey analysis and coding strategy

Question number	Content	Score processing
h3101	Respondents' attention to economic and financial information	Assign scores to the five options according to the level of attention, with scores ranging from 1 to 5 (and divide by 5 when calculating the final score)
h3103	Whether respondents believe high returns come with high risks	Option 1: Correct, score is 1. If any other option is chosen, the score is 0
h3105	Calculation of principal and interest for 100 Yuan at an annual interest rate of 4%	Option 2: Correct, score is 1. If any other option is chosen, the score is 0
h3106	With an annual interest rate of 5% and an inflation rate of 3%, the value of 100 Yuan after one year	Option 1: Correct, score is 1. If any other option is chosen, the score is 0
h3107	Respondents' lottery choices	Option 2: Correct, score is 1. If any other option is chosen, the score is 0
h3110	Overall understanding of stocks, bonds, and funds	Assign scores to the five options according to the level of attention, with scores ranging from 1 to 5 (and divide by 5 when calculating the final score)
h3111	Risk assessment of stocks and funds	Option 1: Correct, score is 1. If any other option is chosen, the score is 0
h3112	Risk assessment of main board stocks and growth enterprise board stocks	Option 2: Correct, score is 1. If any other option is chosen, the score is 0
h3113	Risk assessment of equity funds and bond funds	Option 1: Correct, score is 1. If any other option is chosen, the score is 0
h3114	Risk assessment of government bonds and corporate bonds	Option 2: Correct, score is 1. If any other option is chosen, the score is 0
h3115	Do respondents believe that investing in multiple financial assets carries less risk than investing in just one type of financial asset?	Option 1: Correct, score is 1. If any other option is chosen, the score is 0

the household participates in financial risk investment" as the dependent variable, the Probit model is used for model fitting. Since both Tobit and Probit models are nonlinear models, all reported regression results are marginal effects.

6.4.4 Empirical Analysis

6.4.4.1 Descriptive Statistical Analysis

As shown in Table 6.2, the mean of "Proportion of Risk Financial Assets" is 0.0754, and the mean of "Participation in Risk Investment" is 0.154. This indicates that residents have a relatively low level of investment in risk financial products. The mean value of "Financial Knowledge" is only 1.953 (out of a maximum of 10.5), suggesting that, overall, respondents have a relatively low level of financial knowledge. In summary, respondents' levels of participation and understanding of the financial market are both relatively low.

In the total sample, there are 24,152 households that have not experienced demolition, while there are 2183 households that have gone through demolition. Among them, 1046 households received monetary compensation, and 1137 households received housing compensation. Additionally, there is a category in the questionnaire for demolition households that received both types of compensation. Due to the research scope and the relatively small sample size in this category, it will not be considered in this chapter (see Table 6.3).

Table 6.2 Descriptive statistics of total sample

Variable	N	Mean	Standard deviation	Min	Max
Relocation experience	26,335	0.133	0.339	0	1
Relocation experience (monetary compensation)	26,335	0.0284	0.166	0	1
Relocation experience (housing compensation)	26,335	0.0261	0.160	0	1
Percentage of risky financial assets	26,335	0.0754	0.214	0	1
Engagement in risk investment	26,335	0.154	0.361	0	1
Trust level	26,335	3.961	0.934	1	5
Risk preference	26,335	4.251	1.389	1	5
Years of education	26,335	3.430	1.684	1	9
Physical condition	26,335	2.613	1.016	1	5
Urban–rural variable	26,335	0.318	0.466	0	1
Number of housing units	26,335	1.221	0.538	0	27
Social insurance	26,335	0.976	0.152	0	1
ln (annual total income)	26,335	10.62	1.526	-2.288	15.42
ln (family assets)	26,335	12.57	1.983	0	17.22
Financial knowledge	26,335	1.953	1.309	0	10.40

Table 6.3 Relocation experience

Relocation situation	Frequency (households)	Percentage (%)
No relocation experience	24,152	91.71
Experienced relocation (monetary compensation)	1046	3.97
Experienced relocation (housing compensation)	1137	4.32
Total	26,335	100

6.4.4.2 Descriptive Statistical Analysis of Demolition Situations

As shown in Table 6.4, after distinguishing the types of compensation for demolition, it can be observed that there are some differences in participation in the financial market among different demolition groups. Regarding the "proportion of risk assets," households with no demolition experience have a mean of 0.075. In contrast, households that experienced monetary compensation for demolition have a mean of 0.094, and households that received housing compensation have a mean of 0.102. This indicates that, in the total sample, households that have experienced demolition invest more in risk financial assets compared to those without demolition experience. Within the demolition groups, households that received housing compensation tend to maintain a higher level of investment in risk financial assets compared to those that received monetary compensation.

Additionally, it is worth noting that the "urban–rural variable" means of families with demolition experience are smaller. Within the demolition groups, families that received housing compensation have smaller means compared to those that received monetary compensation. Since this variable is assigned as "rural = 1, urban = 0," it implies that families with demolition experience are more likely to have urban household registrations compared to families without demolition experience. Moreover, families that received housing compensation are more likely to have urban household registrations compared to those that received monetary compensation. This may be correlated with the urbanization process and government demolition plans in China.

Under the influence of mental accounting, individuals tend to allocate their wealth into different mental accounts. For "windfall gains," people are more inclined to place them in a special mental account, making the wealth in this account more likely to be spent. Financial risk investments serve as an important channel for utilizing this type of wealth. However, for households facing demolition, we must first define what constitutes a "windfall gain." Taking the example of monetary compensation for demolition, if the compensation received after demolition is not sufficient to purchase a house similar to the previous one in the local area, then families experiencing demolition not only do not receive a "windfall gain," but may even experience a decrease in their overall wealth. Therefore, in studying the impact of demolition experiences with monetary compensation on family risk investments, it is essential to determine whether the compensation reaches a certain threshold, constituting a so-called "windfall gain."

Table 6.4 Differentiated compensation types

Variable	No relocation experience		Relocation experience (monetary compensation)				Relocation experience (housing compensation)			
	Mean	Standard deviation	Mean	Standard deviation	Minimum	Maximum	Mean	Standard deviation	Minimum	Maximum
Asset proportion	0.075	0.214	0.094	0.238	0	1	0.102	0.246	0	1
Risk investment	0.157	0.364	0.193	0.395	0	1	0.192	0.394	0	1
Trust level	3.950	0.931	3.966	0.948	1	5	4.002	0.897	1	5
Risk preference	4.225	1.407	4.357	1.269	1	5	4.409	1.192	1	5
Years of education	3.499	1.747	3.486	1.534	1	9	3.411	1.459	1	8
Physical condition	2.592	1.017	2.592	0.982	1	5	2.541	0.974	1	5
Urban–rural variable	0.323	0.468	0.153	0.360	0	1	0.042	0.201	0	1
Number of houses	1.203	0.492	1.213	0.483	0	4	1.360	0.747	1	8
Social insurance	0.973	0.163	0.986	0.119	0	1	0.990	0.097	0	1
ln (income)	10.60	1.560	10.98	1.363	0	14.86	10.92	1.294	0.56	15.4
ln (assets)	12.50	1.984	13.29	1.905	4.2	17.22	13.28	1.980	4.04	17.2
Financial knowledge	2.154	1.375	2.101	1.230	0	8.200	2.196	1.297	0	9.20

Table 6.5 Compensation for demolition

Variables	Mean	P25	P50	P75	Standard deviation	Minimum value	Maximum value
Demolition compensation	295,441.7	27,000	100,000	312,000	622,525.4	0	15,000,000
House value	411,935.3	45,000	140,000	350,000	1,473,056	0	50,000,000

Unit CNY (Chinese Yuan)

As shown in Table 6.5, the distribution of demolition compensation is extremely uneven. For example, in the case of monetary compensation, the mean is approximately 300,000 Yuan, yet it is close to the 75th percentile. This means that the majority of families' received demolition compensation is "averaged out" and far from constituting a "windfall gain." Therefore, to examine the real impact of demolition experiences with monetary compensation on family risk investments from the perspective of mental accounting, this chapter sets the regression condition as "compensation greater than the median," which is 100,000 Yuan, in order to exclude, as much as possible, households with amounts too small to constitute a "windfall gain." Similarly, to control conditions, for families that received housing compensation, the study also excludes samples where the "equivalent market value of the house" is less than 100,000 Yuan.

6.5 Demolition Experience and Participation in Household Finance Risk Asset Investment

Based on the previous definitions of demolition experience types and participation in risk financial asset investment, we first examine whether household demolition experience significantly affects their likelihood of participating in risk financial asset investment. Table 6.6 presents the estimation results of the Probit model and Tobit model. In columns (1) and (3), Probit models are estimated separately for situations where compensation is distinguished and not distinguished. These models assess the impact of different demolition experiences and other factors on the likelihood of households participating in risk investments.

For the model that does not distinguish compensation situations, after controlling for all household and homeowner characteristic variables, demolition experience has a significant positive effect on household investment in risk financial assets. The marginal effect of demolition experience is 0.022, and it is statistically significant at the 5% level. This indicates that households with demolition experience have a 2.23% higher likelihood of participating in risk financial asset investment.

In the model distinguishing compensation situations, the marginal effect of experiencing demolition with housing compensation is 0.025, significant at the 10% level.

Table 6.6 Impact of demolition experience on household financial investment

Variables	Distinguish compensation Situation		Without distinguishing compensation situation	
	(1)	(2)	(3)	(4)
	Risk investment or not probit	Percentage of risk assets tobit	Risk investment or not probit	Percentage of risk assets tobit
Experience of demolition and relocation with monetary compensation (compensation > 100,000)	0.0413**	0.133**		
	(0.0210)	(0.0545)		
Experience of demolition and relocation with house compensation (compensation > 100,000)	0.0245*	0.0841**		
	(0.0153)	(0.0420)		
Whether experienced housing demolition and relocation			0.0223**	0.0749***
			(0.00885)	(0.0258)
Financial knowledge	0.0169***	0.0392***	0.0169***	0.0405***
	(0.00270)	(0.00772)	(0.00259)	(0.00741)
Trust level	– 0.0248***	– 0.0646***	– 0.0239***	– 0.0609***
	(0.00384)	(0.0113)	(0.00368)	(0.0109)
Risk preference	– 0.0432***	– 0.126***	– 0.0425***	– 0.124***
	(0.00249)	(0.00775)	(0.00240)	(0.00747)
Years of education	0.0314***	0.0936***	0.0321***	0.0952***
	(0.00194)	(0.00597)	(0.00189)	(0.00581)
Physical condition	– 0.00240	0.00482	– 0.00367	0.00110
	(0.00383)	(0.0112)	(0.00367)	(0.0108)
Urban–rural variable	– 0.131***	– 0.437***	– 0.131***	– 0.435***
	(0.0131)	(0.0407)	(0.0127)	(0.0394)
Number of houses	0.00503	0.00363	0.000482	– 0.00606
	(0.00649)	(0.0177)	(0.00609)	(0.0167)
Social insurance	0.0623***	0.199***	0.0519***	0.155***
	(0.0212)	(0.0636)	(0.0204)	(0.0606)
Income	0.0449***	0.127***	0.0450***	0.128***
	(0.00346)	(0.0102)	(0.00334)	(0.00987)
Total assets	1.04e–08***	2.29e–08***	1.08e–08***	2.37e–08***
	(1.23e–09)	(3.17e–09)	(1.20e–09)	(3.08e–09)
Sample size	10,350	9850	11,013	10,484

Note *, **, *** indicate significance at the 10%, 5%, and 1% levels respectively. The table reports marginal effects, with standard errors in parentheses

This implies that households experiencing demolition with housing compensation are 2.45% more likely to participate in the risk financial market compared to other households, validating Hypothesis 4. Furthermore, households experiencing demolition with monetary compensation greater than 100,000 Yuan have a 4.13% higher likelihood of participating in the risk financial market compared to other households, confirming Hypothesis 2.

Additionally, the study incorporates homeowner and household characteristics to control for factors influencing household participation in risk financial asset investment, such as human capital and family conditions. Taking column (3) as an example, the estimation results show that household assets and income have a positive relationship with the likelihood of household participation in risk investment. Families with social insurance have a higher likelihood of investing in risk financial products. Compared to urban households, rural households have a lower probability of participation, which may be related to differences in income, assets, education levels, and knowledge levels between urban and rural households. Variables like education years, homeowner risk preference, trust in strangers, and others also significantly affect the likelihood of household participation in risk financial investment. Finally, the marginal effect of financial knowledge is statistically significant at the 1% level, indicating that for every one-unit increase in the financial knowledge score, the likelihood of household participation in risk financial assets increases by 1.67%.

6.6 Relationship Between Demolition Experience and the Proportion of Household Finance Risk Asset Investment

Columns (2) and (4) in Table 6.6 present the Tobit models with "Proportion of Risk Financial Assets" as the dependent variable, distinguishing compensation categories and not distinguishing compensation categories, respectively. For the model not distinguishing compensation categories, after controlling for all household and homeowner characteristic variables, the marginal effect of demolition experience is significant at the 1% level. This indicates that demolition experience not only encourages household participation in risk financial investment but also increases the proportion of investment in risk assets. Similarly, residents with higher education levels tend to invest more in risk assets. An increase in financial knowledge also leads to a higher proportion of household investment in risk assets. The results of the other control variables are consistent with the previous findings.

For the model distinguishing compensation categories, after controlling for other variables, the marginal effect of demolition experience with housing compensation is significant at the 5% level. This suggests that experiencing demolition with housing compensation significantly increases household investment in risk financial assets, validating Hypothesis 3. Additionally, the marginal effect of experiencing monetary compensation demolition implies that this category of households has a risk financial asset proportion that is 13.3% higher than other households, confirming Hypothesis 1.

6.7 Robustness Test

To prevent potential biases due to variable selection for control, the study conducted a robustness test by adding four control variables: internet use, age squared, gender, and region, to the original model. For internet use, yes = 1, no = 0. For region, 1 = Eastern region, 2 = Central region, 3 = Western region. For gender, male = 1, female = 0. After adding these control variables, the research results did not exhibit significant differences from the previous findings. Refer to Table 6.7 for details.

6.8 Reflections Based on Research Conclusions

Demolition of homes not only affects the fate of individuals and families but also has implications for the overall stability and development of society. For individuals, incorrect handling of demolition compensation may bring significant impacts to households. For society, improper resettlement of demolished families may lead to an increase in social conflicts and have negative consequences. Therefore, the impact of home demolition on household financial risk asset investment carries profound research significance.

This chapter, based on the theories of mental accounting and housing wealth effect, analyzed the 2017 CHFS data and found that compensation for housing demolition and high compensation amounts significantly increased the likelihood of households investing in financial risk assets. Additionally, it raised the proportion of household financial risk asset investment. The underlying logic is that the more compensation a household receives for housing demolition, the greater their disposable income. Under the influence of mental accounting, the high compensation is perceived as "windfall income," leading to a decrease in its psychological valuation. This encourages households to engage in more financial investments. For households compensated with housing, the properties can serve as collateral to generate additional income. Therefore, households with more properties are more likely to invest in risk assets. Previous literature also suggests that families with their own homes and higher wealth levels are better equipped to withstand risks, and thus, the proportion of investment in risk assets tends to be higher (Wu et al. 2010). Considering the above, it's evident that households subject to demolition hold a higher risk tolerance for housing compensation categorized as "windfall income." Therefore, under the influence of mental accounting, profit motives will promote these households to increase participation in the financial market and raise the proportion of risk asset usage.

Table 6.7 Robustness test of models with additional control variables

Variables	Distinguish compensation situation		Without distinguishing compensation situation	
	(1)	(2)	(3)	(4)
	Risk investment or not probit	Percentage of risk assets tobit	Risk investment or not probit	Percentage of risk assets tobit
Experience of demolition and relocation with monetary compensation (compensation > 100,000)	0.0375*	0.119**		
	(0.0204)	(0.0541)		
Experience of demolition with house and relocation compensation (compensation > 100,000)	0.0231*	0.0736*		
	(0.0151)	(0.0422)		
Whether experienced demolition and relocation			0.0225**	0.0703***
			(0.00883)	(0.0259)
Financial knowledge	0.0120***	0.0285***	0.0116***	0.0288***
	(0.00270)	(0.00775)	(0.00258)	(0.00745)
Trust level	– 0.0192***	– 0.0496***	– 0.0184***	– 0.0458***
	(0.00385)	(0.0114)	(0.00369)	(0.0109)
Risk preference	– 0.0365***	– 0.110***	– 0.0355***	– 0.107***
	(0.00256)	(0.00789)	(0.00247)	(0.00760)
Years of education	0.0251***	0.0795***	0.0254***	0.0801***
	(0.00200)	(0.00606)	(0.00194)	(0.00589)
Physical condition	0.00245	0.0148	0.00177	0.0126
	(0.00394)	(0.0116)	(0.00377)	(0.0111)
Urban–rural variable	– 0.107***	– 0.363***	– 0.107***	– 0.360***
	(0.0134)	(0.0419)	(0.0130)	(0.0405)
Number of houses	0.00521	0.00674	0.00110	– 0.00246
	(0.00636)	(0.0176)	(0.00598)	(0.0166)
Social insurance	0.0584***	0.175***	0.0483**	0.131**
	(0.0209)	(0.0633)	(0.0200)	(0.0603)
Income	0.0383***	0.110***	0.0386***	0.111***
	(0.00338)	(0.0101)	(0.00328)	(0.00975)
Total assets	8.15e–09***	1.73e–08***	8.47e–09***	1.81e–08***
	(1.24e–09)	(3.23e–09)	(1.21e–09)	(3.14e–09)

(continued)

Table 6.7 (continued)

Variables	Distinguish compensation situation		Without distinguishing compensation situation	
	(1)	(2)	(3)	(4)
	Risk investment or not probit	Percentage of risk assets tobit	Risk investment or not probit	Percentage of risk assets tobit
Age squared	5.75e−06**	3.19e−05***	5.65e−06**	3.21e−05***
	(2.39e−06)	(7.00e−06)	(2.30e−06)	(6.75e−06)
Gender	− 0.0189**	− 0.0495**	− 0.0197***	− 0.0563***
	(0.00762)	(0.0222)	(0.00734)	(0.0214)
Central region	− 0.0319***	− 0.0999***	− 0.0305***	− 0.0943***
	(0.00905)	(0.0273)	(0.00875)	(0.0264)
Western region	− 0.0433***	− 0.131***	− 0.0408***	− 0.118***
	(0.00869)	(0.0268)	(0.00835)	(0.0257)
Internet usage	− 0.142***	− 0.436***	− 0.146***	− 0.450***
	(0.00926)	(0.0294)	(0.00881)	(0.0281)
Sample size	10,146	9656	10,984	10,461

Note *, **, *** indicate significance at the 10%, 5%, and 1% levels respectively. The table reports marginal effects, with standard errors in parentheses

Based on the research conclusions above, the following recommendations are proposed:

Firstly, government departments should disseminate financial knowledge to demolished households and implement corresponding policies to enhance their financial literacy and capabilities. Encourage them to follow diversified investment strategies, optimize household financial asset allocation, and reduce and try to avoid the influence of mental accounting in their household economic decisions, thus avoiding irrational behavior.

Secondly, communities should pay special attention to the demolished household population. Organize a series of activities, popularize relevant financial investment cases, create a conducive learning atmosphere, and guide them to navigate away from the excessive influence of mental accounting on household financial market participation.

Finally, financial institutions can design financial products at different levels to meet the investment needs of this group. Simultaneously, they should also conduct various forms of financial education, enhance the overall financial literacy of the demolished household population, make rational decisions regarding household assets, and guard against household financial risks.

References

Bernheim BD, Garrett DM (2003) The effects of financial education in the workplace: evidence from a survey of households. J Public Econ 87(7–8):1487–1519

Calvet LE, Campbell JY, Sodini P (2009) Fight or flight? Portfolio rebalancing by individual investors. Q J Econ 124(1):301–348

Chen Y, Gu J, Shi Y (2014) Housing wealth, credit constraints, and urban household education expenditure: evidence from CFPS2010 Data. Econ Res 49(S1):89–101

Kivetz R (1999) Advances in research on mental accounting and reason-based choice. Mark Lett 10(3):249–266

Li A, Ling W, Fang L et al (2007) The implicit structure of chinese psychological accounts. Acta Psychol Sin 4:706–714

Li A, Hao M, Li L et al (2012) A new perspective on consumer decision analysis: dual-channel mental accounting theory. Adv Psychol Sci 20(11):1709–1717

Luo W, Liang J (2020) Financial literacy and household risk asset investment decision: an empirical study based on CHFS 2017 data. Financ Theory Pract 11:45–56

Thaler R (1985) Mental accounting and consumer choice. Mark Sci 4(3):199–214

Wu W, Wang Y, Liang H (2006) Overconfidence, limited participation, and asset price bubbles. Econ Res 4:115–126

Wu W, Yi J, Zheng J (2010) Investment structure of Chinese resident families: an empirical analysis based on lifecycle, wealth, and housing. Econ Res 1:72–82

Yuan W, Huang R (2018a) Housing demolition and household financial risk asset investment. Finance Econ Res 4:143–153

Yuan W, Huang R (2018b) This money is different: household consumption under demolition impact—analysis of the regulatory effects of household wealth and health. Bus Res 3:67–75

Zhang H, Yin Z (2016) Financial knowledge and financial exclusion of Chinese families: an empirical study based on CHFS data. Financ Res 7:80–95

Chapter 7
Age-Period-Cohort Effects on Financial Health of Household

Household financial behavior is an essential component of economic cycles and the functioning of financial systems. Encouraging household financial investment and safeguarding financial health are crucial forces for unleashing the potential of domestic demand and ensuring the healthy development of the economic and financial sectors. However, in recent years, with the increasingly prominent characteristics of small-scale and aging households in China, more individuals and families need to take responsibility for managing household finances and using financial tools effectively to achieve their development goals. The traditional mutual assistance in forming economic resources within families is gradually being replaced by market relationships, placing higher demands on individuals and families for financial awareness and capability.

In 2015, the Center for Financial Services Innovation (later renamed Financial Health Network) in the United States first introduced the concept of financial health. The Chinese Academy of Financial Inclusion (CAFI) released the "Inclusive, Healthy, and Responsible—Development Report on Inclusive Finance in China (2019)", which provided the first domestic interpretation of financial health. Specifically, financial health refers to the financial status of individuals, families, and enterprises. It indicates the extent to which they can smoothly manage daily income and expenses, handle financial shocks prudently, make comprehensive investments for future development, and possess certain financial capabilities. This can help them overcome financial vulnerabilities, enhance financial resilience, and better cope with challenges and risks.

In 2017, General Secretary Xi Jinping pointed out at the National Financial Work Conference that preventing systemic financial risks is the fundamental theme of financial work. Recent surveys have shown that Chinese financial consumers' financial health has exhibited various deficiencies, with increasing instances of unhealthy financial behavior. From 2012 to 2021, the annual scale of repayments by Chinese residents increased from 5 trillion yuan to 14 trillion yuan. The debt-to-income ratio of residents rose from 24.5 to 28.2%. In 2021, the debt-to-income ratio reached

S. Zhao and D. Zhao, *The Household Finance Issues in China*,
https://doi.org/10.1007/978-981-97-0706-5_7

124.4%. High levels of debt restrict residents' liquidity assets such as bank savings and cash holdings. It also leads to a crowding-out effect on consumption, increasing the likelihood of systemic financial risks and economic downturns. In recent years, the government has formulated a series of related policies and measures to help people enhance their ability to cope with economic crises. In 2016, the State Council issued the "Promotion Plan for the Development of Inclusive Finance (2016–2020)", which significantly improved financial support for initial entrepreneurs, including low-income urban populations, disadvantaged groups, rural impoverished populations, entrepreneurial farmers, students in vocational colleges and universities, and disabled workers. The integration and promotion of the new rural cooperative medical care system and the urban resident medical insurance system also provided guarantees for residents to reasonably reduce "precautionary savings" and securely allocate family assets. This not only promotes greater participation of families in the formal financial market but also prevents vulnerable groups from resorting to inappropriate financial self-rescue measures during crises. This ultimately contributes to individual and family financial health. Families constitute the largest micro-group in the financial system. Financial health, as an advanced form of inclusive finance development, focuses on further enhancing the financial resilience of the main bodies and their ability to withstand risks, building on existing financial services. Therefore, conducting timely systematic empirical research is of great practical significance in providing a reliable basis for enhancing family financial health.

Overall, research on Chinese family financial health is relatively lacking and has not comprehensively presented the diversity and complexity of current Chinese family financial health. In the new era, it is worth asking: What level is Chinese family financial health at, given the slowdown in economic growth and changes in population age structure during the period of social transformation? What trends have been observed in recent years? What factors have influenced these changes? Exploring the changing trend of financial health over time not only helps us better understand the transition of family life cycles but also provides a clearer understanding of the heterogeneous characteristics of financial health status in different age structures and cohort groups.

The changes in contemporary family financial health may result from both changes in the life cycle and the impact of significant social transformations. Based on this, this chapter places the dynamic changes in financial health within the framework of age-period-cohort analysis. It specifically addresses the following three questions: First, what trend does financial health exhibit as individuals age? Second, how does the promotion of inclusive financial policies during the period of social transformation affect the level of financial health in resident families? Third, since 1930, what imprint have major historical events and social transformations left on the construction of financial health for different cohort groups? Based on these three changing trends, corresponding theoretical hypotheses will be proposed. Empirical tests will be conducted using data from the China Household Finance Survey for the years 2013, 2015, 2017, and 2019. Addressing these three questions from a temporal perspective allows for the study of changing trends in financial health in resident families, understanding the development of financial health capabilities among different population groups, and discerning the role that major historical events have played in their individual growth processes. This holds significant research value in constructing a theory of financial health from the perspective of the family life cycle.

7.1 The Emergence and Connotation of Financial Health Concept

The conceptual framework of financial health consists of eight measurement indicators related to four dimensions: on the expenditure side, it includes having income greater than expenses and timely payments; on the savings side, it involves having sufficient liquidity and long-term savings; in terms of borrowing, it encompasses manageable debt and a high-quality credit score; and in planning, it pertains to having appropriate insurance and advance financial planning. These indicators integrate various aspects of the subject's performance into a coherent whole, namely, financial health (Parker et al. 2016). Assessing people's financial lives holistically, from withstanding shocks to achieving goals, financial health is the best indicator for measuring the subject's financial capability. Although different researchers or institutions do not have a unified definition of financial health, discussions on the financial health status of demographic and socio-economic groups, such as gender and race, and the application of financial health as a utility tool in various aspects like client financial consulting, corporate financial capacity assessment, and government financial condition measurement, have extended the concept's connotation from individuals to enterprises and even more organizations and groups, gradually elevating it from a practical tool to a development concept (Mo 2022).

In 2020, CAFI proposed that financial health is a concept related to family well-being or sustainable enterprise development. The measurement of how families or enterprises use financial services requires considering how they meet their daily and long-term needs, as well as assessing their ability to withstand financial shocks. In 2021, CAFI released the report "China's Women's Financial Health is Accelerating Development", discussing the current status of women's financial health and the need for financial capacity building. The research found that women outperform men in daily expense management and financial resilience, while men have a slight advantage in investing for the future and financial capability. However, the comprehensive scores for both men and women indicate that the overall financial health of respondents is in a suboptimal state.

Before the concept of financial health was proposed, some studies, although not explicitly stated, involved multiple dimensions of financial health.

(1) Regarding income and expenditure, researchers pointed out that there exists a dynamic equilibrium relationship between the income and consumption of urban and rural residents in China. Urban residents' income has a greater long-term impact on consumption, while the increase in income for rural residents has a

significant impact on consumption levels, whether in the long or short term (Ma and Guo 2011). Additionally, there are issues with low consumption proportions and unreasonable allocation of financial assets in Chinese households (Wei et al. 2013).

(2) In terms of debt, durable goods consumption significantly increases household debt, while families with higher levels of medical and education expenses have a stronger savings motive and are less inclined to smooth consumption through debt (Zhu and Xia 2018).

(3) The cornerstone of family security requires a stable cash flow. Currently, data shows that nearly half of Chinese households' savings are precautionary, i.e., additional savings made by residents to guard against the impact of future uncertainties on consumption (Leland 1968). Factors such as income uncertainty, liquidity constraints, social security, and higher education reform all have a significant impact on family consumption and saving behavior (Yang and Chen 2009; Gan et al. 2018).

(4) Household financial investment behavior promotes the willingness to purchase commercial insurance, thereby reducing the need for precautionary savings (Lu and Yang 2022). Participating in medical insurance and pension insurance reduces the savings rate of residents. In recent years, China has continuously promoted the participation of resident families in medical insurance and pension insurance. The continuous expansion of the basic medical security network and basic pension insurance coverage for the entire population has effectively provided protection for enhancing family risk management capabilities, with a particular emphasis on immunization efficiency. This has also increased the future planning and development capabilities of families, ensuring the maximization and sustainability of the financial well-being of resident families. These intertwined factors mutually influence each other, collectively promoting the continuous development of the level of financial health in Chinese families.

7.2 Empirical Research on Financial Health

Given that financial health is a newly proposed concept in recent years, existing empirical research is still in its initial stages. Therefore, limited studies primarily focus on exploring the current status and influencing factors of financial health among different demographic groups. For instance, Zhang Heng (2020) took productive farmers as an example and analyzed the issues of consumer financial health in credit business from the perspectives of supply and demand subjects, as well as the institutional challenges they face (Zhang 2020). Liu and Sun (2021) pointed out in their study that the financial literacy of the household head has a significant positive impact on household financial health, and this positive impact is significant only in households with female heads, indicating that this positive effect varies by the gender of the household head (Liu and Sun 2021). For young families, factors such as age, gender, marital status of the household head, as well as family characteristics like family size and financial product investments, all have significant impacts on household financial health. The average value of the financial health index for young Chinese families remains relatively stable across all age groups. They perform well in dimensions such as daily income and expenditure, as well as assets and liabilities. However, there are areas of deficiency in managing liquid assets, providing unexpected protection, and ensuring retirement security (Fang and Chen 2022).

7.3 Theoretical Analytical Framework from a Life Course Perspective

The life course theory requires connecting individual life experiences with social history and structure to elucidate personal lives (Li et al. 1999). It reconstructs the concept of "age" from three perspectives: life time, social time, and historical time, transcending individual levels. Specifically, life time refers to the actual age, i.e., the life stage an individual is in. Social time refers to the appropriate timing for playing specific roles, reflecting the influence of social and cultural factors on individual development. Historical time refers to the year of birth, emphasizing situating individuals in historical contexts and focusing on the impact of specific historical events and social environments on individuals. These three dimensions of time effectively integrate the individual, social, and historical levels around the core concept of age, forming an analytical framework for the theory of life course (Bao 2005).

7.3.1 Age Effects on Financial Health

It is generally believed that age effect reveals individual life cycle characteristics. Since people's wealth perceptions and financial behaviors are closely tied to specific ages or stages in their life experiences and role transitions, they are influenced by age changes. Exploring age effects can help us better understand the transformation of family life cycles and provide a clearer insight into the heterogeneous characteristics of financial health under different age structures.

In the current process of economic development in China, a large number of young people are attracted to economically developed areas, facing a continuous rise in the pressure of life. The phenomenon of income and expenditure imbalance is particularly prominent. Young household heads are in the early stage of asset accumulation, often having relatively less wealth and a strong demand for real estate (Zhu et al. 2012). The proportion of household debt in total assets is often relatively large. At the same time, financial planning is far from being a daily behavior. With age, the financial planning ability of resident families tends to show an inverted "U" shape, increasing first and then decreasing. Improving financial literacy can promote families to reduce excessive debt, make rational use of credit markets to smooth consumption throughout their lives, thereby positively impacting household financial well-being (Wu et al. 2018). Against the backdrop of extended life expectancy, the improvement of health status for elderly individuals and the extension of their life cycles also mean that the age structure in the original life cycle theory assumptions has changed. Especially for the "young old" group who have just retired, they have lower time costs and more abundant wealth accumulation, showing a more positive attitude towards financial asset allocation. This allows the level of household financial health to reach a certain height. Of course, with the gradual increase in age, the preference of elderly household heads for risk avoidance gradually becomes apparent. Compared to the allocation of financial assets such as funds and stocks, the proportion of household savings gradually increases. Therefore, we propose the hypothesis of age effect on household financial health (Wang et al. 2017).

Hypothesis 1 With the increase in the age of the household head, the level of household financial health continues to rise and may reach its peak in the "young old" stage.

7.3.2 Period Effects on Financial Health

Period effects focus on the universal impact of social changes during a specific historical period or data collection point. It is the collective effect of changes in the background of an era on the population across all age groups. Studying period effects allows us to better explore the trends in the financial health of resident families under the background of economic reform and modernization, thereby enhancing our understanding of the relationship between economic growth, changing times, and the financial well-being of resident families.

In the past decade, under the combined influence of government macro-control and the implementation of long-term effective economic policies, China's economic level has significantly improved, and per capita income has seen substantial growth. Taking the years from 2013 to 2019, which are the focus of this chapter, as an example, China's total GDP increased from 56 trillion yuan to nearly one hundred trillion yuan, and per capita disposable income of residents exceeded 30,000 yuan. The coverage of the social security system continues to expand, and the level of protection continues to rise. According to data from the Ministry of Human Resources and Social Security of China, from 2013 to 2019, the income of the basic pension insurance fund in China showed a stable growth trend. Compared to 2013, in 2019, the national income from basic pension insurance was 5.5 trillion yuan, and the number of participants in urban employee basic pension insurance was 1.35 times that of six years ago. The number of participants in unemployment insurance and medical insurance was 1.25 times and 2.37 times that of eight years ago, respectively (Statistical Bulletin on the Development of Human Resources and Social Security 2013). Under this growth trend, the financial health level of Chinese residents should also continue to develop in a positive direction. Economic progress, as an external social environmental change, has a direct impact on the income consumption, assets and liabilities, and participation in social security of Chinese resident families, thereby influencing the improvement of the level of household financial health. Therefore, the author proposes the hypothesis of the period effect on household financial health.

Hypothesis 2 The level of household financial health gradually increases with period changes.

7.3.3 Cohort Effects on Financial Health

Based on socialization theory and life course theory, specific historical events or social environments can have specific impacts on the same cohort of people, emphasizing the collective influence of early individual growth environments and social factors. A cohort can be viewed as a structural category, and the unique environment and conditions of the same cohort from birth to death actually provide a record of structural changes and social transformations. Similarly, the common living conditions and resources of the same cohort may have a unique shaping effect on their experiences (Keyes et al. 2010). By studying cohort effects, we can indirectly understand how historical events have influenced people's behavior in household finance.

One of the theories frequently used to explain cohort effects is the theory of cumulative advantage/disadvantage. It emphasizes that certain characteristics (such as wealth, health, or status) unique to individuals when they are young will show systematic trends over time (Dannefer 2003). Life course scholars view cumulative advantage/disadvantage as a stratification process, in which the advantages/disadvantages experienced by people in different cohorts in their early years accumulate, leading to favorable/unfavorable outcomes.

Since the late 1970s, the adjustment of China's socio-economic structure has made those who have experienced this transformation beneficiaries. As mentioned earlier, this leads to an expectation that, over the course of life, residents' financial health is composed of cumulative advantages, meaning individuals who perform better in factors such as wealth endowment, educational level, and financial literacy benefit more in the later stages of their lives, thus there may be intergenerational differences (Chen 2018).

For those born before 1960, most did not receive formal higher education, and they not only experienced wars and natural disasters but also faced the most severe economic difficulties in China. Therefore, their savings motivation is most significant. Most of these individuals accumulated wealth throughout their lives, and their desire for consumption is minimal.

For cohorts born between 1960 and 1990, most received good education during their childhood and adolescence. The tremendous social changes led to the rapid arrival of new things and disruptions became the norm in their growth process.

Compared to earlier cohorts, this group has stronger consumption demands and lower savings intentions.

Especially for cohorts born after the 1970s, the tremendous economic pressure of raising children in the family, the negative correlation between the proportion of children and the participation rates in medical insurance and pension insurance, will directly reduce the level of household financial health. It is worth noting that the later-born cohorts have a stronger risk preference. Families in these cohorts invest more in risky assets, and the pressure of housing and car loans increases the possibility of household debt (Shen and Shi 2020). Therefore, we propose the cohort effects hypothesis of household financial health.

Hypothesis 3: On the cohort dimension, the overall level of financial health of cohorts born in different eras shows a downward trend.

7.4 Development of Age-Period-Cohort Analysis Method

The Age-Period-Cohort (APC) analysis method assumes that individual differences are jointly influenced by three factors: age, period, and cohort. Therefore, it is necessary to grasp the effects of age, period, and cohort by analyzing age data from different survey points and birth cohorts (Tian 2017). However, in actual research, distinguishing age, period, and cohort effects faces some difficulties. In multi-period cross-sectional data, age effects and cohort effects may be mixed together. When the age-period-cohort analysis approach and the APC multi-category model were first proposed, the issue of collinearity between age, period, and cohort was not truly addressed (Mason et al. 1973). Among these three factors, knowing any two factors will uniquely determine the third factor, that is, there exists complete collinearity between the three variables (period = age + birth cohort). If all three factors are simultaneously included in a regular linear analysis model, the model's estimated coefficients cannot obtain a unique solution, making it impossible to differentiate age effects, period effects, and cohort effects.

This chapter uses the Intrinsic Estimator (IE) method proposed by Yang et al. (2004) to address the problem of complete collinearity, in order to obtain stable APC model coefficient estimates (Yang et al. 2004). The two-factor model is also a method to obtain unique solutions for APC model parameters, that is, in the age-period-cohort three-factor model, selecting two of them to establish either an age-period model, an age-cohort model, or a period-cohort model. After simplifying the three-factor model into a two-factor model, there is no longer a linear relationship between the model variables. Researchers often construct both two-factor and three-factor models at the same time to observe the true influencing factors of the target variable (Su and Peng 2014).

In summary, research on financial health in China is still in the early stages of development. Especially in the field of household finance, a large number of previous studies hardly introduced the concept of financial health when discussing issues.

Some individual studies analyze the financial health performance of surveyed households in combination with different influencing factors, but there is a lack of attention to the dynamic trends of household financial health in recent years. Decision-making in household finance not only concerns short-term asset allocation but also reflects long-term financial planning and development goals. Paying attention to the dynamic trends of financial health is not only conducive to understanding the financial situation of individual households but also helps grasp the trends of socio-economic development. Therefore, in this chapter, we use multi-period cross-sectional data from the China Household Finance Survey and attempt to analyze the performance of household financial health under different age, period, and cohort effects from the perspective of life course theory using the Age-Period-Cohort (APC) model, providing a scientific basis for a deeper understanding of the development of financial health in Chinese households.

7.5 Empirical Analysis Based on China Household Finance Survey Data

7.5.1 Data

This chapter uses data from the China Household Finance Survey (CHFS), which is a nationwide sampling survey project conducted by the China Household Finance Survey and Research Center of Southwestern University of Finance and Economics. The survey aims to collect relevant information about household finance at the micro level. The main contents include population characteristics and employment, assets and liabilities, income and consumption, social security and insurance, and subjective attitudes, providing a comprehensive and detailed description of aspects such as household economy and financial behavior. By combining data from four periods in 2013, 2015, 2017, and 2019, this study will explore the age-period-cohort effects on household finance health in China.

7.5.2 Variables

Overall, domestic studies related to financial health evaluate the financial health of subjects by measuring and scoring various dimensions such as daily expenditure management, financial resilience, future planning, and financial capabilities. The construction of the indicator system generally includes subjective and objective parts, but specific measurement indicators vary depending on the research question and subjects. According to the connotation of financial health and referring to existing research methods, this study will measure household financial health from five dimensions: daily expenditure management, asset-liability management, liquidity management, unexpected protection management, and retirement security management. Each dimension indicator adopts a 100-point scale, with a passing score set at 60. After determining the passing line for each dimension using the dual threshold method, the sample mean for the province in which the household is located is calculated.

In the dimension of expenditure management, the proportion of total family income to total family expenditure in the past year is calculated. The passing line is set to 1, meaning that if income and expenditure are equal, the household receives 60 points. This score is then compared with the sample mean of the province. For the dimension of asset-liability management, the proportion of total family debt to total family assets is calculated. The sample mean for the province is used as a dual threshold. If the proportion of total family debt is equal to the provincial sample mean, the household receives 60 points. Specific scores are calculated according to the corresponding scoring rules. In the dimension of liquidity management, based on previous research, a household that has enough liquid funds to cover three months of living expenses receives 60 points. The dimension of unexpected protection management primarily evaluates whether the household has sufficient protection to cope with unexpected shocks. The specific measurement method calculates the participation rate of household members in social medical insurance, other medical insurance, commercial health insurance, or commercial life insurance. If the participation rate of household members is equal to the provincial sample mean, it is scored as 60 points. In the dimension of retirement security management, the participation rate of household members in social pension insurance, enterprise supplementary pension insurance, or annuities is calculated. Planning for the future also reflects the family's retirement security, and a certain degree of relief in the family's retirement burden is beneficial to household financial health. By using equal weighting to calculate the scores of the five dimensions, a financial health index variable is obtained. The total score is 100 points, with higher scores indicating better performance in household financial health.

Regarding the variables related to the Age-Period-Cohort (APC) model, Age (A) refers to the age of the household head. The age range in the study sample is 20–79 years old. Period (P) represents the year of data collection, and Cohort (C) represents the birth cohort of the sample. In addition, the model includes individual characteristic variables such as gender, marital status, years of education, and financial literacy of the household head, as well as family characteristic variables such as family size and indirect financial literacy, as control variables.

Financial literacy is assessed based on the responses provided by the household head to questions pertaining to interest rates, inflation, and risk-related financial matters. Consistent with established research methodologies, respondents are awarded 2 points for a correct answer regarding interest rates and inflation calculations, 1 point for an incorrect answer, and 0 points if they are unable to perform the calculation. For queries related to stock and fund risks, participants receive 3 points for a correct response, 2 points for an incorrect one, 1 point if they have not heard of stocks or funds before, and 0 points if they have no knowledge about them at all. The cumulative score obtained from these assessments determines the level of financial literacy.

Indirect financial literacy is measured by the number of people in the family engaged in financial-related industries. Specifically, if someone in the family is engaged in work in industries such as finance, real estate, leasing, and business services, the family is considered to have a relatively high level of indirect financial literacy (Zhuang 2022). The minimum value is 0, and the maximum value is 3. Since the sample size is small, samples with values of 2 and 3 are combined with samples with a value of 1 to obtain a virtual variable for family indirect financial literacy, where 1 indicates a relatively high level of family indirect financial literacy. The specific details of the control variables are shown in Table 7.1.

7.5.3 Models

The APC model considers the temporal factors affecting a certain social phenomenon in three dimensions: age, period, and cohort. This allows for a better understanding of the effects of each dimension on the dependent variable. In this study, the age, period, and cohort effects reflect the degree of variation in household financial health caused by different ages, survey periods, and birth cohorts. Based on the endogenous factor method proposed by Yang et al., the following logarithmic linear APC model is constructed:

$$FH_{ij} = \mu + \alpha_i + \beta_j + \gamma_k + X_{ij\delta} + \varepsilon_{ij}$$

where, FH_{ij} represents the financial health index score of family i in age group j. α_i represents the financial health age effect of age group i, β_j represents the financial health period effect of period j, γ_k represents the financial health cohort effect of cohort k. μ is the model intercept term. ε_{ij} is the random disturbance term of the model.

Additionally, the study will further construct two-factor models of age-period and age-cohort to analyze the effect changes of household financial health. The endogenous factor parameter estimation method requires the data to satisfy the condition of age + cohort = period, and in most studies, the data is grouped into 5-year intervals. However, since the data used in this study does not meet the grouping condition in terms of period span, the data will only be grouped in the two-factor model.

Table 7.1 Descriptive statistics of control variables

Variable	Definition	Sample Size	Min	Max	Mean	Standard Deviation
Gender	Female = 0, Male = 1	69,307	0	1	0.72	0.45
Marital status	Unmarried, Separated, Divorced, Widowed = 0, Married, Cohabiting, Remarried = 1	69,308	0	1	0.81	0.39
Years of education	No formal education = 0, Primary school = 6, Junior high school = 9, High school = 12, Vocational/ Technical school = 12, Associate's degree/Higher vocational school = 15, Bachelor's degree = 16, Master's degree = 19, Doctoral degree = 22	69,308	0	22	9.31	4.20
Financial literacy	Score for financial-related issues like interest rates, inflation, risk, etc., with a maximum score of 7	69,308	0	7	2.66	2.29
Family size	Total Household Population	69,308	1	20	3.00	1.56
Indirect financial literacy	Low Indirect Financial Literacy in the Family = 0, High Indirect Financial Literacy in the Family = 1	69,308	0	1	0.04	0.19

7.6 Measurement Results of Various Dimensions of Financial Health and Composite Financial Health Index of Chinese Families

Table 7.2 displays the measurement results of various dimensions of household financial health and the composite financial health index. In all samples, the average score of the financial health index is 65.69, slightly higher than the passing score of 60. According to the classification of the Financial Health Network for the performance of the main financial health index, an average score of 0–39 indicates that the subject is in a financially vulnerable state, with few or almost no reported healthy results in various dimensions. An average score of 40–79 indicates that the subject is in a financially coping state, with some reported healthy results in certain measurement indicators. An average score of 80–100 indicates that the subject is in a financially healthy state, with all measurement indicators reporting healthy results. From Table 7.2, it can be seen that some measurement indicators in the five dimensions of household financial health perform well. Therefore, overall, Chinese household financial health is basically in a state of financial coping, with room for improvement in performance in individual dimensions.

In terms of daily income and expenditure management, most sample households have an average score higher than the passing line, indicating that the majority of households have higher annual income than expenses. However, the overall mean is slightly below 60 points, indicating that there are still some sample households with higher annual expenses than income, resulting in a lower score in the dimension of

Table 7.2 Descriptive statistics of household finance health dimension indicators

Financial health dimension	Minimum value	1st Quartile	Median	3rd Quartile	Maximum value	Mean	Sample size
Daily expenditure management	0	18.26	65.26	100	100	56.83	69,308
Asset and liability management	0	97.30	100	100	100	90.87	69,307
Liquid capital management	0	3.24	13.95	92.03	100	36.29	69,308
Accidental protection management	0	61.14	100	100	100	81.34	69,283
Retirement protection management	0	39.68	69.87	100	100	63.13	69,291
Financial health index	0	53.19	65.93	80	100	65.69	69,280

daily income and expenditure management. In the dimension of asset and liability management, the average score for all sample households reaches 90.87 points, with the vast majority of households performing well in debt management. Most sample households perform poorly in the dimension of liquidity management. The cash and current deposits held by families cannot cover three months of living expenses. The average score for all sample households is only 36.29, indicating that more than half of the households have low scores in liquidity management, with only a few sample households reaching the passing line. In the dimension of unexpected protection management, the overall sample performs well, with an average score of 81.34, second only to the score performance in the dimension of asset and liability management. The average score for retirement protection management reaches the passing line, and this indicator performance is closely related to the number of minors in the family. In addition to the insufficient planning for future retirement in the family, the impact of family members without relevant retirement protection due to age on the participation rate of family retirement protection may also be the reason for the relatively low average score in this indicator.

7.7 Analysis of Age-Period-Cohort Model for Household Financial Health in China

Table 7.3 reports the results of the analysis of household financial health using the Age-Period-Cohort (APC) model (endogenous factor method). Figure 7.1 shows the age effect on household financial health. Overall, household financial health gradually increases in middle age and reaches its highest point around the age of 60 before gradually declining. From the ages of 20–45, household financial health shows some fluctuations, but there is no clear upward or downward trend. After the age of 45, the age effect curve begins to show growth, reaching its peak in the age range of 55–65, which is the highest point in the entire age range. After the age of 65, the household financial health index begins to show a continuous decline. Residents often plan their asset allocation based on their income throughout their life cycle. As Wu et al. (2010) found, the investment structure of resident households exhibits a "bell-shaped" structure in terms of risk as it changes with age (Wu et al. 2010). The effectiveness of investment portfolios also demonstrates a clear inverted "U-shaped" age effect, with household investment efficiency reaching its highest point around the age of 59 (Zhou 2021). In households where the head is between 55 and 65 years old, the accumulation of income from the older generation and the stable employment income of the younger generation after adulthood will contribute to the good financial condition of the family. At the same time, the reduction in risk preference and the accumulation of financial knowledge will also encourage families to consciously develop rational financial plans to achieve long-term development goals.

Further analyzing the scores of the measurement indicators in the five dimensions at different age stages, as shown in Figs. 7.2 and 7.3, it is evident that sample

Table 7.3 Results of APC analysis of family financial health

Independent variable	Dependent variable	
	Household Financial health	
	Coefficient	Standard deviation
Gender (female)	0.0224^{***}	0.0023
Spouse (none)	0.0640^{***}	0.0029
Years of education	0.0131^{***}	0.0003
Financial literacy	0.0183^{***}	0.0008
Household size	-0.0383^{***}	0.0052
Indirect financial literacy	0.0472^{***}	0.0005
Age	Yes	Yes
Period	Yes	Yes
Cohort	Yes	Yes
Intercept	4.0298^{***}	0.0023
AIC	10.6722	–
BIC	– 445,628	–

Note *, **, and *** indicate significance at the 10%, 5%, and 1% levels, respectively

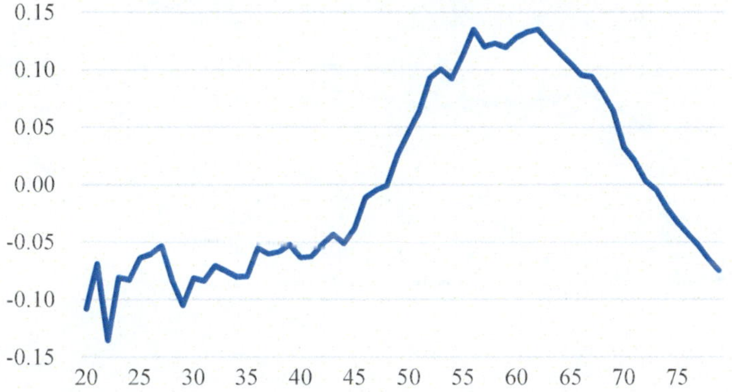

Fig. 7.1 Age effect of family financial health

households demonstrate a simultaneous increase in scores in the dimensions of accidental protection management and pension protection management as age advances. In 2013, the basic national medical insurance system was initially established in China, and other medical insurance and commercial medical insurance were still in the developmental stage. The construction of the social security system was still in full swing. Therefore, it can be seen that in 2013, the scores for accidental protection management and pension protection management were relatively low. However, it is still noticeable that sample households reached their peak scores in these two dimensions at around 60 years of age. Afterward, the scores remained relatively stable, with slight fluctuations or a slight downward trend. Hence, the fluctuations in financial health in terms of age effects are mainly influenced by the performance of scores in the dimensions of accidental protection and pension protection. Additionally, the trough in scores for pension protection management at the age range of 30–44 may be attributed to the growth in family population size driven by childbirth behavior during this age range, indirectly leading to a decline in the participation rate of pension insurance.

From Fig. 7.4, it can be observed that the household finance health index continues to increase with the change of time periods. However, there is a slight downward trend from 2017 to 2019. Looking at the scores in each dimension (see Fig. 7.5), the scores for household debt management remain at a high level across different time periods. In contrast, sample households perform poorly in the dimension of liquidity management, with average scores in all periods falling below 40 points. Unlike the gradual increase in scores for accidental protection and pension protection management over time, the score for expenditure management does not show a

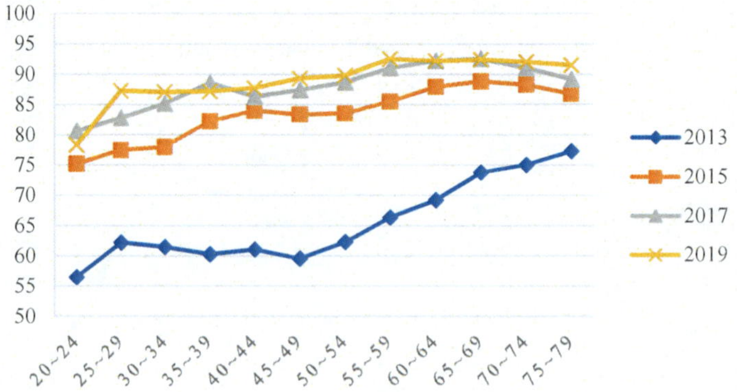

Fig. 7.2 Accident protection management scores by age

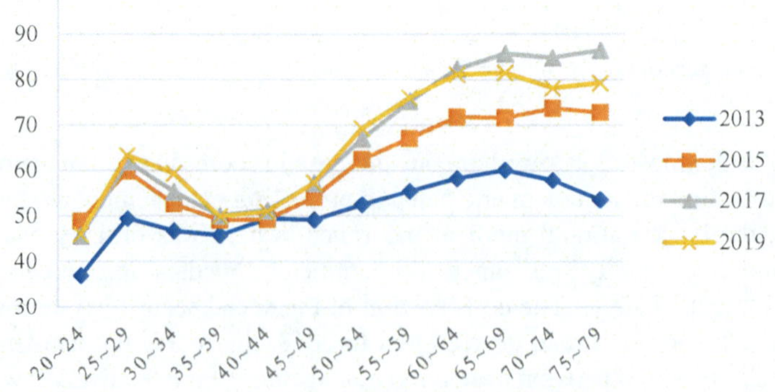

Fig. 7.3 Elderly security management scores by age

clear upward trend. Instead, it fluctuates within the range of 50–60 points. The calculation of expenditure management involves the total income and total expenses of the household, representing the income not used for consumption, which constitutes savings according to the national economic accounting system. China's savings rate has consistently been much higher than in other countries. Since the 2008 international financial crisis, the savings rate has decreased, and since 2016, it has even been slightly lower than the optimal savings rate. It is expected that the overall savings rate in China will continue to decline in the future (Chen and Liang 2022). With the combined effect of a slowdown in economic growth, a decrease in short-term savings, and a decrease in confidence in long-term financial goals, the proportion of total expenses to total income in households has increased. This has led to a decrease in the score for expenditure management. In the absence of any significant trend changes in other dimension indicators, this indirectly contributed to the decrease in household finance health score in 2019.

According to the results in Fig. 7.6, there is a slight decrease in household finance health in the birth cohorts from 1934 to 1959, and it remains stable in the cohorts

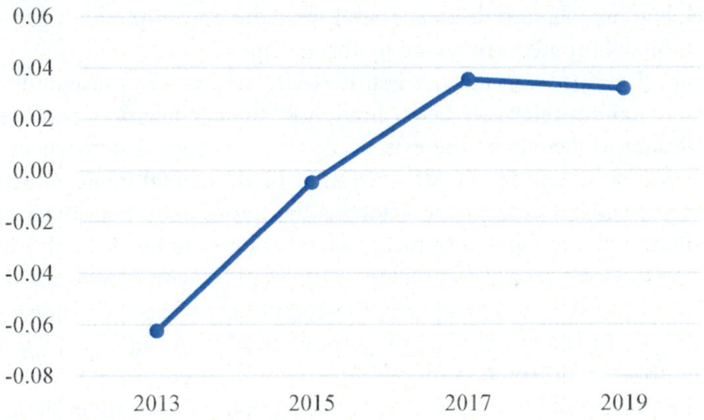

Fig. 7.4 Period effects on household financial health

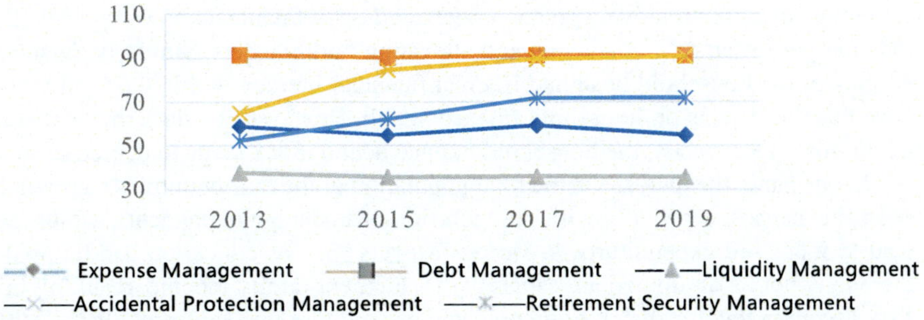

Fig. 7.5 Changes in scores for various dimensions of household financial health over time

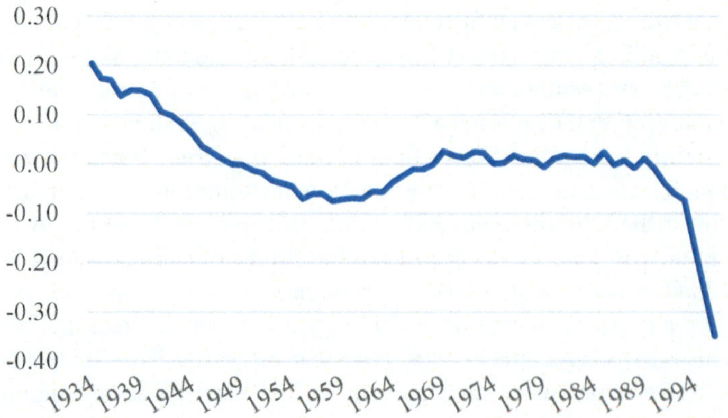

Fig. 7.6 Household financial health cohort effect

born from 1960 to 1990. However, it is worth noting that due to the smaller sample size of cohorts born after 1994, the household finance cohort effect sharply decreases after 1994, leading to a sample bias. Therefore, there may not be enough information to support the cohort effect reflected by this group.

In terms of control variables, when it comes to gender, households with male heads tend to exhibit relatively better household finance health. Upon specific analysis of different dimensions, there is no apparent gender difference in the scores of all dimensions except for the dimension of liquid capital management. Existing studies indicate that women have a longer life expectancy and lower risk preferences. Additionally, compared to men, female household heads tend to place more emphasis on the long-term development of the family, which gives them a stronger motivation to save (Liu 2013). Hence, this might be a reason why households with female heads do not have sufficient preparation in terms of liquid capital. Compared to households with no spouses, households with married heads tend to have relatively higher household finance health indices. Spouses not only provide emotional support but also positively impact the stability of income sources and expenditure balance in the family. An increase in the educational years of the household head has a significant positive effect on household finance health. With higher levels of education, there is a relatively greater understanding of financial knowledge, leading to better performance in managing and allocating family assets. Similarly, financial literacy of the household head and indirect financial literacy within the family also have positive effects on household finance health. However, the data shows that as the family size expands, the household finance health index tends to decrease.

On one hand, the increase in the total population of the family implies a growth in overall expenses, especially with the inclusion of underage dependents, which can lead to increased expenditures in various aspects such as education. Additionally, there may not be an immediate capability to augment family income, resulting in a lower score in the dimension of income and expenditure management. On the other hand, the increase in underage dependents in the family can affect future family planning, specifically reflected in the decrease in the participation rate in retirement insurance, indirectly impacting the family's score in retirement security management.

7.8 Verification of the Two-Factor Model for Household Financial Health in China

Table 7.4 presents the results of the two-factor model analysis for age-period and age-cohort effects on household financial health. It can be observed that the influence of various control variables on household financial health is generally consistent with the regression results of the three-factor model. Furthermore, after grouping the age and birth cohort variables, the results of the two-factor model show a similar trend to the analysis results of the age-period-cohort model (using endogenous factor method). In both the age-period model and the age-cohort model, the household financial health index continues to increase with age and reaches its peak in the 60–69 age group, followed by a gradual decline. Regarding period effects, household financial health shows a year-on-year growth, but compared to 2017, there was no significant increase in 2019. Moreover, there was a slight decrease in the coefficient performance. According to the assumed results, household heads born in the 1960s and 1970s are in middle age and may have relatively higher financial literacy, which positively affects the level of household financial health. However, contrary to expectations, the grouped cohort effects show a more pronounced overall downward trend, and the 1990s cohort exhibits a lower level of financial health. This result may be closely related to the family life cycle, where earlier birth cohorts have accumulated assets and risk avoidance orientations that contribute to better performance in the financial health index. When the fit results of the two-factor model are close to those of the three-factor model, the two-factor model is considered superior (Clayton and Schifflers 1987). It can be concluded that the level of household financial health is primarily influenced by age and period effects. Overall, the results of the two-factor model further confirm the analysis results of the age-period-cohort three-factor model.

7.9 Realistic Analysis and Development Suggestions for Household Financial Health Level in China

The current research on household financial health in China is still in its early stages. Based on data from the national sampling surveys conducted in 2013, 2015, 2017, and 2019 by CHFS, an examination of the trends in the financial health of Chinese households was conducted in terms of age, period, and cohort. Through the endogenous factor method, age, period, and cohort effects were effectively separated, enabling an estimation of the evolutionary trends in financial health across three dimensions.

Table 7.4 Analysis results of the two-factor model for household financial health

	Dependent variable			
Independent variable	Household financial health			
	Age-period		Age-cohort	
	Coefficient	Standard deviation	Coefficient	Standard deviation
Gender (female)	0.0222***	0.0023	0.0274***	0.0023
Spouse (none)	0.0662***	0.0029	0.0647***	0.0030
Education years	0.0129*	0.0003	0.0130***	0.0003
Financial literacy	0.0181***	0.0005	0.0173***	0.0005
Family size	– 0. 0387***	0.0008	– 0.0429***	0.0008
Indirect financial literacy	0.0469***	0.0052	0.0468***	0.0052
Age	Yes	Yes	Yes	Yes
Period	Yes	Yes	No	No
Cohort	No	No	Yes	Yes
Intercept	4.0443***	0.0042	4.0413***	0.0041
AIC	10.6938	–	10.77	–
BIC	– 445,116	–	– 439,874.4	–

Note *, **, and *** indicate significance at the 10%, 5%, and 1% levels, respectively

The research findings indicate that the level of household financial health in China exhibits significant age effects, steadily increasing with age, and maintaining a relatively high level between ages 55 and 65, followed by a gradual decline. With China's economy transitioning towards higher quality development, residents' awareness of household wealth management is growing. The trend of population aging implies that the influence of age structure on financial market participation behavior, as per the original life-cycle theory, is delayed. In terms of period effects, the level of household financial health has been increasing year by year, but a slight decline was observed between 2017 and 2019. This may be attributed to the impact of slowing economic growth, leading to a decrease in short-term savings rates and an increase in the proportion of consumption expenditure in total household income, resulting in a lower score in the expenditure management dimension. The cohort effect results can be explained by the cumulative advantage theory, indicating that the differential impact of early historical events on cohort groups accumulates over time. Consequently, individuals benefit more in the later stages of their life, leading to a steady decline in household financial health levels. Additionally, the model results also indicate that larger family sizes correspond to lower financial health scores. Variables such as gender, marital status, education level, financial literacy, and indirect financial literacy all have a significant positive impact on household financial health.

Overall, the financial health level of Chinese residents is significantly influenced by age and period effects, with an average score above the passing line of 60. A small proportion of households have achieved high financial health status (above 80).

The majority of households in our sample perform excellently in asset and liability management, with household debt within manageable and controllable limits. The scores for accident protection and retirement protection management both meet the passing standard, indicating that the implementation of relevant policies on medical insurance and pension insurance not only provides personal life security and enhances risk resistance but also indirectly promotes the improvement of household financial well-being and resilience.

In terms of daily expenditure management, there is a significant disparity among households, with some households having expenditure levels lower than the average of sample households in their respective provinces. Against the backdrop of demographic transition, the elderly burden on families may further increase. This necessitates families to strike a balance between income and expenditure while having policy safeguards in place, and to make rational future plans based on their own financial conditions.

In the dimension of managing liquid assets, the majority of households have low scores. This performance is related to the relatively high proportion of precautionary savings among Chinese residents, which may have a certain impact on household financial resilience. Previous studies have found that precautionary savings can explain at least 20–30% of the per capita financial asset accumulation of Chinese residents. However, at the same time, the rapidly developing mobile payment methods in recent years can not only reduce the savings rate by alleviating liquidity constraints, credit constraints, and expanding social networks but also mitigate the impact of precautionary savings on health risks, medical risks, unemployment risks, income risks, and other factors (Yin et al. 2022). In summary, there is still significant room for improvement in the financial health level of Chinese households. Various measurement dimension indicators are intertwined, collectively constituting the performance of the financial health index. Therefore, the enhancement of household financial health levels should be considered from multiple perspectives.

As an advanced form of inclusive finance development, further strengthening the construction of financial health capabilities is needed for the high-quality development of inclusive finance. At the individual level, attention should be paid to financial consumers, and financial education should be conducted for different population groups at different life stages to enhance their financial literacy and financial health awareness. This will empower individuals or families to make financial decisions, strengthen their confidence in their long-term financial conditions, and provide full empowerment for the improvement of financial well-being and financial resilience. At the policy level, a multi-level policy framework should be established to provide policy guarantees for the development of financial health. Further improvement of relevant policies and laws and regulations, strengthened supervision of financial markets, and reduction of external risks that may impact households should be undertaken. Additionally, it is necessary to establish a sound evaluation index and assessment system related to financial health, providing comprehensive and scientific measurement standards for the development of financial health. This will better serve as a tool to measure the financial conditions of households or other entities and help researchers more accurately grasp the financial health status of subjects.

References

Bao LP (2005) An exploration of the time perspective in life course theory. Sociol Stud (4):120–133+244–245

Chen DN (2018) The impact of population aging on household financial asset allocation: a study based on CHFS household survey data. J Central Univ Finance Econ 7:40–50

Chen W, Liang J (2022) Study on changes, trends, and influences of China's savings rate. Southwest Finance 2:27–41

Clayton D, Schifflers E (1987) Models for temporal variation in cancer rates II: age-period-cohort models. Stat Med 6:469–481

Dannefer D (2003) Cumulative advantage/disadvantage and the life course: cross-fertilizing age and social science theory. J Gerontol B Psychol Sci Soc Sci 58(6):S327–S337

Fang S, Chen Y (2022) Research on the financial health level and influencing factors of young families: based on the 2017 China household finance survey. Chin Youth Soc Sci 41(5):106–115

Gan L et al (2018) Income inequality, liquidity constraints, and Chinese household savings rate. Econ Res 53(12):34–50

Keyes KM, Utz RL, Robinson W, Li GH (2010) What is a cohort effect? Comparison of three statistical methods for modeling cohort effects in obesity prevalence in the United States, 1971–2006. Soc Sci Med 70(7):1100–1108

Leland HE (1968) Saving and uncertainty: the precautionary demand for saving. Quart J Econ 82(3):465–473

Li Q et al (1999) Social change and individual development: paradigms and methods of life course research. Sociol Res 6:1–18

Liu W (2013) The impact of gender ratio changes on savings rate: an empirical study based on data from 84 countries. Dissertation, Fudan University

Liu P, Sun L (2021) Financial literacy and household financial health research: a study based on the 2017 China household finance survey. Res World 10:16–25

Lu Z, Yang Y (2022) Empirical study on the impact of household financial investment behavior on consumption expenditure of urban and rural residents. Rural Finan Res 10:41–51

Ma M, Guo L (2011) Empirical analysis of long-term equilibrium and short-term fluctuation in income and consumption of urban and rural residents in China. Stat Decis 3:125–127

Mason KO, Mason WM, Winsborough HH et al (1973) Some methodological issues in cohort analysis of archival data. Am Sociol Rev 38(2):242–258

Mo X (2022) The practical significance of financial health concept. China Finance 11:86–88

Parker S, Castillo N, Garon T et al (2016) Eight ways to measure financial health: center for financial services innovation

Shen TT, Shi GF (2020) Population age structure, financial market participation, and household asset allocation: an analysis based on CHFS data. Mod Fin (J Tianjin Univ Finance Econ) 40(5):59–73

Su J, Peng F (2014) Recent advances in parameter estimation methods for age-period-cohort models. Stat Decis 23:21–26

This data is compiled and calculated through the publicly available data from the National Bureau of Statistics and the Statistical Bulletin on the Development of Human Resources and Social Security in 2013

Tian F (2017) Reverse growth: a decade of changes in the socioeconomic status of migrant workers (2006–2015). Sociol Stud 32(3):121–143+244–245
Wang C et al (2017) The influence of age structure on household asset allocation and its regional differences. Int Finance Res 2:76–86
Wei X et al (2013) The impact of social security improvement on consumption-investment choices of Chinese household. Pract Underst Math 43(2):29–39
Wu W et al (2010) Investment structure of Chinese resident households: an empirical analysis based on lifecycle, wealth, and housing. Econ Res S1:72–82
Wu WX et al (2018) Financial literacy and household debt: an analysis based on microdata from Chinese resident families. Econ Res 53(01):97–109
Yang R, Chen B (2009) Higher education reform, precautionary savings, and household consumption behavior. Econ Res 44(8):113–124
Yang Y, Fu WJ, Land KC (2004) A methodological comparison of age-period-cohort models: the intrinsic estimator and conventional generalized linear models. Sociol Methodol 34(1):75–110
Yin Z et al (2022) The impact of mobile payments on China's household savings rate. Fin Res 9:57–74
Zhang H (2020) Institutional dilemmas and recommendations for financial health of inclusive finance recipients: a case study of productive farmers. Rural Finance Res 12:46–51
Zhou C (2021) Lifecycle and effectiveness of household investment portfolio—accumulation of investment experience or decline in cognitive ability? Southern Econ 6:101–118
Zhu W, Xia Y (2018) A study on the consumer debt behavior of Chinese household. Econ Res 44(10):67–81
Zhu T et al (2012) Asset selection of Chinese middle-aged and young families: an empirical study based on human capital, real estate, and wealth. Explor Econ Issues 12:170–177
Zhuang J (2022) Social relationship network, education level, and financial literacy of Chinese residents—a study based on CHFS. Sociol Rev 4:151–167

Chapter 8
The Influence of Risk Attitude and Borrowing Behavior on Entrepreneurship

Innovation and entrepreneurship are powerful drivers of economic development and essential engines for national and social progress. Since the introduction of the national "mass entrepreneurship and innovation" development strategy in 2014, the entrepreneurial market in China has grown rapidly, with a significant increase in the number of self-employed individuals and new businesses. According to data from the State Administration for Market Regulation, in the first three quarters of 2020, the number of new market entities nationwide reached 18.45 million, with an average daily increase of 67,600. As of September 2020, the total number of registered market entities nationwide reached 134 million, maintaining a year-on-year growth rate of 3.3% despite the complex environment brought about by the COVID-19 pandemic (State Administration for Market Regulation 2020). Various forms of entrepreneurship, such as online platforms, e-commerce, and micro-businesses, have emerged, injecting new vitality into economic development.

Recognizing the paramount significance of entrepreneurship in driving socio-economic development, the academic community has conducted extensive research on entrepreneurial behavior, proposing various analytical frameworks. Gartner (1985) highlighted that entrepreneurial behavior is influenced by individual, organizational, entrepreneurial process, and external environment factors (Gartner 1985). Timmons et al. (1977) further emphasized the diversity of entrepreneurial subjects, suggesting that research should be conducted at multiple levels and dimensions, including individual, group, industry, enterprise, and society (Timmons et al. 1977). Based on this, domestic scholars have primarily focused their analysis of factors influencing entrepreneurship on social capital and risk attitudes, (Lv and Guo 2018) discussing the conditions for entrepreneurial behavior from various angles such as external environment, personal traits, credit constraints, and social capital. Specifically, a favorable external environment provides the breeding ground for entrepreneurial sprouting. Cultures that respect and recognize entrepreneurs not only foster individuals' enthusiasm to engage in entrepreneurial activities but also enhance their entrepreneurial capabilities by facilitating the perception of entrepreneurial

S. Zhao and D. Zhao, *The Household Finance Issues in China*,
https://doi.org/10.1007/978-981-97-0706-5_8

opportunities and acquisition of technical skills (Zhang and Yang 2003). In terms of research on personal characteristics, it has been found that there are significant differences in entrepreneurial behavior between men and women in urban and rural settings. Men are the main force in urban entrepreneurship, while women dominate in rural areas (Chen 2015). The level of education has a significant impact on entrepreneurial behavior under different motivations. Higher education levels reduce the likelihood of individuals participating in "survival-type" entrepreneurship but increase the probability of engaging in "opportunity-type" entrepreneurship (Song and Zhang 2010). The individual's health condition is also one of the background risks affecting entrepreneurial behavior. Deteriorating health conditions lead individuals to reduce the holding of financial assets, especially risky assets, and transfer assets to safer productive assets and real estate, demonstrating a tendency to avoid entrepreneurship (Lei and Zhou 2010). Having medical insurance can enhance an individual's risk-bearing capacity, reduce fear of future uncertainties, and promote participation in entrepreneurial activities (Zhang 2017). Due to the existence of the threshold for entrepreneurial capital, wealth accumulation is significantly correlated with entrepreneurial behavior. The study found that those with a higher net asset accumulation and weaker financial constraints are more likely to engage in entrepreneurship. There is a crowding-out effect between entrepreneurial behavior and financial investment activities. Individual investments in stocks, bonds, and other financial sectors will reduce the amount of assets available for entrepreneurship, thereby reducing the likelihood of participation in entrepreneurship (Chen and Xiao 2018).

While previous discussions on the conditions for entrepreneurship have focused on different aspects, the risk attitude of entrepreneurs and the source of entrepreneurial capital are two crucial factors in the analysis of entrepreneurial behavior. Research around risk attitude suggests that the daring spirit of entrepreneurship is a necessary trait for entrepreneurs. Research focused on the objective conditions of entrepreneurship, namely the perspective of financial constraints, emphasizes that entrepreneurial activities require sufficient startup capital and whether there is adequate financial support. However, there have been relatively fewer studies that integrate both perspectives into the same framework, and the analysis has mostly concentrated on rural credit constraints, (Cheng and Luo 2009; Peng and Liu 2016) paying less attention to the borrowing participation of urban and rural residents through different channels and purposes, as well as the impact of different types of borrowing on entrepreneurial activities. Based on this, this chapter primarily analyzes the mechanism of the impact of individual risk attitudes and borrowing behavior on residential entrepreneurship.

8.1 Concept and Connotation of Entrepreneurship

Entrepreneurship is seen as an act of career transition, different from wage employment, with founding a business or self-employment as its main features (Evans and Jovanovic 1989). However, establishing a new organization is not a necessary condition for entrepreneurship, especially for the group of naturally self-employed farmers, this criterion lacks applicability. Therefore, some scholars suggest including farmers with high operating costs and large production scale in the broad category of entrepreneurship. This is because, through the adjustment of the operating scale, farmers have effectively updated their original production methods. It is worth noting that in this chapter, the so-called entrepreneurial activities mainly adhere to the narrow definition of entrepreneurship, considering entrepreneurship as one of the types of occupations.

Entrepreneurship is typically viewed as an economically high-risk activity. While entrepreneurs operate and earn profits, they also bear risks such as entrepreneurial failure and price uncertainty of goods. Early entrepreneurship analyses often start from individual traits, discussing the relationship between entrepreneurs' risk attitudes and entrepreneurial activities. The most representative risk aversion theory holds that entrepreneurs, different from others, engage in entrepreneurship primarily due to their risk preferences and desire for achievement. Under the same market wage level, individuals with different risk attitudes choose different occupations. Groups with a preference for risk-taking are willing to switch careers at a lower threshold wage and are therefore more likely to become entrepreneurs, whereas risk-averse individuals tend to seek stable income in employment relationships (Kihlstrom and Laffont 1979).

The risk aversion theory provides a certain explanation for entrepreneurial activities. However, Isvăn and Kretzwei supplemented from the perspectives of financial constraints and initial wealth, arguing that whether one can obtain sufficient operating capital is the primary constraint on entrepreneurship (Eswaran and Kotwal 1986). Individuals with limited initial wealth, strong credit constraints, and limited access to informal financing are often excluded from the entrepreneurship market due to insufficient capital. In addition, the amount of capital directly affects the scale and mode of entrepreneurial operations. With an increase in capital, individuals are more inclined to reduce direct labor participation and take on management roles.

8.2 The Relationship Between Risk Attitude and Entrepreneurial Activities: Research and Hypotheses

Risk attitude generally refers to the subjective attitude individuals or entities hold towards the uncertainty between the objectives and outcomes of production activities. It manifests as the willingness to accept or avoid such uncertainty, reflecting a psychological state regarding its acceptance (Luo and Zhang 2016). Previous research has mainly utilized two approaches to measure risk attitude at the micro-level. One is to calculate the degree of risk attitude using questionnaires or scales, such as the Choice Dilemma Questionnaire (CDQ) (Kogan and Wallach 1964), Risk Attitude Scales (RAS) (Longair 1997), Domain-Specific Risk Taking (DOSRT) scales, (Nicholson and Soane 2005) or directly assess individuals' risk inclination using single-item questions. The second approach employs behavior, like seat belt usage, smoking, or insurance purchases, as proxy variables for risk attitude in discussing its impact on entrepreneurship.

Research on the mutual influence between risk attitude and entrepreneurship has a long history, but the conclusions are often controversial. In the 1940s, Knight (1942) found a positive relationship between the degree of risk attitude and entrepreneurship, suggesting that individuals with a higher risk preference are often more proactive in entrepreneurship (Knight 1942). Kihlstrom and Laffont (1979) proposed the risk aversion theory of entrepreneurship, arguing that risk-averse individuals prefer earning wages as employees rather than starting their own businesses because their economic return expectations are lower (Kihlstrom and Laffont 1979). However, opponents argue that individual-level risk attitude tendencies are unstable and do not substantially impact entrepreneurial activities. They posit that there is no significant difference in risk attitudes between entrepreneurs and non-entrepreneurs, and the former simply appear more optimistic about risks and may make seemingly riskier choices (Caliendo et al. 2009). In the context of Chinese society, researchers have only recently started to focus on the relationship between risk attitude and entrepreneurship. Due to differences in target groups and social conditions, the conclusions of studies based on Western countries need further validation. Lv and Guo (2018) analyzed the relationship between individual risk attitude and household entrepreneurship in the context of Chinese society. They found that although the influence of individual risk attitude on entrepreneurship varies slightly in social structures with different levels of strength, it generally has a positive impact. Individuals who prefer risk are more likely to become entrepreneurs (Lv and Guo 2018).

However, Chen (2009) study of migrant workers returning to their hometowns for entrepreneurship found that risk-averse migrant workers have lower investment return expectations, engage in smaller-scale and less challenging hometown entrepreneurship, and display more entrepreneurship behavior compared to risk-seeking individuals (Chen 2009). Other researchers have defined two concepts, risk preference and risk tendency, based on "personal traits" and "behavioral tendencies" respectively. They found that risk preference as a stable personal trait does not significantly affect entrepreneurship, while exhibiting a high risk tendency in behavioral decision-making significantly increases the likelihood of individual participation in entrepreneurship. Risk perception plays a bridging role in this influencing process (Ma and Qin 2010). Previous research has provided a wealth of empirical evidence for the study of risk attitude, and although there are significant differences in the results for different groups, the basic significance of the impact of risk attitude on entrepreneurship has been recognized. Therefore, starting from the study of risk attitude, the following hypotheses are proposed.

Hypothesis 1 Risk attitude has a positive impact on entrepreneurial activities. The higher the degree of risk preference, the greater the likelihood of engaging in entrepreneurial activities.

8.3 The Relationship Between Borrowing Participation and Entrepreneurial Activities: Research and Assumptions

Borrowing participation refers to economic transactions between individuals and other economic entities, including economic exchanges with other individuals, banks, or businesses. This economic exchange can flow in both directions, with the focus of this research being on the inflow of funds, where individuals borrow money from other economic entities. Existing research generally categorizes borrowing into formal and informal borrowing based on the degree of regulation and constraints imposed by the funding provider. Formal borrowing involves obtaining loans from formal financial intermediaries like banks, typically requiring a structured approval process. Informal borrowing, on the other hand, involves obtaining funds from informal sources or from friends and family, which is relatively more flexible in its arrangement (Shang 2019). Starting from the perspective of financial constraints and initial wealth, the ability to obtain sufficient funding is crucial for entrepreneurial activities. While household wealth is often seen as a primary source of entrepreneurial capital, borrowing becomes an important source when family wealth alone cannot support entrepreneurial endeavors. Therefore, researchers consider borrowing participation as a significant factor in analyzing entrepreneurship.

A substantial amount of research on formal borrowing and entrepreneurship has confirmed a positive relationship between the two. Formal borrowing not only assists entrepreneurs in overcoming financing difficulties but also provides support for expanding production operations and enhancing market competitiveness (Zhang and Hao 2015). However, it is worth noting that due to the various constraints associated with formal borrowing, many potential entrepreneurs find it challenging to obtain ample and fair lending services from mainstream financial institutions, which inhibits their likelihood of engaging in entrepreneurship (Liu and Qian 2018). In recent years, some domestic scholars have shifted their focus to explore the impact of informal borrowing on entrepreneurship. Some believe that, in the presence of widespread credit constraints, informal borrowing can reduce the difficulty of obtaining funds. By helping individuals gain access to new technologies, improve education levels, and secure health, among other avenues, it enhances the capacity to withstand risks, thereby promoting entrepreneurial activities (Su and Hu 2013). Informal borrowing is also considered as a substitute or complement to formal borrowing. By providing alternative financial services, informal borrowing alleviates the constraints brought about by the lagging development of formal finance, thus encouraging households to engage in entrepreneurial activities such as starting businesses or self-employment. This influence is particularly pronounced in regions where formal credit is underdeveloped (Ma and Yang 2011). Li and Zhang (2016) found through a comparison of households with and without credit constraints that informal borrowing, characterized by simple operating procedures, flexible repayment terms, and comprehensive borrower information, attracts individuals to consider it as a crucial source of entrepreneurial funding (Li and Zhang 2016). In comparison, formal borrowing holds greater significance for entrepreneurship. While many households use informal borrowing to obtain entrepreneurial capital, lending based on kinship, geographical proximity, or industry relationships is costly, less secure, and poses a higher risk of default, making it unsuitable for market-oriented economic activities. Furthermore, an excessively large scale of informal borrowing may bring financial risks and debt crises to entrepreneurs (Tian and Jin 2018).

Regarding the impact of borrowing on entrepreneurial activities, there are currently two different interpretations. The first believes that obtaining loans increases personal wealth, providing operational funds for entrepreneurial activities, leveraging financing effects, and reducing participation costs for financially risky activities (Cocco 2005; Heaton and Lucas 2000). The second focuses on the negative impact of borrowing on entrepreneurship, suggesting that borrowers tend to have higher risk aversion. For example, taking housing loans as an example, as the proportion of housing loans in family expenses increases, the likelihood of family entrepreneurship decreases (Bracke et al. 2013).

Given that current research does not distinguish between these two effects of borrowing, the differential impact of borrowing on entrepreneurship may be significantly related to the purpose of the funds. Therefore, based on the relationship between borrowed funds and entrepreneurial activities, this chapter further distinguishes between borrowing for business operations and borrowing for consumption activities. Business-oriented borrowing aids entrepreneurs in meeting their working capital needs and overcoming financing barriers, exerting positive financing or leverage effects on entrepreneurial activities. According to the initial wealth theory, in an imperfect financial market, households with a preference for future consumption are less likely to accumulate the initial capital necessary for entrepreneurship. The likelihood of entrepreneurship is reduced due to the constraints of capital. Borrowing funds used predominantly for education, housing, vehicles, and medical expenses, among other consumption areas, not only fails to bring immediate returns like entrepreneurial activities but may also increase individual debt pressure upon repayment, thereby suppressing entrepreneurship (Li and Sun 2019). The lack of financing and insufficient own capital deters households with a high consumption inclination from choosing entrepreneurship. The sources and purposes of borrowed funds interact with each other, resulting in various combinations. This further deepens the discussion on the implications of borrowing participation and its impact on entrepreneurship within complex societal contexts. According to the channels and purposes of borrowing, borrowing participation is further subdivided into formal business, formal consumption, informal business, and informal consumption. This chapter then explores their impact on entrepreneurial behavior and proposes the following assumptions.

Hypothesis 2 Regardless of the type of borrowing channel, individuals obtaining operational loans are more likely to enhance the feasibility of entrepreneurial activities.

Hypothesis 3 Regardless of the type of borrowing channel, individuals obtaining non-operational loans may reduce the feasibility of entrepreneurial activities.

Hypothesis 4 Comparing participation in formal borrowing channels with participation in informal borrowing channels, the former has a greater impact on entrepreneurial activities.

8.4 Empirical Study Based on the 2015 China Household Finance Survey

8.4.1 Data

The data used in this chapter comes from the third round of the China Household Finance Survey conducted nationwide in 2015 by the China Household Finance Survey and Research Center of Southwestern University of Finance and Economics. The 2015 survey adopted a three-stage stratified and proportional sampling method according to population size, covering 29 provinces (autonomous regions, municipalities directly under the Central Government), 351 counties (districts, county-level cities), and 1396 villages (residential committees) nationwide. A total of 37,289 families provided information on assets and liabilities, income and expenditure, insurance and security, family demographic characteristics, and employment, providing strong data support for studying micro-level financial behavior. The study excluded samples under 15 years old and over 70 years old, ultimately retaining 20,664 observations with potential entrepreneurial possibilities. Among them, males accounted for 59.78%, while females accounted for 40.22%.

8.4.2 Variables

8.4.2.1 Entrepreneurial Activity

Entrepreneurship, as one of the individual's occupational types, has a distinct "self-employment" characteristic compared to other occupational types. In this chapter, individuals with the current occupational status characterized by "self-employment" are considered entrepreneurs. Specifically, the measurement is conducted through the question in the questionnaire: "What is the nature of the first or second job you are currently engaged in?" The answer options are: (1) Employed by others or units (with a formal labor contract); (2) Temporary work (without a formal labor contract); (3) Farming; (4) Operating an individual or private enterprise, self-employment, opening an online store; (5) Freelancing; (6) Other six types. According to the occupational characteristics, individuals who choose the status type of any job as "Operating an individual or private enterprise, self-employment, opening an online store" are defined as entrepreneurs, while other cases are considered non-entrepreneurs. In the

Table 8.1 Regional distribution of entrepreneurs

	Eastern	Central	Western	Total
Entrepreneurship (%)	15. 04	12. 90	12. 13	13. 70
	(1496)	(720)	(623)	(2839)
Non-entrepreneurship (%)	84. 96	87. 10	87. 87	86. 30
	(8451)	(4860)	(4514)	(17,825)

2015 survey sample, there were 2,839 interviewed entrepreneurs, accounting for 13.7% of the total population. The entrepreneurial proportion in the eastern region was 15.04%, relatively lower in the central region and western region, which were 12.90% and 12.13% respectively. The proportion of urban registered entrepreneurs was 15.02%, while the proportion of rural registered entrepreneurs was 13.05% (see Table 8.1).

8.4.3 Risk Attitude

Risk attitude is one of the core explanatory variables in this chapter. In the 2015 China Household Finance Survey, respondents were directly asked about their investment risk attitude with the question: "If you have funds for investment, which type of investment would you prefer?" The options were: (1) High-risk, high-return projects; (2) Slightly high-risk, slightly high-return projects; (3) Medium-risk, medium-return projects; (4) Slightly low-risk, slightly low-return projects; (5) Unwilling to take any risk. After reverse coding the options, the variable "Risk Attitude" was obtained, with values ranging from 1 to 5. A higher numerical value indicates a stronger risk preference for the investor.

8.4.4 Participation in Borrowing

Participation in borrowing is another core explanatory variable in this chapter. Based on the source of borrowing, it is divided into formal participation and informal participation. On this basis, it is further categorized into operational borrowing and consumption borrowing based on whether the borrowing is applied to entrepreneurial activities. These two dimensions are combined to form four categories of borrowing participation.

Specifically, formal borrowing is measured by the question in the questionnaire: "Do you have any bank loans that have not been repaid for production and operation, education, housing, car purchase, or land?" It only includes those who have already obtained loans and excludes those who intend to apply or are in the process of applying. Informal borrowing is measured by the question: "Do you have any private loans that have not been repaid for production and operation, education, vehicle purchase, land, housing, medical treatment, or other reasons?" The questionnaire also specifically inquires about the purpose of each loan, including eight categories such as agricultural operation, industrial and commercial operation, education, vehicle purchase, housing, medical treatment, other non-financial assets, and other reasons. The first two are defined as for operational purposes, while the latter six are defined as for consumption purposes. This results in four variables: formal operational borrowing participation, formal consumption borrowing participation, informal operational borrowing participation, and informal consumption borrowing participation. The presence of this type of borrowing participation is coded as 1, otherwise it is coded as 0.

8.4.5 Control Variables

There are many factors that influence entrepreneurship. Referring to previous studies, age, gender, marital status, education level, self-rated health, logarithm of household assets, and region were selected as control variables to reduce bias in the explanatory analysis. It is worth noting that with the continuous improvement of the financial market, there are increasing numbers of risky investment channels available to the public. Investing in risky assets not only meets individual preferences for risk but also reduces the funds available for entrepreneurship. This should not be overlooked in the analysis of entrepreneurship. Therefore, this chapter includes holding high-risk assets as a control variable in the model. After removing samples with missing data, the final sample size is 20,664. Descriptive statistics of variables are shown in Table 8.2.

8.4.6 Model Construction

Given that the explanatory variable, whether residents engage in entrepreneurship, is a binary variable, a Logistic model is selected for analysis. The model is set up as follows:

$$\begin{aligned}\text{Logit}(\text{Entre}_i = 1) = \beta_0 + \beta_1\text{Risk} + \beta_2\text{Borr\_ZJ} + \beta_3\text{Borr\_ZX} + \beta_4\text{Borr\_FJ} \\ + \beta_5\text{Borr\_FX} + \beta_6\text{Control} + \varepsilon\end{aligned}$$

where, Entre_i indicates whether an individual participates in entrepreneurial activities.; Risk represents risk preference.; Borrowing Participation includes four types: formal operational borrowing, formal consumption borrowing, informal operational borrowing, and informal consumption borrowing, denoted by Borr_ZJ, Borr_ZX,

Table 8.2 Descriptive statistics of variables

Variable	Code	Percentage	Variable	Code	Percentage
Entrepreneurial activity	Yes	13.74	Marital status	Married	89.07
	No	86.26		Unmarried	10.93
Sex	Male	40.25	Formal borrowing for business	Yes	4.38
	Female	59.75		No	95.62
Age	≤ 29	9.09	Formal borrowing for consumption	Yes	12.88
	30–39	19.08		No	87.12
	40–49	31.43	Informal borrowing for business	Yes	7.55
	50–59	25.47		No	92.45
	≥ 60	14.93	Informal borrowing for consumption	Yes	12.94
Education level	≤ Elementary school	29.82		No	87.06
	Junior high school	32.26	Holding high-risk assets	Yes	14.39
	Senior high school	18.37		No	85.61
	≥ College degree	19.55			
	Minimum value	Maximum value	Mean	Standard deviation	
Risk attitude	1	5	2.08	1.215	
Self-rated health	1	5	3.57	0.921	
Logarithm of household assets	2.30	16.81	12.68	1.536	

Borr_FJ, and Borr_FX respectively. Control represents the control variable set.ε represents unobserved variables in the model affecting entrepreneurship.

Table 8.3 Entrepreneurship proportion under different risk attitudes

	Not entrepreneurship	Entrepreneurship	Total
Risk aversion (%)	84.71	12.59	65.47
	(10,841)	(1562)	(12,403)
Risk neutrality (%)	82.59	17.41	22.36
	(3501)	(738)	(4239)
Risk preference (%)	82.94	17.06	12.18
	(1915)	(394)	(2309)
Total (%)	85.78	14.22	100
	(16,257)	(2694)	(18,951)

8.4.7 Empirical Results and Analysis

8.4.7.1 Differences in Entrepreneurship Participation Under Different Risk Attitudes

To better compare the differences in entrepreneurship participation under different risk attitudes, the risk attitude variable is coded according to previous literature into three categories: risk aversion, risk neutrality, and risk preference. The statistical results show that the proportions of Chinese residents with risk aversion, risk neutrality, and risk preference are 65.47%, 22.36%, and 12.18%, respectively. It can be considered that risk aversion is still a major characteristic of Chinese residents in financial asset allocation. The groups with neutral and risk-seeking attitudes towards risk have similar proportions of entrepreneurship, at 17.41% and 17.06% respectively, which are higher than the 12.59% entrepreneurship rate for risk-averse individuals (see Table 8.3).

8.4.7.2 Differences in Entrepreneurship Rates Under Different Borrowing Participation Types

Borrowing can provide entrepreneurs with liquid capital, but the impact of different types of borrowing participation on entrepreneurship rates is not consistent. There is a strong correlation between entrepreneurship rates and the purpose of borrowing. The proportion of entrepreneurial activities obtaining operational loans is significantly higher than those who do not, with those obtaining formal operational loans and informal operational loans having entrepreneurship rates 21.80% and 14.26% higher, respectively. However, the proportion of entrepreneurship after obtaining informal consumption loans is lower, 5.42% lower than those who did not obtain them. Although the entrepreneurship rate of formal consumption borrowers is slightly higher than that of non-borrowers, the difference between the two is only 3.94%,

Table 8.4 Entrepreneurship proportion with different borrowing participation

	Formal-business	Formal-consumption	Informal-business	Informal-consumption
Obtained (%)	36.35	17.17	26.92	9.02
Not obtained (%)	14.55	13.23	12.66	14.44

which is much lower than the difference in entrepreneurship rates between formal operational borrowers and non-borrowers (see Table 8.4).

8.4.7.3 Differences in Entrepreneurship Rates Among Different Groups

The proportion of entrepreneurship varies across different age groups, educational levels, and marital statuses. Specifically, the entrepreneurship rate initially rises and then declines with age. The age group of 30–39 has the highest proportion of respondents engaging in entrepreneurial activities, with 19.30% of respondents choosing self-employment. The entrepreneurship rate for respondents aged 50 and above significantly decreases, reaching only 11.15%. For those aged 60 and above, the entrepreneurship rate drops even further to around 5%. In terms of educational attainment, respondents with a high school education have the highest participation in entrepreneurship, nearly three times that of respondents with primary school education or below. However, respondents with an associate degree or higher education have an entrepreneurship rate of only 10.68%. Married individuals have an entrepreneurship rate of 14.11%, which is 3.44% higher than unmarried individuals. There are significant differences in entrepreneurship rates among respondents with different self-rated health levels. The higher the self-rated health, the higher the entrepreneurship rate. The entrepreneurship rate for those with relatively poor self-rated health is less than half of those with relatively good self-rated health. Health is an important factor influencing entrepreneurial activities (see Table 8.5).

8.5 Model Analysis of Risk Attitude, Borrowing Participation, and Entrepreneurship Activity

8.5.1 Basic Analysis Results

After incorporating various factors into the regression model, the author analyzed their impact on entrepreneurship. We report the regression analysis results of risk attitude, borrowing participation, and entrepreneurship activity (See Table 8.6). Model 1 only considers the impact of risk attitude on entrepreneurship. From Model 2 to

Table 8.5 Entrepreneurship proportions for different groups

		Entrepreneurship		Non-entrepreneurship	
	Grouping	Percentage (%)	Sample Size	Percentage (%)	Sample Size
Age	≤ 29	16.03	356	83.97	1841
	30–39	19.30	799	80.70	3351
	40–49	15.81	1046	84.19	5661
	50–59	11.15	506	88.85	4467
	≥ 60	5.28	132	94.72	2505
Education level	≤ Primary school	7.93	488	92.07	5669
	Junior high school	17.55	1169	82.45	5492
	High school	19.74	749	80.26	3045
	≥ College degree	10.68	431	89.32	3605
Marital status	Married	14.11	2596	85.89	15,802
	Unmarried	10.67	241	89.33	2017
Self-rated health	Poor	7.51	202	92.49	2489
	Average	12.27	983	87.73	7029
	Good	16.61	1654	83.39	8304

Model 5, various types of borrowing are introduced into the equation. Finally, risk attitude and borrowing participation types are simultaneously included in Model 6. Each model includes control variables.

The results of Model 1 show a positive relationship between risk attitude and entrepreneurship activity. For each level increase in preference, the proportion of individuals engaging in entrepreneurship increases by 5.10%. This result validates Hypothesis 1: there is a positive relationship between risk attitude and entrepreneurship activity, with a higher preference for high risk indicating a higher likelihood of entrepreneurship. In Model 2, formal business loans are included, and it is found that obtaining this type of loan significantly increases the likelihood of engaging in entrepreneurship. The likelihood of participants engaging in entrepreneurial activities after obtaining formal business loans is 2.57 times that of non-recipients. Model 3 introduces formal consumer loans, which mainly refer to loans obtained from formal institutions like banks for purposes such as education, housing, and car purchases. However, this type of loan does not show a significant impact on entrepreneurship activity. Model 4 includes non-formal loans for business purposes. Similar to formal business loans, obtaining non-formal channel loans that support business activities also significantly increases the likelihood of entrepreneurship. The likelihood of participants engaging in entrepreneurship after obtaining such loans is 2.73 times that of non-recipients. Model 5 focuses on the impact of non-formal channel consumer loans on entrepreneurship. The results show that obtaining consumer loans from

Table 8.6 Logistic regression model analysis of risk attitudes, borrowing participation, and entrepreneurial activities

	(1) Risk attitude	(2) Formal business	(3) Formal consumption	(4) Informal business	(5) Informal consumption	(6) Overall model
Risk attitude	1.051***					1.033
	(0.02)					(0.02)
Formal business		2.566***				2.054***
		(0.20)				(0.18)
Formal Consumption			0.914			0.934
			(0.06)			(0.06)
Informal business				2.728***		2.630***
				(0.19)		(0.20)
Informal consumption					0.567***	0.499***
					(0.04)	(0.04)
≤ 29						
30–39 years old	1.061	1.027	1.041	1.031	1.039	1.034
	(0.09)	(0.09)	(0.09)	(0.09)	(0.09)	(0.09)
40–49 years old	0.791***	0.767***	0.761***	0.765***	0.759***	0.776***
	(0.07)	(0.07)	(0.06)	(0.07)	(0.06)	(0.07)
50–59 years old	0.555***	0.524***	0.509***	0.527***	0.504***	0.558***
	(0.05)	(0.05)	(0.05)	(0.05)	(0.05)	(0.05)
≥ 60 years old	0.366***	0.345***	0.324***	0.344***	0.312***	0.371***
	(0.04)	(0.04)	(0.04)	(0.04)	(0.04)	(0.05)
Male	1.010	0.993	1.015	1.007	1.016	0.990
	(0.05)	(0.05)	(0.05)	(0.05)	(0.05)	(0.05)
Primary school and below						
Junior high school	1.502***	1.490***	1.477***	1.511***	1.454***	1.529***
	(0.10)	(0.10)	(0.09)	(0.10)	(0.09)	(0.10)
High school	1.338***	1.325***	1.318***	1.367***	1.290***	1.383***
	(0.11)	(0.10)	(0.10)	(0.11)	(0.10)	(0.11)
College degree and above	0.362***	0.369***	0.365***	0.380***	0.349***	0.383***
	(0.04)	(0.04)	(0.04)	(0.04)	(0.03)	(0.04)
Married	1.110	1.076	1.105	1.087	1.113	1.101
	(0.10)	(0.09)	(0.09)	(0.09)	(0.09)	(0.09)
Urban	0.833***	0.886***	0.843***	0.903***	0.824***	0.898***
	(0.05)	(0.05)	(0.05)	(0.06)	(0.05)	(0.06)
Self-rated health	1.124***	1.128***	1.122***	1.150***	1.109***	1.140***
	(0.03)	(0.03)	(0.03)	(0.03)	(0.03)	(0.03)

(continued)

Table 8.6 (continued)

	(1) Risk attitude	(2) Formal business	(3) Formal consumption	(4) Informal business	(5) Informal consumption	(6) Overall model
Family assets	1.870***	1.831***	1.894***	1.875***	1.886***	1.820***
	(0.04)	(0.04)	(0.04)	(0.04)	(0.04)	(0.04)
High-risk assets	0.782***	0.816***	0.802***	0.810***	0.785***	0.795***
	(0.05)	(0.06)	(0.05)	(0.05)	(0.05)	(0.06)
Eastern region						
Central region	1.220***	1.200***	1.239***	1.161***	1.266***	1.145***
	(0.07)	(0.07)	(0.07)	(0.06)	(0.07)	(0.07)
Western region	1.110*	1.053	1.127*	1.071	1.144*	1.045
	(0.06)	(0.06)	(0.06)	(0.06)	(0.06)	(0.06)
Sample size	18,777	20,463	20,463	20,463	20,463	1878
Wald test value	1325.13	1586.34	1441.42	1584.33	1498.32	1589.80
Log-likelihood ratio	– 6767.69	– 7125.51	– 7188.11	– 7091.99	– 7157.22	– 6598.04
Pseudo R^2	0.12	0.13	0.12	0.13	0.13	0.14
BIC	13,702.67	14,419.76	14,544.97	14,352.72	14,483.20	13,402.74

Note $^{*}p < 0.05$, $^{**}p < 0.1$, $^{***}p < 0.01$. The values in the table are odds ratios (standard errors)

non-formal channels significantly reduces the likelihood of participants engaging in entrepreneurship, with a decrease of up to 43%. The regression results from Model 2 to Model 5 confirm Hypothesis 2 of this study: regardless of the source of borrowing, obtaining loans for business purposes that directly support production and operation activities contributes to the feasibility of entrepreneurial activities. However, in contrast to Hypothesis 3, participation in consumer lending activities shows completely opposite results depending on the source of borrowing: formal channel consumer lending does not have a significant impact on entrepreneurship, while obtaining loans for consumer purposes from relatives, friends, or non-formal institutions has a significant inhibitory effect on entrepreneurship.

Model 6 reports the overall regression results of the model. After incorporating all independent variables, the Bayesian Information Criterion of the model decreases, indicating a higher explanatory power. After including all variables, although risk attitude still has a positive effect on entrepreneurship, it is no longer statistically significant. This is slightly different from the conclusion in Hypothesis 1 that risk attitude has a positive relationship with entrepreneurship activity. Unlike the risk attitude variable, after introducing control variables, the impact of various types of borrowing participation on entrepreneurship is consistent with individual models, but the coefficients fluctuate. After obtaining formal business, non-formal business, and non-formal consumer loans, the likelihood of entrepreneurship is 2.05 times, 2.63 times, and 0.50 times that of non-borrowers, respectively. This indicates that obtaining loans directly for production and operation activities in the form of financial support safeguards participation in entrepreneurship. However, participating in debt as a liability has a negative impact on entrepreneurship activity. This conclusion only applies to consumer loans obtained from non-formal channels. This may be closely related to the differences in the groups participating in the two types of loans. Through the analysis of the sample, it is found that among the 2685 samples participating in formal consumer loans, 80% of the income falls within the top 50% of the overall population. In contrast, among those participating in non-formal consumer loans, the highest income group is in the 50–75% range. The former group with stronger economic strength has greater repayment capacity, and the constraint of debt on entrepreneurship is relatively limited. For the middle and lower income groups, even if it is informal lending, it will increase the financial pressure and reduce the enthusiasm for participating in entrepreneurship.

In summary, focusing on the comprehensive impact of risk attitude and borrowing participation on entrepreneurship, it is found that the significance of risk attitude in influencing entrepreneurship disappears with the introduction of borrowing participation. This means that risk attitude can indeed explain the differences in participation in entrepreneurship to a certain extent, but the influence of borrowing participation is stronger. Under equal capital conditions, individuals with a preference for high risk will have greater enthusiasm for participating in entrepreneurship. However, whether entrepreneurship activities can be implemented depends on the acquisition of entrepreneurial capital. Although formal borrowing has advantages in reliability, its complex review process limits its coverage to a limited number of entrepreneurs. Most individuals still need to seek non-formal borrowing to further enhance the feasibility and sustainability of entrepreneurship.

Looking at different age groups, the 16–29-year-old cohort exhibits the highest propensity for entrepreneurial engagement. However, as individuals surpass the age of 40, their enthusiasm for entrepreneurship gradually wanes. Specifically, compared to the 16–29 age group, the incidence rates of entrepreneurship decrease by 22.4%, 44.2%, and 62.9% in the age groups of 40–49, 50–59, and above 60 respectively. It should be noted that although there is a higher likelihood of entrepreneurial activity among individuals aged between 30 and39 in our sample, this conclusion cannot be generalized to the overall population due to various factors at play.

Furthermore, it is currently observed that those under thirty are most proactive in pursuing entrepreneurial endeavors. As work experience accumulates over time, career transition costs gradually escalate which subsequently diminishes one's inclination towards leaving their current profession for entrepreneurship.

Moreover, gender does not exhibit significant disparities in terms of entrepreneurial participation contrary to previous findings suggesting males' greater predisposition towards business initiation. This shift can be attributed to increasing marketization levels and evolving social status of women which have led to more equalized opportunities for entrepreneurship across genders; thus rendering gender no longer a pivotal factor impeding female entrepreneurial pursuits.

In terms of education level, respondents with a junior high school education have the highest likelihood of entrepreneurship. The incidence rate of entrepreneurship for this group is 52.9% higher than that of respondents with primary school education or below. On the other hand, the group with the highest level of education has the lowest incidence rate of entrepreneurship, which is only 38.3% of the primary school group. This is consistent with the findings of other scholars that higher education levels are less likely to lead to entrepreneurship. The dividend from education has allowed individuals with higher education levels to obtain good positions. Entrepreneurship means giving up stable jobs with higher current income, which comes with higher opportunity costs. There is no significant difference in entrepreneurial participation between married and unmarried individuals. Compared to rural residents, urban residents have a 10.2% lower likelihood of participating in entrepreneurial activities. This differs from the phenomenon presented in the descriptive analysis, which showed a higher proportion of entrepreneurship in urban areas. This may be largely due to the significant differences in entrepreneurial activities between urban and rural residents, largely influenced by financial constraints. When considering only household registration differences, urban household registration has a higher proportion of entrepreneurship. However, after the model controls for the natural logarithm of family assets, rural residents show a stronger willingness to participate in entrepreneurial activities. One's confidence in their own physical health significantly affects entrepreneurship. For each unit increase in self-rated health level, the incidence of entrepreneurship increases by 14.0%. Good physical condition is a guarantee for entrepreneurship. Based on this, individuals can participate in various stages of entrepreneurship with higher production and operation efficiency. Family assets have a very significant impact on entrepreneurial activities. For each unit increase in the natural logarithm of family assets, the incidence of entrepreneurship is 1.82 times that of the previous level.

Holding high-risk assets shows a crowding-out effect on entrepreneurial activities. After holding high-risk assets, the incidence of entrepreneurship decreases by 21.5%. Although individuals who purchase high-risk assets such as stocks and funds in asset allocation also show a higher risk preference, they do not show enthusiasm for entrepreneurship because their risk preference is satisfied by participating in high-risk asset activities. Instead, their participation in entrepreneurship decreases due to reduced liquidity. Entrepreneurial behavior is also closely related to the external economic policy environment.

Regionally, after controlling for other conditions, especially family wealth, the incidence of entrepreneurship in the central region is 14.5% higher than that in the eastern region. This contradicts the phenomenon in descriptive statistics where the proportion of entrepreneurship in the eastern region is the highest. This is because entrepreneurship is largely constrained by startup capital, and family wealth levels show significant regional differences. Therefore, in descriptive statistics, the proportion of entrepreneurship in the eastern region is much higher than that in the central region. However, at the same level of wealth, individuals in the central region have more entrepreneurial activities. This phenomenon can be understood from two perspectives: entrepreneurial demand and entrepreneurial costs. The eastern region has a higher level of economic development and can provide more employment opportunities. There is no need for survival-driven entrepreneurship. Entrepreneurship in the east also faces higher costs in terms of housing, production, and labor, presenting greater challenges for entrepreneurship activities.

8.5.2 Why Does Risk Attitude Lose Explanatory Power

Unlike previous studies that concluded that individuals with a preference for risk have a higher probability of entrepreneurship, in Model 6, the influence of risk attitude on entrepreneurship is not significant. To further clarify which factors affect the effectiveness of risk attitude, Model 7 introduces the interaction between risk attitude and various types of borrowing participation.

The results in Table 8.7 indicate that whether one can obtain operational loans from formal financial institutions has significant implications for risk attitude. The key to implementing entrepreneurship lies in acquiring entrepreneurial capital. Under realistic entrepreneurial conditions, risk attitude can influence entrepreneurial activities. For groups that can obtain loans, especially formal operational loans, a preference for high risk can demonstrate a positive impact on entrepreneurship.

8.5.3 Comparison of Urban–Rural Differences in Impact Effects

To further verify the robustness of the analytical model, this chapter discusses the samples divided into urban and rural categories according to household registration status. The results show that risk attitude has a certain positive impact on entrepreneurship, but it is not significant in rural areas. Obtaining operational loans can significantly increase the likelihood of entrepreneurial activities. The impact in urban areas is much greater than in rural areas. Consumer-type loans can reduce individual participation in entrepreneurial activities. Both formal and informal consumer loans in urban areas reduce the likelihood of participating in entrepreneurial activities. However, in rural areas, only informal consumer loans significantly inhibit entrepreneurship. Entrepreneurial households in rural areas typically engage in small-scale, long-term entrepreneurial activities. They lack highly recognized collateral and find it difficult to obtain loans from formal institutions. Therefore, entrepreneurial activities in rural areas exhibit a stronger dependence on informal borrowing. Overall, risk attitude has a certain positive impact on entrepreneurship, but the influence is relatively small. Operational loans have a significantly positive effect on entrepreneurial activities. The conclusion that informal consumer loans have a significantly negative effect on entrepreneurship is credible. However, further discussion is needed regarding the differential performance of risk attitudes and formal consumer loans in urban and rural areas.

Table 8.7 Interaction analysis between risk attitude and types of lending participation

	(1)	(6)	(7)
	Risk attitude	Overall model	Interaction term
Risk attitude	1.051***	1.033	1.021
	(0.02)	(0.02)	(0.02)
Formal operation		2.054***	1.444***
		(0.18)	(0.28)
Formal consumption		0.934	1.089
		(0.06)	(0.15)
Informal operation		2.630***	2.154***
		(0.20)	(0.33)
Informal consumption		0.499***	0.523***
		(0.04)	(0.08)
Formal operation × Risk attitude			1.151**
			(0.08)
Formal consumption × Risk attitude			0.939
			(0.05)
Informal operation × Risk attitude			1.095
			(0.06)
Informal consumption × Risk attitude			0.975
			(0.06)

Note * $p < 0.05\%$, ** $p < 0.1$, *** $p < 0.01$. The values in the table are odds ratios (standard errors)

8.6 The Relationship Between Risk Attitude, Borrowing Behavior, and Residents' Entrepreneurship

This chapter analyzes the data from the 2015 China Household Finance Survey to discuss the impact of risk attitude and borrowing behavior on entrepreneurial activities. The study finds that risk attitude affects individual participation in entrepreneurship. When considering the type of borrowing participation, risk attitude has a positive effect, but only in urban areas, and its explanatory power is very limited. Borrowing participation, on the other hand, is of great significance for entrepreneurship. Loans for production and operation purposes have a positive effect on entrepreneurship. Whether obtained through formal or informal channels, they significantly increase the likelihood of individuals engaging in entrepreneurial activities. However, consumer loans for non-entrepreneurial purposes have a negative impact on entrepreneurship, especially loans from informal channels, which significantly reduce the occurrence of entrepreneurship. Furthermore, respondents aged 16–29, those with middle or high school education, and those with higher family assets have a higher likelihood of entrepreneurship. Respondents with a university education or above have a lower likelihood of entrepreneurship. Under consistent conditions, individuals living in central regions show higher entrepreneurial enthusiasm compared to those in the eastern regions.

It is worth noting that there is no significant difference between formal and informal lending in their impact on urban entrepreneurship. However, the influence of informal lending on entrepreneurial activities in rural areas is significantly stronger than formal lending. This is closely related to the disparity in financial services. While the development of the financial system has facilitated access to formal lending, restrictions such as review mechanisms and collateral requirements limit its prevalence. This is especially true for rural areas with relatively underdeveloped financial institutions, where obtaining formal credit is even more challenging. In contrast, informal lending, coupled with adaptability to local cultures, allows for flexible exchange of information and rapid access to funds, effectively overcoming the challenges of insufficient capital in entrepreneurship. Based on the analysis in this chapter, it is observed that the influence of risk attitude, as a subjective factor, on entrepreneurial activities is relatively limited. This may be related to the prevailing risk-averse attitude among residents. According to survey results, over 60% of residents hold an aversion to risk. This not only reflects a lack of confidence in risk investment activities among the general public but also indicates a relatively low level of knowledge and information about the financial market. Faced with the prevailing conservative risk choices among residents, in the future guidance of entrepreneurship, efforts can be made from both institutional guarantees and financial support to change the inherent attitude towards entrepreneurial risk. Specific measures may include strengthening the promotion of financial knowledge and reducing information asymmetry, both of which can effectively leverage the positive effects of risk attitude on entrepreneurship.

Furthermore, the impact of lending participation, as an objective factor, on entrepreneurial activities varies significantly depending on the channel. To promote participation in entrepreneurship through formal lending, special attention must be paid to the application and issuance of production and operation loans. In order to mitigate bad loans, banks require applicants to provide movable or immovable collateral when granting business loans. They also require applicants to provide business certificates. While this is beneficial for sustaining the activities of existing entrepreneurs, it still presents a high threshold for entrepreneurs in the initial stages. Additionally, in urban and rural areas, there is still ample room for the effectiveness of formal lending to be developed. Improving the accessibility of formal loans, particularly focusing on the development of business loans in rural areas, can bring more vitality to entrepreneurship and innovation. Informal lending is also an essential aspect that cannot be ignored in entrepreneurial analysis. It not only supplements the shortcomings of formal lending but also serves as an important source of entrepreneurial funding. Efforts should be made to standardize informal lending and unleash its potential in the entrepreneurial field, which is an urgent task at present.

The analysis in this chapter also reveals that there is still significant room for the development of entrepreneurship guidance for individuals with higher education levels. Despite the favorable policies for innovation and entrepreneurship for individuals with higher education levels in various regions under the background of promoting innovation and entrepreneurship, there has not been a significant increase in the participation of this group in entrepreneurship. How to assist this group in participating in entrepreneurship should be a focus of future discussions. Finally, the gap between the stronger entrepreneurial enthusiasm in central regions and the relatively lower entrepreneurship due to wealth constraints deserves attention. In future entrepreneurial research, it is necessary to continue to focus on and address the differentiated demands in different regions.

As sociologist Coleman pointed out, the outcomes of individual actions also affect others, meaning that individual actions are also influenced by macro structures. The combination of micro actions produces macro-level results, meaning that individual actions lead to macro-level changes (Coleman 2008). Therefore, although this study focuses on the micro-financial behavior and entrepreneurial activities of individuals, it is also of great significance for understanding the current employment structure, methods, challenges in Chinese society, and the corresponding design of social policies. With the transformation and upgrading of China's social industrial structure, the role of traditional industries in absorbing labor has weakened, especially after the COVID-19 pandemic, which has caused many companies to struggle. In the post-pandemic era, solving the employment problem has become an important livelihood issue related to social stability and development. At the same time, with the rise of the internet society, it has provided individual actors with rich market information platforms and extensive social interaction space. This new fundamental social infrastructure is gradually becoming solid, providing many new opportunities for individuals to engage in "entrepreneurship" and employment. These research findings emphasize the construction of a multi-level, multi-channel financial resource supply system and the improvement of the basic financial institutional infrastructure, which is of great significance for stimulating social innovation, promoting social employment, and solving livelihood problems.

References

Bracke P, Hilber C, Silva O (2013) Homeownership and entrepreneurship: the role of commitment and mortgage debt. IZA Discussion Papers

Caliendo M, Fossen FM, Kritikos AS (2009) Risk attitudes of nascent entrepreneurs—new evidence from an experimentally validated survey. Small Bus Econ 32(2):153–167

Chen B (2009) An empirical study on the impact of risk attitude on returning home for entrepreneurship. Manage World 3:84–91

Chen Q (2015) Heterogeneous impact of risk preferences on entrepreneurial choices: an empirical study based on RUMIC 2009 data. Population Econ 2:78–86

Chen Z, Xiao Z (2018) Innovation, entrepreneurship institutional environment, entrepreneurial behavior, and family asset selection. World Econ Dig 4:20–35

Cheng Y, Luo D (2009) Entrepreneurial choices of farmers under credit constraints: an empirical analysis based on the Chinese household survey. Chin Rural Econ 11:25–38

Cocco JF (2005) Portfolio choice in the presence of housing. Rev Financ Stud 18(2):535–567

Coleman JS (2008) Foundations of social theory. Social Sciences Academic Press, Beijing

Eswaran M, Kotwal A (1986) Access to capital and agrarian production organization. J Econ 96(382):482–498

Evans DS, Jovanovic B (1989) An estimated model of entrepreneurial choice under liquidity constraints. J Polit Econ 97(4):808–827
Gartner WB (1985) A conceptual framework for describing the phenomenon of new venture creation. Acad Manag Rev 10(4):696–706
Heaton J, Lucas D (2000) Portfolio choice and asset prices: the importance of entrepreneurial risk. J Financ 55(3):1163–1198
Kihlstrom RE, Laffont JJ (1979) A general equilibrium entrepreneurial theory of firm formation based on risk aversion. J Polit Econ 87(4):719–748
Knight FH (1942) Profit and entrepreneurial functions. J Econ Hist 2(S1):126–132
Kogan N, Wallach MA (1964) Risk taking: a study in cognition and personality. J Risk Res 8(2):157–176
Lei X, Zhou Y (2010) Asset allocation choices of Chinese families: health status and risk preferences. Finan Res 1:31–45
Li K, Sun Z (2019) Consumption inclination and entrepreneurial choice: perspectives of financial constraints and social relationships. J Univ Electron Sci Technol China (Soc Sci Edn) 1:1–8+29
Li Y, Zhang B (2016) Research on the impact mechanism of informal finance on rural household entrepreneurship. Econ Sci 2:93–105
Liu Y, Qian W (2018) The influence of formal and informal finance on household entrepreneurial decision-making and performance: a perspective based on substitution effect. Econ Perspect 2:41–47
Longair M (1997) Ways forward: the RAS questionnaire. A&G 38(3):19–22
Luo M, Zhang X (2016) Entrepreneurial risk tolerance and its avoidance: a literature review. Lujia Manag Rev 1:53–64
Lv J, Guo P (2018) Social relationships, heterogeneity in risk preferences, and family entrepreneurship. Financ Dev Res 10:22–28
Ma K, Qin R (2010) Research on the relationship between individual risk propensity and entrepreneurial decision: the mediating role of risk perception. Forecasting 1:42–46
Ma G, Yang E (2011) Social networks, informal finance, and entrepreneurship. Econ Res 3:83–94
Nicholson N, Soane E (2005) Personality and domain-specific risk taking. J Risk Res 8(2):157–176
Peng K, Liu X (2016) Farmer's income increase, accessibility of formal credit, and non-agricultural entrepreneurship. Manage World 7:88–97
Shang H (2019) The impact mechanism of financial support on consumption upgrading: a comparison of formal finance, informal finance, and internet finance. Bus Econ Res 12:157–161
Song Y, Zhang Q (2010) Institutional factors, personal characteristics, and entrepreneurial behavior: Chinese experience. China Soft Sci 1:12–16
State Administration for Market Regulation (2020) 18.45 million new market entities registered nationwide in the first three quarters. State administration for market regulation website, 2020–10–30
Su J, Hu Z (2013) Threshold characteristics and regional differences in the poverty reduction effect of rural informal financial development: an analysis based on panel smooth transition models. Chin Rural Econ 7:58–71
Tian L, Jin X (2018) The influence of mainstream and non-mainstream finance on household entrepreneurship: an investigation based on data from 28,143 household surveys in CHFS project. J Chongqing Univ (Soc Sci Edn) 2:24–35
Timmons JA, Smollen LE, Dingee AL (1977) New venture creation: a guide to small business development. Irwin Professional Publishing
Zhang L (2017) The impact of urban residents' basic medical insurance on family entrepreneurial decision-making. Contemp Econ Manag 1:89–97
Zhang Y, Yang J (2003) An empirical study on entrepreneurial behavior of entrepreneurs. Econ Manag 20:19–26
Zhang H, Hao Z (2015) Social capital and financial constraints in household entrepreneurship: a study based on rural financial survey data. Zhejiang Soc Sci 7:15–27+155

Chapter 9
Financial Exclusion and Entrepreneurship Under the Influence of Financial Literacy

Abstract The outbreak of the COVID-19 pandemic at the end of 2019 posed severe challenges to the national economy and social operations, profoundly impacting China's employment situation. "Stabilizing employment" has become one of the important tasks for economic development at all levels of government. The 20th National Congress report of the Communist Party of China clearly stated the need to "implement a strategy of giving top priority to employment, strengthen policies prioritizing employment, and provide opportunities for everyone to achieve self-development through diligent work." This highlights the core essence of focusing on people in employment efforts.

The outbreak of the COVID-19 pandemic at the end of 2019 posed severe challenges to the national economy and social operations, profoundly impacting China's employment situation. "Stabilizing employment" has become one of the important tasks for economic development at all levels of government. The 20th National Congress report of the Communist Party of China clearly stated the need to "implement a strategy of giving top priority to employment, strengthen policies prioritizing employment, and provide opportunities for everyone to achieve self-development through diligent work." This highlights the core essence of focusing on people in employment efforts.

Attention to the issue of entrepreneurship and the study of its influencing factors have important practical significance and theoretical value. From the perspective of the entrepreneurial environment, although the promotion of inclusive finance has accelerated the continuous innovation of financial products and services, creating a favorable financial environment for mass entrepreneurship and innovation, it is still imperfect. This prevents market participants from freely entering and exiting the financial market, and fund lending is not entirely determined by the expected repayment ability of the fund demander. Wang et al. (2013) found through a survey of 1547 households that 55.1% of the households were subject to savings exclusion, and 88.1% were subject to credit exclusion. A large number of households find it difficult to enjoy regular financial services (Wang et al. 2013). Even in financially developed regions like Beijing, residents are still subject to financial exclusion

S. Zhao and D. Zhao, *The Household Finance Issues in China*,
https://doi.org/10.1007/978-981-97-0706-5_9

(Zhu and Ning 2017). Financial exclusion also has a significant inhibitory effect on the entrepreneurship rate (Tao et al. 2021). Existing studies have found that even if some market entities are expected to have good repayment potential, due to low existing assets, a lack of necessary social relationships, or insufficient payment of the "financial rent" threshold, they cannot obtain financial services in a reasonable and appropriate manner (Li and Li 2020). This hinders the possibility of household entrepreneurship and negatively affects the operational performance of enterprises after entrepreneurship, mainly manifested in the reduction of financial resource allocation efficiency and the expansion of financial risk. This has become a shackle on economic development and social progress.

In fact, the success or failure of entrepreneurship is not only constrained by the entrepreneurial environment but also influenced by the literacy and abilities of the entrepreneur. Financial literacy is an important indicator reflecting individual abilities. Compared to education and previous work experience, financial literacy more reflects people's understanding of financial knowledge and their ability to use it to effectively allocate resources for financial security (Wang and Yang 2014; Yin et al. 2015). The improvement of financial literacy helps to reduce the likelihood of individuals or families experiencing financial exclusion, thereby influencing entrepreneurial behavior. Most of the entrepreneurship mentioned in existing literature refers to entrepreneurial decision-making, that is, how to promote entrepreneurial activities. However, the discussion on post-entrepreneurial performance, that is, the operational performance of enterprises after entrepreneurship, is lacking. In fact, starting a business does not necessarily mean entrepreneurial success. The development of entrepreneurial activities often means that entrepreneurs face more constraints and greater risks in their operations. Therefore, while focusing on entrepreneurial decision-making, the analysis of post-entrepreneurial performance is more conducive to understanding the current situation of household entrepreneurship in China. It provides a reference for improving the enthusiasm and motivation of entrepreneurs and enhancing the actual results and quality of entrepreneurial activities.

This chapter attempts to explore how financial literacy plays a regulatory role in the process of financial exclusion affecting household entrepreneurial decision-making and entrepreneurial performance. Two noteworthy points in this chapter are: first, based on the use of instrumental variables to overcome endogeneity, it attempts to explore the impact of financial exclusion on household entrepreneurship and entrepreneurial performance at the micro level, providing empirical support for the current domestic research on financial exclusion from a micro perspective. Second, unlike previous studies that solely focus on whether entrepreneurship occurs, this chapter also considers entrepreneurial performance. It not only pays attention to "whether or not," but also discusses "good or not." This further explores the practical significance of financial literacy in alleviating financial exclusion, promoting inclusive finance, and improving socio-economic conditions.

9.1 Entrepreneurship Under the Influence of Business Environment and Individual Factors

Entrepreneurship is an innovative behavior. In 1934, American economist Joseph Schumpeter proposed in his book "The Theory of Economic Development" that "innovation" is the process of recombining existing production factors into the production system through means such as introducing a new product, adopting a new method, opening a new market, obtaining a new raw material, or adopting a new organizational form, thereby generating a new production function.

Existing research generally analyzes entrepreneurial behavior from two perspectives. The first perspective primarily examines the influence of economic, political, and cultural factors on entrepreneurship through factors such as liquidity constraints, government institutional inhibitions on entrepreneurial intent, (Chen 2015; Zhu and Ge 2018) the promotion of market environments on entrepreneurial behavior, (Torrini 2005) and the regional differences in cultural environments affecting entrepreneurial activities (Zhao et al. 2012). The second perspective starts from the individual level, discussing factors such as individual or family wealth levels, social networks, risk attitudes, and financial literacy (Wu et al. 2014; Liu et al. 2020; Chen 2009; Song et al. 2020) that influence entrepreneurial behavior. Overall, entrepreneurship is the process by which market actors recombine various production factor resources, open up new production fields, or innovate in business forms to maximize their own interests.

The success of entrepreneurship is closely related to the abundance of elements provided by the entrepreneurial environment and the ease of obtaining these elements. However, unlike developed countries, entrepreneurs in developing countries face issues of financial exclusion, (Li et al. 2010) making it difficult for Chinese residents to allocate resources through formal financial channels during the entrepreneurial process. On the other hand, it is related to the entrepreneur's outstanding organizational ability, ability to judge risks and opportunities, and ability to recombine production factor resources. Financial literacy to some extent reflects the entrepreneur's organizational and judgment capabilities. Experimental studies on European enterprises have shown that providing training programs aimed at improving financial literacy to entrepreneurs can significantly enhance their management capabilities, thereby increasing the company's profits and sales. Therefore, a favorable entrepreneurial environment and the personal abilities of entrepreneurs play an irreplaceable role in entrepreneurial behavior and performance, and attention to financial exclusion and financial literacy is conducive to deepening the explanatory power of innovation development theory.

9.2 Study on Financial Exclusion and Its Impact on Entrepreneurship

Obtaining effective financial services can promote the occurrence of entrepreneurial behavior. Since the concept of financial exclusion was proposed in the 1990s, it has been widely studied by many scholars. Its most basic characteristic is that some groups cannot access necessary financial products and services through appropriate channels. The concept of financial exclusion originated from financial geography. Leyshon and Thrift (1995) studied the impact of the actual distance between residents and financial service outlets on the accessibility of financial services for residents. The research pointed out that impoverished populations face difficulties in accessing financial services and products and proposed the concept of financial exclusion (Leyshon and Thrift 1995). Kempson and Whyley (1999) expanded the concept of financial exclusion, pointing out that besides the influence of geographical factors, the origins of financial exclusion also include factors such as assessment exclusion, conditional exclusion, price exclusion, market exclusion, and self-exclusion (Kempson and Whyley 1999). Gloukoviezoff (2007) pointed out that financial demanders' experience of financial exclusion is a form of social exclusion. Financial exclusion includes not only geographical factors, but also financial products and services such as funds, insurance, and securities (Gloukoviezoff 2007).

Existing research on financial exclusion of rural households is mainly conducted from two levels: macro and micro. At the macro level, existing research mainly focuses on regional development and urban–rural dualism. Research has found that there are significant differences in financial scale and accessibility between urban and rural areas and different regions. This further amplifies income disparities between urban and rural areas and income imbalances between eastern, central, and western regions through threshold effects and exclusion effects (Xu and Tian 2008; Tian 2011). At the micro level, existing research mainly focuses on the impact of financial exclusion on individuals and families, such as the impact of financial exclusion on household financial participation and resident employment behavior, (Sun and Lin 2018) as well as attention to the causes of financial exclusion, such as the influence of social networks, personality traits, family wealth levels, and financial literacy on financial exclusion (Ding et al. 2021; Li et al. 2010; Yin et al. 2015). Overall, financial exclusion mainly limits the channels through which some groups can access necessary financial products and services, thereby influencing the behavioral choices and decisions of this group.

Entrepreneurship is the process of reorganizing and integrating various production factors. When encountering financial exclusion, some entrepreneurs are excluded from the basic avenues of obtaining production factors, making it impossible for them to obtain support from the formal financial system, and they are more likely to face liquidity constraints (Cai et al. 2018). This in turn affects the entrepreneurial behavior of entrepreneurs and their performance after entrepreneurship. Based on this, this chapter proposes the following hypothesis.

Hypothesis 1 Financial exclusion has a negative effect on entrepreneurial decision-making and entrepreneurial performance.

9.3 Research on Financial Literacy and Its Impact on Entrepreneurship

A 2014 World Bank survey revealed that a lack of knowledge about financial products and services seriously hinders access to household finance accounts. While the rapid development of inclusive finance in China has significantly improved financial accessibility, financial exclusion still persists, with some families remaining excluded from the formal financial system. Research by Hou (2017) found that certain groups experience financial exclusion due to a lack of corresponding financial knowledge and the inability to access financial information (He et al. 2017). Therefore, individuals and families with higher financial literacy are less likely to be affected by financial exclusion.

In addition to the focus on the phenomenon of financial exclusion, scholars both domestically and internationally have increasingly emphasized the crucial role of financial literacy in financial investments. Corr (2006) argued that financial knowledge has an increasingly significant impact on people's lives, and the level of financial knowledge is a crucial factor in determining whether individuals can be integrated into the financial system (Corr 2006). Zeng et al. (2015) discovered that families with higher levels of financial knowledge are more likely to participate in financial markets and have a more diverse range of financial asset investments (Zeng et al. 2015). Entrepreneurship, as a form of venture capital, is a result of family asset allocation. The level of financial literacy influences family participation in the financial market and the proportion of risk asset allocation. It also affects entrepreneurial behavior through its impact on credit financing (Hastings and Tejeda-Ashton 2008; Lv and Wu 2017). Existing studies have shown that improving financial literacy can effectively enhance preferences for household borrowing channels, improve the demand for formal household credit, and increase the availability of formal household credit (Su and Kong 2019; Jia et al. 2021).

Furthermore, financial literacy's impact on entrepreneurial behavior exhibits urban–rural disparities. Compared to urban households, the marginal utility of financial literacy is stronger for rural households. Under consistent levels of financial literacy, rural households are more likely to choose entrepreneurship (Zhao et al. 2015). Overall, there has been in-depth research in China on the relationship between financial literacy and entrepreneurial behavior. However, upon review, two points are evident: first, previous research has focused more on the impact of financial literacy on family entrepreneurial decisions, with less attention paid to its influence on the sustainability of entrepreneurship. Second, prior studies have primarily concentrated on the impact of financial literacy on household financing constraints and participation in financial markets, while overlooking its effect on family entrepreneurship that is excluded from the financial market. Based on this, the following hypotheses are proposed in this chapter:

Hypothesis 2 Financial literacy has a positive effect on entrepreneurial decisions and performance.

Hypothesis 3 Financial literacy mitigates the negative impact of financial exclusion on family entrepreneurship.

9.4 Empirical Analysis Based on the 2019 China Household Finance Survey

9.4.1 Data

The data used in this chapter is sourced from the 2019 "China Household Finance Survey" (CHFS). This survey employed a combination of stratified, three-stage proportional to size (PPS) sampling method, and focused sampling design. It covered 29 provinces (autonomous regions, municipalities directly under the central government), 170 cities, 345 districts and counties, and 1360 villages (residential) committees. The sample size amounted to 34,643 households, providing highly representative data. It is the first high-quality national financial condition database in China. The study excluded data with missing values, as well as data where the age of the household head was less than 18 years or greater than 80 years, resulting in a final sample of 17,735.

9.4.2 Variables

9.4.2.1 Dependent Variables

Entrepreneurial Decision: The household head's occupational status is used to distinguish entrepreneurial activity. Engaging in salaried work is considered non-entrepreneurial, while the opposite is regarded as entrepreneurial. A binary variable is constructed based on the question "Does the household engage in industrial and commercial production and operation projects?" where 'yes' is assigned a value of 1, and 'no' is assigned a value of 0. Entrepreneurial performance primarily refers to the economic benefits generated from household entrepreneurial activities. The study selects net profit from the main ongoing entrepreneurial project as the measurement indicator. The scope of entrepreneurial activities is defined as industrial and commercial production and operation activities, including individual businesses, leasing, transportation, online shops, and business operations, but excluding traditional agricultural production and operation such as farming, forestry, and animal husbandry.

9.4.2.2 Independent Variables

Financial Exclusion. It refers to the inability of certain groups to access or use financial services and products necessary for their normal social life, including banking transactions, savings, and credit. Three types of financial exclusion are considered: banking transaction exclusion, savings exclusion, and credit exclusion. There is currently no unified method for measuring financial exclusion. Institutions such as the Financial Services Authority in the UK and the British Bankers' Association use the possession of a financial account to describe the financial exclusion status of residents. This is also the method adopted by most literature that studies financial exclusion at the household level. Zhang and Yin (2016) use the possession of corresponding accounts as a measurement indicator (Zhang and Yin 2016). In this chapter, we adopt a similar approach by using the binary variable "whether or not the household has a financial account" to measure financial exclusion. If a household lacks a current deposit account, it is considered excluded from banking transactions; if it lacks a fixed deposit account, it is considered excluded from savings; and regarding credit, being denied a bank loan or needing a bank loan but not applying for one indicates credit exclusion. As long as one of these three forms of financial exclusion exists, the household is considered to experience financial exclusion, with a value of 1, otherwise, it is assigned a value of 0.

Financial Literacy. Following the practices of previous studies, this research assesses respondents' financial literacy through three questions in CHFS2019 related to interest calculation, understanding inflation, and awareness of investment risks. First, respondents' answers are differentiated to determine whether they answered incorrectly or could not answer or did not know. This represents different levels of financial knowledge. Based on this, two binary variables are constructed: the first binary variable measures whether the answer is correct (incorrect = 0, correct = 1); the second binary variable measures whether the respondent answered directly or not, with not knowing or being unable to calculate counted as an indirect answer (indirect answer = 0, direct answer = 1). We conducted factor analysis on the six binary variables, extracting a common factor, which is defined as financial literacy. KMO test and Bartlett's sphericity test pass, indicating that factor analysis on the six binary variables is reasonable. The Cronbach's Alpha coefficient is 0.733, suggesting good reliability in measuring financial literacy (see Table 9.1).

9.4.2.3 Control Variables

Drawing from existing research findings, this chapter selects five variables, namely gender, age, marital status, political affiliation, and educational attainment, to reflect

Table 9.1 Factor analysis results

	Factor loadings
Correct answer on interest rate questions	0.859
Unknown/unable to calculate on interest rate questions	0.632
Correct answer on inflation questions	0.702
Unknown/unable to calculate on inflation questions	0.061
Correct answer on investment questions	0.335
Unknown/unable to calculate on investment questions	0.001
KMO value	0.671
Bartlett sphericity test	$X^2 = 19{,}593.64$, $P < 0.001$
Cronbach's alpha coefficient	0.733

individual characteristics. Family income, household asset status, savings rate, family wealth, and housing situation are chosen to represent household economic features. Additionally, dummy variables for urban and provincial levels are included to mitigate the potential impact of regional disparities. Descriptive statistics for the variables used are presented in Table 9.2.

9.4.3 Models

The study begins by analyzing the impact of financial exclusion and financial literacy on household entrepreneurship decisions. Since the dependent variable is binary, a Probit model is employed:

$$\mathrm{Prob}(\mathrm{Fi} = 1 || \mathrm{E_i}, \mathrm{K_i}) = \Phi(\alpha 0 + \alpha \mathrm{E_i} + \alpha \mathrm{K_i} + \varepsilon_i) \tag{9.1}$$

Next, an analysis of entrepreneurial performance is conducted. Due to the stage-specific nature of entrepreneurial performance, a Tobit model is utilized:

$$\ln(\mathrm{Entrepreneurial\_Income}) = \alpha 0 + \alpha 1\mathrm{Ei} + \alpha \mathrm{Ki} + \varepsilon \mathrm{i} \tag{9.2}$$

Given that approximately 20% of entrepreneurial households in the sample do not generate profits and only maintain a balanced income and expenditure, implying a substantial number of zeros in the household entrepreneurial returns, a Tobit censored regression model is used, with 0 set as the left-censored value. In the model, E_i represents the explanatory variables, including subjective factors and financial literacy, while K_i and X_i represent the control variables, and εi denotes the error term.

Table 9.2 Variable definition and descriptive statistics

	Variable definition	Frequency	Percentage (%)	Mean	Standard Deviation	Min	Max
Entrepreneurial decision	Entrepreneurship = 1	2591	14.61				
	Non-Entrepreneurship = 0	15,140	85.39				
Entrepreneurial performance	Net profit of the main project			557,506.8	1,483,333	0	8,000,000
Logarithm of entrepreneurial performance	Logarithm of net profit of the main project			11.66	1.80	2.30	15.89
Financial exclusion	No relevant financial account = 1	15,352	86.56				
	Has relevant financial account = 0	2383	13.44				
Financial literacy	Financial literacy			0.0001	0.91	− 1.60	0.91
Age	Head of household's age			49.00	15.32	18.00	80.00
Gender	Male = 1	8736	49.26				
	Female = 0	8999	50.74				
Marital status	Married = 1	1903	10.73				
	Unmarried = 0	15,832	89.27				
Educational level	Elementary school and below = 1	3250	18.33				
	Junior high school and high school = 2	7260	40.94				
	Associate degree = 3	3753	21.16				
	Bachelor's degree and above = 4	3472	19.58				
Political identity	Party member = 1	3427	19.31				

(continued)

Table 9.2 (continued)

	Variable definition	Frequency	Percentage (%)	Mean	Standard Deviation	Min	Max
	Non-party member = 0	14,308	80.69				
Housing status	Self-owned housing = 1	14,931	84.27				
	Non-self-owned housing = 0	2788	15.73				
Family annual income	Family annual income			142,113.40	333,314.95	0.00	12,122,418.00
Family annual income (logarithmic)	Logarithm of family annual income			11.21	1.36	0.56	16.31
Urbanicity of the family	First-tier and new first-tier cities = 1	6680	37.67				
	Second-tier cities = 2	2762	15.57				
	Third-tier cities and below = 3	8293	46.76				
Region of the family's residence	Eastern region = 1	8283	46.77				
	Central region = 2	3251	18.33				
	Western region = 3	5019	28.30				
	Northeast region = 4	1182	6.60				

9.4.4 Instrumental Variables

Financial literacy, as an intrinsic capability, may potentially lead to endogeneity issues in the model. On one hand, higher financial literacy generally enhances the ability to access financial resources, thereby mitigating the inhibitory effects of financial exclusion, which subsequently affects household entrepreneurship decisions and performance. On the other hand, the process of choosing entrepreneurship and integrating factors during entrepreneurship itself may also elevate financial literacy, thus alleviating financial exclusion faced by enterprises. Therefore, it is necessary to discuss the endogeneity of the regression equation. The study adopts the average financial literacy in the community where the household resides as the instrumental variable for financial literacy, following the approach of previous literature. Generally, a household's financial literacy is influenced by the level of financial development in the community and the atmosphere for financial knowledge acquisition. A favorable environment for financial development and learning will subtly influence the households in the region. However, the average financial literacy in the community will not directly impact the economic behavior of individual households, making this instrumental variable selection reasonable.

9.5 Impact of Financial Exclusion and Financial Literacy on Entrepreneurship Decisions and Performance

Table 9.3 presents the regression results of the impact of financial exclusion and financial literacy on household entrepreneurship. Models 1 and 2 are Probit regression results for household entrepreneurship decisions, while Models 4 and 5 are Tobit regression results for household entrepreneurship performance. The results of Models 1 and 4 show that financial exclusion has a significant negative impact on both household entrepreneurship decisions and performance. The estimated coefficient of financial exclusion in Model 1 is -0.109, significant at the 1% level, indicating that households experiencing financial exclusion are 51.6% less likely to choose entrepreneurship compared to those not affected by financial exclusion. In Model 4, the estimated coefficient of financial exclusion is -0.438, significant at the 5% level, confirming Hypothesis 1.

Models 2 and 5 demonstrate that financial literacy significantly promotes household entrepreneurship decisions and performance. The marginal effects of financial literacy on entrepreneurship decisions and performance are 0.011 and 0.277, respectively, both significant at the 1% level. This indicates that financial literacy can stimulate household entrepreneurship and enhance the enterprise performance during the survival period. Hypothesis 2 is confirmed.

The model variations demonstrate the inhibitory effect of financial literacy on financial exclusion. After adding financial literacy (Model 2), the marginal effect of financial exclusion decreases from − 0.109 to − 0.102. The result turns significantly

Table 9.3 Financial exclusion, financial literacy, and household entrepreneurship

	Entrepreneurship decision			Entrepreneurship performance		
	Model 1	Model 2	Model 3	Model 4	Model 5	Model 6
Financial exclusion	– 0.098***	– 0.092***	– 0.379***	– 0.367***	– 0.249	– 0.153
	(0.010)	(0.010)	(0.053)	(0.177)	(0.176)	(0.183)
Financial literacy		0.011***	0.158***		0.285***	0.417***
		(0.003)	(0.036)		(0.045)	(0.155)
Age	– 0.005***	– 0.005***	– 0.023***	– 0.012***	– 0.013***	– 0.013***
	(0.000)	(0.000)	(0.001)	(0.004)	(0.004)	(0.004)
Gender	0.014***	0.014***	0.071***	– 0.002	– 0.004	– 0.005
	(0.005)	(0.005)	(0.024)	(0.076)	(0.075)	(0.075)
Marital status	0.086***	0.086***	0.402***	0.496***	0.502***	– 0.506***
	(0.010)	(0.010)	(0.045)	(0.147)	(0.145)	(0.142)
Education level						
Elementary school and below = 1	—	—	—	—	—	—
Junior high school and high school = 2	0.009	0.006	– 0.004	0.056	0.033	0.010
	(0.009)	(0.009)	(0.042)	(0.132)	(0.130)	(0.131)
Associate degree = 3	– 0.037***	– 0.042***	– 0.244***	0.173	0.109	0.031
	(0.010)	(0.011)	(0.051)	(0.154)	(0.152)	(0.155)
Bachelor's degree and above = 4	– 0.067***	– 0.073***	– 0.443***	0.250	0.144	0.043
	(0.011)	(0.011)	(0.058)	(0.170)	(0.169)	(0.175)
Political affiliation	– 0.052***	-0.052***	– 0.247***	– 0.080	– 0.078	– 0.077
	(0.008)	(0.008)	(0.036)	(0.120)	(0.119)	(0.120)
Housing status	– 0.005	– 0.005	– 0.019	– 0.130	– 0.119	– 0.110
	(0.007)	(0.007)	(0.033)	(0.097)	(0.096)	(0.097)
Family income	0.011***	0.011***	0.042***	0.331***	0.318***	0.310***
	(0.002)	(0.002)	(0.011)	(0.024)	(0.024)	(0.025)
Family location (city)						
Third– tier city and below	—	—	—	—	—	—
First–tier and new first–tier city	– 0.014**	– 0.016**	– 0.093**	0.596***	0.601***	0.603***
	(0.006)	(0.006)	(0.038)	(0.089)	(0.088)	(0.088)
Second-tier city	0.007	0.007	0.21	0.676*	0.709*	0.723*
	(0.008)	(0.008)	(0.032)	(0.113)	(0.112)	(0.113)

(continued)

Table 9.3 (continued)

	Entrepreneurship decision			Entrepreneurship performance		
	Model 1	Model 2	Model 3	Model 4	Model 5	Model 6
Region of family residence						
Western	—	—	—	—	—	—
Eastern	0.039***	0.039***	0.193***	0.369***	0.383***	0.389***
	(0.006)	(0.006)	(0.035)	(0.094)	(0.093)	(0.093)
Central	0.049***	0.049***	0.242***	0.466***	0.494***	0.506***
	(0.007)	(0.007)	(0.032)	(0.102)	(0.101)	(0.172)
Northeastern	0.034***	0.034***	0.169***	0.502***	0.496***	0.493***
	(0.012)	(0.012)	(0.055)	(0.176)	(0.174)	(0.172)
N	17,183	17,183	15,757	1937	1937	1937
Pseudo R^2/R^2	0.059	0.061		0.047	0.052	
Wald x^2 (11)			796.71**			425.98**
F value			573.03			32.91

Note Values reported in parentheses are standard errors; ** $p < 0.05$, *** $p < 0.01$

positive at the 5% level, indicating that households with higher financial literacy are less affected by the negative impact of financial exclusion on entrepreneurship decisions. With the inclusion of financial literacy (Model 5), the marginal effect of financial exclusion on entrepreneurship performance decreases from -0.375 to -0.248. The influence of financial exclusion on entrepreneurship performance becomes insignificant, indicating that financial literacy significantly reduces the negative impact of financial exclusion on entrepreneurship performance. Hypothesis 3 is verified.

Models 3 and 6 in Table 9.3 are the endogeneity test regression results for entrepreneurship decisions and performance after adding instrumental variables. The p-values of the Wald endogeneity tests in Models 3 and 6 are both less than 0.05, rejecting the exogeneity assumption and indicating the existence of endogeneity issues in financial literacy. The first-stage F-values also suggest the absence of weak instrumental variable problems. After incorporating instrumental variables, financial literacy has a significant positive impact on entrepreneurship decisions, and the influence of financial exclusion on entrepreneurship performance becomes insignificant. The results still support the conclusion that financial literacy can mitigate the negative effects of financial exclusion, promote household entrepreneurship decisions, and enhance entrepreneurship performance.

Regarding control variables, higher-income households are more likely to choose entrepreneurship for wealth accumulation and are also more likely to improve enterprise performance during the survival period. At the urban level, although the likelihood of entrepreneurship in first-tier and new first-tier cities is lower compared to households in third-tier and lower cities, the performance level after entrepreneurship is higher. Regionally, compared to households in the western region, those in the eastern, central, and northeastern regions are more inclined to start businesses and obtain better returns. In terms of household head characteristics, young married male household heads are more inclined to choose entrepreneurship. Relatively, this demographic is more likely to possess a greater amount of financial knowledge and higher risk-taking ability.

9.6 The Moderating Effect of Financial Literacy on Household Entrepreneurship Under the Background of Financial Exclusion

To further understand the moderating effect of financial literacy on household entrepreneurship decisions and performance in the context of financial exclusion, Table 9.4 examines the moderating effect of financial literacy by constructing interaction terms between financial exclusion and financial literacy. In Model 1 of Table 9.4, financial exclusion has a significant negative impact on entrepreneurship decisions, while financial literacy has a significant positive impact. The interaction term between financial exclusion and financial literacy is positive, with a coefficient of 0.043, significant at the 5% level. In Model 3 of Table 9.4, the negative effect of financial exclusion on entrepreneurship performance is not significant, while financial literacy has a significantly positive effect. The coefficient is similar to the difference in Table 9.3, but the interaction term between financial exclusion and financial literacy is significant at the 1% level. This means that compared to the sample not affected by financial exclusion, the group experiencing financial exclusion shows a more significant promotion of entrepreneurship through financial literacy when

Table 9.4 Impact of financial literacy on household entrepreneurship in financially excluded samples

	Entrepreneurship decision		Entrepreneurship performance	
	Model 1	Model 2	Model 3	Model 4
Financial exclusion	− 0.078***	− 0.300***	− 0.200	− 0.058
	(0.012)	(0.095)	(0.182)	(0.202)
Financial literacy	0.008***	0.025	0.244***	0.208*
	(0.003)	(0.021)	(0.046)	(0.052)
Financial exclusion × financial literacy	0.043***	0.309**	0.489***	1.027***
Control variables	Control	Control	Control	Control
Pseudo R^2/ R^2	0.061		0.054	
Wald x^2 (12)		2346.84***		461.78***
F value		747.93		85.24

Note Values reported in parentheses are standard errors; ** $p < 0.05$, *** $p < 0.01$

Table 9.5 Robustness test

	Replace key variables		Low income level		Medium income level		High income level	
	Model 1	Model 2	Model 3	Model 4	Model 5	Model6	Model 7	Model 8
Financial exclusion	– 0.103***	– 0.287	– 0.100***	– 0.497*	– 0.051***	– 0.379	0.025	0.129
	(0.010)	(0.176)	(0.012)	(0.208)	(0.018)	(0.300)	(0.031)	(0.357)
Financial literacy	0.008***	0.281***	0.025***	0.119***	0.010***	0.610***	– 0.017***	0.084
	(0.003)	(0.037)	(0.005)	(0.060)	(0.005)	(0.080)	(0.006)	(0.074)
Control variables	Control	Control	Control	Control	Control	Control	Control	Control
N	17,183	1937	5383	531	5897	589	5903	817
R^2	0.049	0.072	0.129	0.52	0.055	0.049	0.091	0.072

Note Values reported in parentheses are standard errors; ** $p < 0.05$, *** $p < 0.01$

making entrepreneurial choices. In other words, entrepreneurs choose entrepreneurship to accumulate wealth by internalizing financial knowledge through enhancing financial literacy and are more likely to promote the development of entrepreneurship performance.

From a micro perspective, it is often challenging to distinguish whether households lack financial accounts due to household income constraints (resulting in no demand for basic financial services) or due to the prevailing financial environment. Therefore, this study employs grouped regression tests on sample households with varying income levels. The findings reveal that financial exclusion significantly hampers entrepreneurship decisions in low and medium-income households, while its impact on the entrepreneurial performance of medium-income households is not significant. Financial exclusion does not have a significant impact on the entrepreneurship decisions and performance of high-income households. One possible explanation is that low and medium-income households are more likely to encounter liquidity constraints during the entrepreneurial process compared to their high-income counterparts, making them more susceptible to the negative effects of financial exclusion. Additionally, financial literacy has a significantly positive influence on low and medium-income households, indicating its potential role in providing support for entrepreneurship within these groups and mitigating the adverse consequences of financial exclusion. High-income households face less financial pressure during entrepreneurship; hence, they are unaffected by significant negative impacts from financial exclusion. Consequently, even after extensively controlling for income levels in variable settings, this study reaffirms that financial exclusion inhibits household entrepreneurship while emphasizing the positive promoting effect of financial literacy (see Table 9.5).

9.7 Discussion

This chapter empirically examines the impact of financial exclusion and financial literacy on household entrepreneurship based on data from the 2019 China Household Finance Survey (CHFS). Firstly, it explores the influence of financial exclusion and financial literacy on household entrepreneurship decisions and performance. It further investigates the impact of financial literacy on household entrepreneurship decisions and performance within the sample that has experienced financial exclusion.

The results indicate: (1) Financial exclusion significantly reduces the likelihood of household entrepreneurship decisions. Families experiencing financial exclusion are less likely to accumulate wealth through entrepreneurship. At the same time, financial exclusion also significantly affects the performance during the entrepreneurship period. (2) Higher levels of household financial literacy effectively alleviate the negative effects of financial exclusion, increasing the likelihood of household entrepreneurship decisions and enhancing entrepreneurship performance. Individuals with higher financial literacy have stronger capabilities in utilizing existing financial resources. Therefore, when facing financial exclusion, financial literacy plays a significant supportive role in entrepreneurial behavior.

Among the production factors required for entrepreneurship, the allocation of financial resources has a significant impact on making entrepreneurship decisions and improving business performance. In recent years, the deepening reform and opening up of the financial sector in China have led to a more rational and efficient allocation of internal and external financial resources. This has gradually formed a market-oriented mechanism for financial risk prevention and disposal, and has also promoted the ability of financial institutions to enhance their services through competition. However, in this process, banks and other financial institutions adopt more conservative operating strategies, such as reducing scale, deleveraging, and streamlining business operations, to avoid reputational risks. This has, to a certain extent, brought about financial exclusion for some regions and populations. Financial exclusion reduces their access to financial services, forcing some groups to choose informal financial channels, or even riskier channels for financing. Therefore, financial exclusion is a major factor inhibiting entrepreneurial activities. The study found that not all families experiencing financial exclusion refrain from participating in entrepreneurial activities. The improvement of financial literacy can effectively alleviate the liquidity constraints faced by entrepreneurs and promote the development of entrepreneurial activities. Moreover, compared to entrepreneurs who have not experienced financial exclusion, those who have faced financial exclusion are more capable of applying financial knowledge to help optimize resource allocation, thereby suppressing the reproduction of inequality in the financial sector.

The discussion on resident entrepreneurship topics has expanded from entrepreneurship decisions to entrepreneurship performance. Analyzing the influencing factors of entrepreneurship decisions helps to understand residents' willingness to start businesses and the macro-level entrepreneurial environment. Meanwhile, discussing the status of entrepreneurship continuity and development directly assesses the actual effects of entrepreneurial activities. The empirical results demonstrate that financial literacy significantly enhances the profitability and performance of entrepreneurs, emphasizing the crucial role of financial literacy in the sustainability of entrepreneurship.

This chapter enriches the study of resident entrepreneurial activities from the perspectives of financial exclusion and financial literacy, providing some enlightening significance for further promoting the construction of an inclusive financial system. On one hand, it is necessary to promote the development of an inclusive financial service system, reduce the degree of financial exclusion, and provide a favorable external environment as much as possible for the startup and sustainability of small and micro enterprises. On the other hand, while promoting the development of an inclusive financial service system, attention should be paid to improving residents' financial literacy, strengthening training and business guidance for entrepreneurs, promoting the sustainable development of entrepreneurs' businesses, and thereby enhancing the driving role of entrepreneurship in employment and economic development.

References

Cai D, Qiu L, Meng X et al (2018) Liquidity constraints, social capital, and family entrepreneurial decision: an empirical study based on CHFS data. Manage World 34(9):79–94

Chen B (2009) Empirical study on the influence of risk attitude on returnees' entrepreneurial behavior. Manage World 3:84–91

Chen G (2015) Regulation and entrepreneurship: micro evidence from China. Manag World 5:89–99+187–188

Corr C (2006) Financial exclusion in Ireland: an exploratory study and policy review. Combat Poverty Agency, Dublin

Ding B, Zhao C, Xi J (2021) The impact of religious beliefs on household financial exclusion: empirical evidence from CHFS 2013. Sociol Rev 9(1):125–143

Gloukoviezoff G (2007) From financial exclusion to overindebtedness: the paradox of difficulties for people on low incomes? In: New frontiers in banking services. Springer, pp 213–245

Hastings JS, Tejeda-Ashton L (2008) Financial literacy, information, and demand elasticity: survey and experimental evidence from Mexico. Nat Bureau Econ Res

He J, Tian Y, Liu T et al (2017) How far is internet finance from farmers? An analysis of internet finance exclusion and influencing factors in underdeveloped rural areas. Financ Trade Econ 38(11):70–84

Jia L, Tan W, Abumunai (2021) Financial literacy, family wealth, and family entrepreneurial decision-making. Southwest Financ (1):83–96

Kempson H, Whyley C (1999) Understanding and combating financial exclusion. Insur Trends 21:18–22

Leyshon A, Thrift N (1995) Geographies of financial exclusion: financial abandonment in Britain and the United States. Transactions of the Institute of British Geographers, pp 312–341

Li J, Li J (2020) Inclusive finance and entrepreneurship: 'Giving a fish' or 'Teaching fishing'? Financ Res 1:69–87

Li T, Wang Z, Wang H et al (2010) Research on financial exclusion of urban residents in China. Econ Res 45(7):15–30

Liu J, He X, Zhang Y (2020) How do farmers succeed in entrepreneurship? An empirical study based on the dual perspectives of human capital and social capital. Sociol Rev 8(3):105–117

Lv X, Wu W (2017) The impact of financial exclusion on household investment portfolios: an analysis based on Chinese data. Shanghai Financ 6:34–41

Song Q, Wu Y, Yin Z (2020) Financial literacy and family entrepreneurship persistence. Sci Res Manag 41(11):133–142

Su L, Kong R (2019) The interactive mechanism of farmers' financial literacy and the development of rural factor markets. Chin Rural Obs 2:61–77

Sun W, Lin H (2018) Financial exclusion, social interaction, and family asset allocation. J Central Univ Financ Econ 3:21–38

Tao Y, Cao Y, Zhang J et al (2021) The impact of digital finance on entrepreneurship—evidence from regional and Chinese family panel studies (CFPS). J Zhejiang Univ (Hum Soc Sci Edn) 1:129–144

Tian L (2011) Research on the urban-rural dualism of financial exclusion in China. China Ind Econ 2:36–45+141

Torrini R (2005) Cross-country differences in self-employment rates: the role of institutions. Labour Econ 12(5):661–683

Wang X, Fu Y, He X et al (2013) Research on the status of financial exclusion of Chinese farmers—based on survey data of 1547 households in 29 counties in 8 provinces of China. Financ Res 7:139–152

Wang Y, Yang S (2014) Recent advances in financial literacy theory. Shanghai Finance (3):26–33+116

Wu X, Wang M, Li L (2014) Does high housing prices in China hinder entrepreneurship? Econ Res 49(9):121–134

Xu S, Tian L (2008) Research on financial exclusion in rural China. Financ Res 7:195–206

Yin Z, Song Q, Wu Y et al (2015) Financial knowledge, entrepreneurial decision-making, and entrepreneurial motivation. Manage World 1:87–98

Zeng Z, He Q, Wu Y et al (2015) Financial literacy and diversity of household investment portfolios. Economist 6:88–96

Zhang H, Yin Z (2016) Financial literacy and financial exclusion of Chinese households: an empirical study based on CHFS data. Financial Research 7:80–95

Zhao P, Wang H, Zhao X (2015) An empirical analysis of the differential impact of human capital on urban and rural family entrepreneurship: based on CHFS survey data. Population Econ 3:89–97

Zhao X, Li H, Rauch A (2012) National (regional) differences in entrepreneurial activities: the interaction of culture and national (regional) economic development levels. Manag World 8:78–90+188

Zhu H, Ge J (2018) Theoretical and empirical study on the impact of government regulation on green entrepreneurship of agricultural enterprises: a case study of agricultural leading enterprises in Jiangxi province. East China Econ Manag 32(11):30–36

Zhu C, Ning E (2017) Does financial exclusion exist in financially developed areas? Evidence from the elderly population in Beijing. Int Finance Res 4:3–13